N. E. W. Chapman M. A. Can

Former Chief Examiner in O-level
Modern Mathematics, London
School Examinations Council
Awarder in O-level Mathematics,
Oxford and Cambridge Board

and

Sometime Head of Mathematics,
Cheshunt Grammar School

Interface
Mathematics

A mainstream course for secondary schools

PUPILS' BOOK 2

First published 1982 by
Hard-Davis Educational Limited
a division of Granada Publishing
Frogmore, St Albans, Hertfordshire AL2 2NF

ISBN 0 247 13176 8

Typeset and printed by Unwin Brothers Ltd,
The Gresham Press, Old Woking, Surrey

Cover and book design by Andrew Haig
Illustrations by Alma R. Duncan and
Sean MacGarry

Granada ®
Granada Publishing ®

Contents

Questions from the O-level papers of various examining boards are indicated as follows:

CB, CC, CD   University of Cambridge Local Examinations Syndicate: Syllabus B, Syllabus C, Syllabus D

JMBB, JMBC   Joint Marticulation Board Syllabus B, Syllabus C

LB, LC, LD   University of London School Examinations Council, Syllabus B, Syllabus C, Syllabus D

051, 052   Oxford Delegacy of Local Examinations, Mathematics 051, 052 (later renumbered 4851, 4852)

OC   Oxford and Cambridge Schools Examination Board

SMP   Oxford and Cambridge Schools Examination Board (School Mathematics Project)

SA, SB   Southern Universities' Joint Board, Syllabus A, Syllabus B

16+   University of Cambridge Local Examinations Syndicate and East Anglian Examinations Board, joint experimental examination at 16+

The author and publishers would like to thank the boards for their permission to reproduce these questions.

I should like to thank my colleague Mrs E. Brown for her work in checking the manuscript and the answers to the examples. I am also grateful to many pupils at various schools, especially Berkhamsted School for Girls, for cheerfully acting as 'guinea pigs'. On these pupils were tried out many of the examples and all the projects, experiments, practical work and games described in the whole of this series of books.

Chapter 1

Gradients

The gradient of a road like the one in the picture is usually given in a form such as 1 in 5 (or 20%). This means that (see Figure 1.1), if A and B are two points on the road,

Figure 1.1

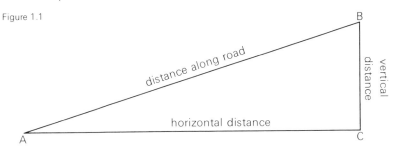

$$\frac{\text{vertical distance between A and B}}{\text{distance along the road from A to B}} = \frac{BC}{AB} = \frac{1}{5} \ (= 20\%)$$

This is the *engineer's gradient*.

If the road is shown on a map, it will appear as the length AC, which is the *horizontal* distance between A and B. The *map gradient* is

$$\frac{\text{vertical distance between A and B}}{\text{horizontal distance between A and B}} = \frac{BC}{AC}$$

which is not the same as the engineer's gradient, although, unless the slope is very steep, the difference between the two is quite small.

In mathematical work, it is the map gradient which is used: in this work

$$\text{Gradient of line AB} = \frac{\text{vertical distance between A and B}}{\text{horizontal distance between A and B}}$$

The abbreviation *grad AB* will be used to denote 'gradient of AB'.

In coordinate work,

$$\text{grad AB} = \frac{y \text{ component of } \mathbf{AB}}{x \text{ component of } \mathbf{AB}}$$

It will be seen that grad AB = tangent of angle AB makes with the horizontal, or with the *x*-axis.

Example 1   Find the gradient of the line l shown in Figure 1.2.

Answer
Choose any two points on l, such as A and B.

Then $\mathbf{AB} = \begin{pmatrix} 4 \\ 2 \end{pmatrix}$, so grad $AB = \dfrac{2}{4} = \dfrac{1}{2}$

If, as we go in the direction of *x* increasing (i.e. from left to right on a normal graph) the line slopes *downwards*, the gradient is given as *negative*.

A horizontal line has gradient 0.

A vertical line is said to have *infinite* gradient.

Example 2   Find the gradient of the line joining P(−2, 5) and Q(4, −3)

Answer
$\mathbf{PQ} = \begin{pmatrix} 6 \\ -8 \end{pmatrix}$, so grad $PQ = \dfrac{-8}{6} = -\dfrac{4}{3}$

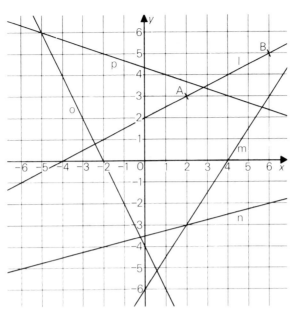

Figure 1.2

Exercise 1.1

1 Find the gradients of the lines m, n, o and p in Figure 1.2.

2 Find the gradients of the vectors

a $\begin{pmatrix} 2 \\ 4 \end{pmatrix}$ **b** $\begin{pmatrix} -3 \\ 6 \end{pmatrix}$ **c** $\begin{pmatrix} -1 \\ -5 \end{pmatrix}$ **d** $\begin{pmatrix} 2 \\ -1 \end{pmatrix}$ **e** $\begin{pmatrix} 8 \\ 0 \end{pmatrix}$

3 Write down the gradients of the lines

a $x = y$,   **b** $y = 6$

What can be said about the gradient of the line $x = 6$?

4 P is $(-2, 5)$, Q is $(4, -3)$, R is $(-1, -3)$, S is $(3, 6)$. Find the gradients of

a PR   **b** PS   **c** QR   **d** QS   **e** RS

5 T is $(-3, 4)$, U is $(3, 5)$, V is $(6, -1)$, W is $(-1, -2)$. Find the gradients of

a TU   **b** TV   **c** TW.   **d** UV   **e** UW   **f** VW.

6 A is (a, b), B is $(a+d, b+2d)$. Find grad AB.

7 C is (c, d), D is $(3c, 5d)$. Find an expression for grad CD.

8 Find the gradient of the line joining the points $(-p, -q)$ and (q, p).

9 Find the gradients of the six lines, each of which joins two of the points $(0, 0)$, $(2, 5)$, $(6, 8)$ and $(4, 3)$.

What kind of quadrilateral is formed by these points?

10 E is $(2, 3)$, F is $(-2, 5+f)$. Find f if grad EF $= \frac{1}{2}$.

11 G is $(-1, 4)$, H is $(3, 7-h)$. Find h if grad GH $= -2$.

12 O is $(0, 0)$, P is $(4, 3)$, R is $(1, 5)$, Q is $(5, q)$. Find q if RQ is parallel to OP, and show that if q has this value, then PQ is parallel to OR.

13 W is $(-2, -3)$, X is $(-1, 2)$, Y is $(2, k)$. Find k if WXY is a straight line.

14 The points $(-5, 6)$, $(-3, a)$ and $(1, 3)$ lie on a straight line. Find a and show that $(a, 1)$ also lies on this line.

Equations of lines

You will be familiar with the equations of at least a few lines, such as $x = y$ and $y = 4$. Each straight line can be regarded as a set of points, such that the coordinates of each point satisfy the equation of the line. For example, the line $x = y$ is a set of points containing $(2, 2)$, $(3, 3)$, $(-5, -5)$, $(4\frac{1}{2}, 4\frac{1}{2})$, $(\sqrt{3}, \sqrt{3})$ amongst an infinite number of others. Since the coordinates of all these points satisfy the equation $x = y$, all these points lie on the line.

Other lines may be regarded as sets of points satisfying other equations: for example the equation $y = 3x - 1$ is satisfied by $(1, 2)$, $(3, 8)$, $(-1, -4)$, $(\frac{1}{3}, 0)$, so the points with these coordinates all lie on the line $y = 3x - 1$.

Exercise 1.2

1 For each of the following equations, find three pairs of values of x and y that satisfy the equation. Plot the points which have these values of x and y for coordinates, and draw the line.

a $y = 2x - 5$	**c** $x = 3y + 1$	**e** $3x + y = 12$
b $x + y = 7$	**d** $2x - y = 3$	**f** $5x + 2y = 10$

2 Find the gradients of all the lines given in Question 1.

3 For each of the following equations, find two pairs of values of x and y which satisfy the equation, and so are coordinates of points on the line given by the equation. Without plotting any points, find the gradient of each line.

a $y = 2x + 3$ c $y = \frac{1}{2}x - 4$ e $y = 1 - 3x$

b $y = 2x + 5$ d $y = \frac{1}{2}x + 1$ f $y = 7 - 3x$

What is the connection between the equation of each line and its gradient?

4   Write down the coordinates of the points where the lines given in Question 3 cross the y-axis. What is the connection between the equation of a line and the y coordinate of the point where it crosses the y-axis?

5   Write down the equations of the lines which have the following gradients, and cross the y-axis at the following points.

a $2, (0, 4)$ c $\frac{1}{2}, (0, -2)$ e $-\frac{1}{4}, (0, \frac{1}{2})$

b $-1, (0, 3)$ d $\frac{2}{3}, (0, 1)$ f $-5, (0, 0)$

6   Rewrite each of these equations in the form $y = mx + c$, where m and c are numbers, and so find the gradient of each line and the point where it crosses the y-axis.

a $x + y = 5$ d $y + 4x = 8$ g $2x + 3y = 9$

b $3x + y = 6$ e $x - 2y = 6$ h $3x - 4y = 12$

c $2x - y = 1$ f $3y + x = 1$

Equations of lines (continued)

After working through the previous exercise it will be clear to you that the equation of any line (other than a vertical line) can be written in the form $y = mx + c$, where m is the gradient of the line and $(0, c)$ is the point where it crosses the y-axis.

To find how to obtain the equations of straight lines from other data, it is best to study the following examples.

Example 3   Find the equation of the line which has gradient 3 and passes through the point $(1, 2)$.

Answer

As the gradient is 3, the equation is $y = 3x + c$, where c has still to be found.

Since $(1, 2)$ lies on the line, the values $x = 1$ and $y = 2$ must satisfy the equation, so $2 = (3 \times 1) + c$. This gives $c = -1$, and the equation is $y = 3x - 1$.

Example 4   Find the equation of the line which has gradient $-\frac{2}{3}$ and passes through the point (3, 4).

Answer

As before, the equation is $y=-\frac{2}{3}x+c$, where c has still to be found.

It is convenient at this stage to rewrite the equation $3y+2x=3c$.

Since (3, 4) lies on the line, $(3 \times 4)+(2 \times 3)=3c$ giving $3c=18$, and the equation is $3y+2x=18$.

Example 5   Find the equation of the line that passes through A(1, 4) and B(2, 7).

Answer

$$\mathbf{AB}=\begin{pmatrix}1\\3\end{pmatrix}\text{ so grad AB}=3.$$

Proceeding as in the previous examples, the equation is $y=3x+c$; substituting the coordinates of A we find $c=1$, and the equation is $y=3x+1$. It is best to use the coordinates of B as a check.

Intersection of two lines

To find the point of intersection of two given lines, their equations are solved simultaneously in the usual way.

Exercise 1.3

In Questions 1 and 2 below, A is (1, 4), B is (2, 7), C is (−2, 3), D is (4, −2).

1   Find the equations of the lines passing through the given points and having the given gradients.

    a A, 2   **c** C, $\frac{1}{2}$ **e** A, $-\frac{1}{4}$ **g** C, $-\frac{1}{2}$

    b B, −1   **d** D, −3   **f** B, $\frac{2}{3}$ **h** D, $\frac{3}{4}$

2   Find the equations of these lines.

    a AC   **b** AD   **c** BC   **d** BD   **e** CD

3   Find the point of intersection of each of the following pairs of lines.

    a $y=x$, $x+y=8$ **d** $x+y=3$, $3x-y=1$

    b $x+y=7$, $y=x+1$ **e** $2x+5y=3$, $3x-2y=14$

    c $x+2y=9$, $2x+y=12$ **f** $3x-y=0$, $6x+2y+4=0$

4 L is $(-1, 3)$, M is $(-2, -5)$ and N is $(4, -2)$. Find the equation of the line through L parallel to MN, and the equation of the line through M parallel to LN. Find the point of intersection of these two lines.

5 L, M and N are as in Question 4, and O is $(0, 0)$. Find the equation of the line through N parallel to LM and that of the line through O parallel to MN. Find the point of intersection of these two lines.

6 P is $(1, 4)$, Q is $(-1, 2)$ and R is $(3, -2)$. Write down the coordinates of S, T and U, the mid-points of QR, RP and PQ respectively. Find the equations of QT and RU, and the coordinates of G, their point of intersection. Show that G lies on PS.

7 Repeat Question 6, but taking P, Q and R as any three points you have chosen.

8 The two lines $y = -2x$ and $x - 2y = 11$ intersect at C, and the line $x - 2y = 11$ cuts the x-axis at D. Calculate the coordinates of C and D.

Calculate the area of the triangle OCD.   (*OC*)

9 The coordinates of the mid-points of the sides of a triangle are $(-2, 3)$, $(3, 5)$ and $(1, -4)$. Find the equations of the sides of the triangle and the coordinates of its vertices.

Inequalities and regions

The line $y = x$ (like any other line) divides the whole coordinate plane into two parts or **regions**. If the point (x, y) lies in the region shaded vertically in Figure 1.3, then $y < x$. The vertically shaded region is the set of points S, where

$$S = \{(x, y): y < x\}.$$

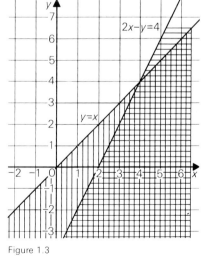

Figure 1.3

Similarly the region not shaded vertically is the set T, where

$$T = \{(x, y): y > x\}.$$

Note that T is not the same as S' (defining $\mathscr{E}$ as {points in the coordinate plane}), since points on the line itself do not belong either to S or to T. If we wish a region to include points on the line we must write $y \leqslant x$, for example, instead of $y < x$.

Figure 1.3 also shows the line $2x-y=4$, which divides the coordinate plane into the regions

$$U=\{(x, y): 2x-y<4\} \text{ and}$$

$$V=\{(x, y): 2x-y>4\},$$

but it is not immediately obvious which is which.

To find which is which, choose any point in the coordinate plane – (0, 0) is a convenient point to choose – and fine whether, a that point, $2x-y$ is more or less than 4. In fact, at (0, 0), $2x-y=0$, which is *less* than 4, so (0, 0) must belong to U. U must therefore be the region which is *not* shaded horizontally, and V must be the region which *is* shaded horizontally.

Regions may overlap or contain one another; for example the doubly shaded region is $S \cap V$, while the completely unshaded region is $T \cap U$.

Exercise 1.4

1 Find the equations of the lines p and q in Figure 1.4. Describe the sets of points which form the following regions.

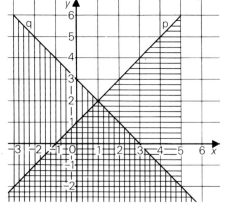

a the region shaded horizontally,
b the region not shaded horizontally,
c the region shaded vertically,
d the region not shaded vertically.

Figure 1.4

Name these regions A, B, C, and D respectively, and describe as the intersections of two sets:

e the region shaded doubly,
f the region not shaded at all,
g the region shaded horizontally but not vertically,
h the region shaded vertically but not horizontally.

2 Repeat Question 1 but with Figure 1.5 and the lines r and s.

3 On graph paper draw the lines whose equations are $x+2y=8$ and $x-y+3=0$. Shade in red the region

$$R=\{(x, y): x+2y<8\},$$

and in green the region

$$G=\{(x, y): x-y+3<0\}.$$

Complete the statements $R'=\{(x, y):$
$\qquad\qquad$ and $G'=\{(x, y):$

Describe as the intersection of two sets

a the region shaded both red and green,
b the unshaded region, together with the lines themselves,
c the region shaded red only, together with one line – which is it?
d the region shaded green only, together with one line – which is it?

4 The vertices of a triangle are (0, 0), (1, 5) and (5, 1). Find the equations of the three sides.

Describe the interior of the triangle as the intersection of three sets.

5 Repeat Question 4, but with the triangle whose vertices are (0, 5), (7, −2) and (−7, −2).

6 Draw the boundary line of the region $\{(x, y): 3x+2y\geqslant6\}$, and shade this region in red.

Draw the boundary line of the region $\{(x, y): y-x\geqslant3\}$, and shade this region in green.

Draw the boundary line of the region $\{(x, y): x+y\leqslant0\}$, and shade this region in blue.

Describe the unshaded region as the intersection of three sets.

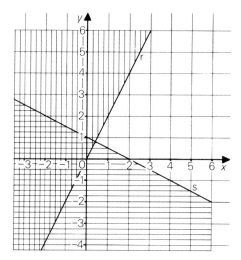

Figure 1.5

7 The regions P, Q and R are defined as follows.

$$P = \{(x, y): x-y>1\}$$
$$Q = \{(x, y): x+y+2<0\}$$
$$R = \{(x, y): x+2y>1\}.$$

Draw the boundary lines and shade P red, Q green and R blue. What can be said about $P \cap Q \cap R$?

Describe the unshaded region as the intersection of three sets.

8 The positive numbers x and y satisfy the inequalities

$$20x+13y>260$$
$$12x+17y<204$$
$$2y>7$$

By drawing appropriate straight-line graphs, using a scale of 1 cm to a unit on each axis, show that there is only one point (x, y), the values of x and y being whole numbers, whose coordinates satisfy all the inequalities simultaneously.

By substituting these values for x and y in the inequalities, show that these inequalities are indeed satisfied.

(OC)

Gradient as a physical quantity

The graph illustrates the motion of a body which has travelled a distance s metres from a fixed point at a time t seconds from a certain instant (Figure 1.6).

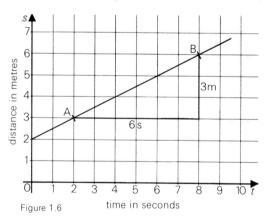

Figure 1.6

The part of the graph between A and B shows that the body travels 3 m in 6 s: thus the speed of the body is $\frac{3}{6}=\frac{1}{2}$ m/s, and this is represented by the gradient of the graph.

If any other two points on the graph, instead of A and B, had been chosen, the result would have been the same: the fact that the graph is a straight line, and that we get the same gradient and the same speed whichever two points are taken, shows that the speed of the body is constant.

Scaled gradient

This graph looks the same as the previous one, but in fact the scale on the distance axis has been changed. The distance travelled in 6 s is now 30 m instead of 3 m, and the speed is $\dfrac{30}{6} = 5$ m/s instead of $\frac{1}{2}$ m/s. The value 5 is called the *scaled gradient* of the

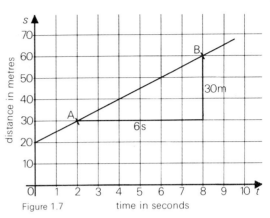

Figure 1.7

graph. It is *not*, of course, equal to the tangent of the angle that the graph makes with the horizontal.

Example 6

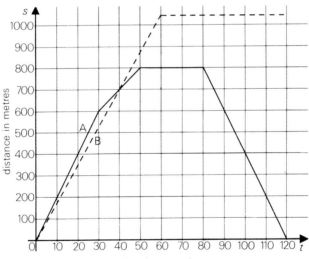

Figure 1.8   time in seconds

Describe the motions of the two bodies whose motions are represented in Figure 1.8. What is the significance of the point where the lines cross?

Answer
Body A travels for 30 s at 20 m/s, covering 600 m; it then travels at 10 m/s for 20 s, covering 200 m; it then stops for 30 s; finally it travels back at 20 m/s, taking 40 s. Body B travels for 60 s at 17.5 m/s; and then stops.

The point where the graphs cross shows where B overtakes A – this is 700 m from the starting point, 40 s after starting.

If the quantity represented on the vertical axis is some quantity other than distance, the gradient still has significance. It represents the rate at which that quantity is increasing. An important example of this occurs when **speed** itself is represented along the vertical axis: the gradient then represents rate of increase of speed, i.e. **acceleration**.

If the quantity represented along the horizontal axis is **not** time, the gradient may still have significance, but such cases will not be considered here.

Exercise 1.5

1 Describe the movements of the two bodies, X and Y, whose motions are represented in Figure 1.9. Explain what is happening at C and at D.

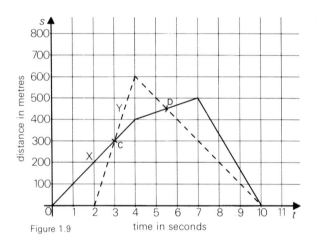

Figure 1.9   time in seconds

The graphs (Figure 1.10) represent the journeys of two lorry-drivers, Ed and Frank. Describe the journey of each, and state where and when they meet.

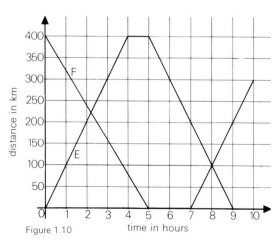

Figure 1.10   time in hours

3   Alf rides his bicycle along a road at 300 m/min for 10 minutes, and then at 200 m/min for 5 minutes. Draw a graph to illustrate this.

Bill, starting at the same time and from the same place as Alf, rides along the same road at 280 m/min. Draw a graph to illustrate the first 15 minutes of Bill's travel, and find when and where he overtakes Alf.

4   Clara sets off at 9 a.m. and drives her car northward at 80 km/h. Dorothy, starting from a point 200 km north of Clara's starting point, sets off at 10 a.m. and drives her car southward at 60 km/h. Draw graphs to illustrate their journeys, and find when and where they meet.

5   George sets out to walk along a footpath: he walks at 2 m/s for 30 minutes and then stops to wait for Herbert, who started 10 minutes later, George has to wait 5 minutes before Herbert reaches him. Draw graphs to illustrate their travels, and find the speed at which Herbert walked.

6   Deeton is 16 km from Eeton. A bus leaves Deeton at 8 a.m. and reaches Eeton at 8.30 a.m. It leaves Eeton again at 8.45 a.m. and reaches Deeton at 9.15 a.m.; it leaves Deeton at 9.30 a.m., and so on all through the day. Draw a graph to illustrate its journeys between 8 a.m. and 11.30 a.m.

A man sets off from Deeton at 8.30 a.m. and walks to Eeton along the same road, reaching it at 11.30 a.m. Draw the graph of his journey, and find when and where he meets or is overtaken by the bus.

7   A and B are two points on a motorway which are 400 km apart. At 9.00 a.m. a motorist leaves A and drives towards B at a steady speed of 90 km/h. At 10.30 a.m. he stops at a service station for 30 minutes and then continues towards B at the former speed of 90 km/h.

Taking scales of 2 cm to 1 hour on one axis and 2 cm to 50 km on the other axis, draw a travel graph of the journey. Find from your graph the time at which the motorist arrives at B.

A second motorist leaves B at 10.00 a.m. and drives at a steady speed of 100 km/h towards A. On the same axes, draw a travel graph of the journey of this motorist, and find from your graph the time at which the two motorists pass each other and their distance from A at that time.

(*OC*)

8   A motorist travelling at a steady speed along a motorway passed a point A at 12.00 noon. At 2.00 p.m. he left the motorway at a junction B which is 160 km from A. At 3.00 p.m. he rejoined the motorway further on at a junction C, a distance of 30 km from B measured along the motorway. He then continued along the motorway at a steady speed of 100 km/h in the same direction as before.

Taking 2 cm to 1 hour on one axis and 2 cm to 50 km on the other, draw the graphs representing the two stages of the motorist's journey on the motorway. Hence find the time at which the motorist arrived at a point D, a distance of 350 km from A measured along the motorway.

A second motorist passed D at 12.00 noon and travelled along the motorway towards A. He did not meet the first motorist on the motorway. Find, by drawing straight line travel graphs or otherwise, the greatest and least steady speeds at which this second motorist could have travelled. *(OC)*

9 Figure 1.11 is the distance–time graph of a train which leaves A at 12.00 and travels to C, stopping on its way at B. The distance from A to B is 3 km and the distance from A to C is 8 km.

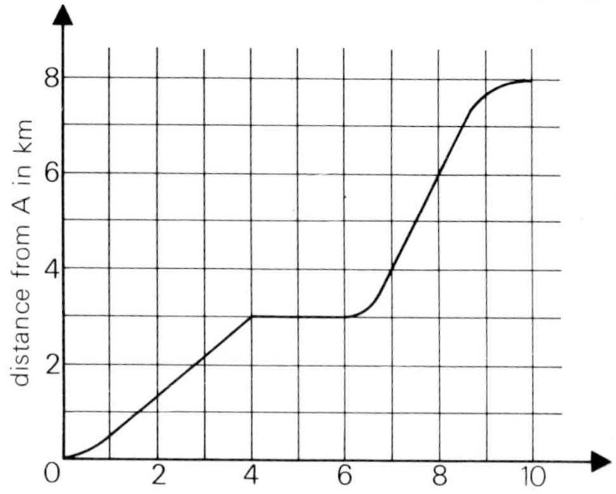

Figure 1.11

a Find the average speed of the train, in kilometres per hour, for the whole journey from A to C.

b Use the graph to estimate the maximum speed of the train.

c An express train, travelling in the opposite direction on a parallel.

10 A train accelerates steadily from rest until its speed is 40 m/s: it travels at this speed for 3 minutes and then decelerates steadily to rest, stopping 5 minutes after it had started. The time spent in decelerating was half the time spent in accelerating. Draw a graph of *speed* against time and find

a the rate of acceleration, in metres per second per second,

b the rate of deceleration, in metres per second per second,

c the length of time during which the speed of the train was more than 30 m/s.

11 A cistern is fitted with three taps; A, which lets water in at 10 litres per minute, B, which lets it in at 40 litres per minute, and C, which lets it *out* at 30 litres per minute.

At 8.00 a.m. the cistern is empty, and A and B are turned on. At 10.00 a.m., B is turned off and C is turned on. Draw a graph plotting time horizontally and volume of water in the cistern vertically, and find at what time the cistern will be empty again if no further changes are made.

When full, the cistern holds 6000 litres. Draw more lines on your graph to find

a the time at which the cistern will be full if B is turned on again at 2.00 p.m., A and C remaining on;

b the time at which B must be turned on if the cistern is to be full at 4.00 p.m., again with A and C remaining on.

Chapter 2

Inverse mappings

You have probably seen this picture before: it appeared at the head of
Chapter 2 in Book 1 to illustrate the relation 'is the owner of' and the
mapping '$x \rightarrow$ car belonging to x' between a domain set of owners and a
range set of cars.

However, the picture will serve equally well to illustrate the relation
'belongs to' and the mapping '$x \rightarrow$ owner of x' between a domain set of
cars and a range set of owners. These are the *inverse relation* and the
inverse mapping to those referred to in the first paragraph.

If a mapping is denoted by f, its inverse is denoted by f^{-1}.

> f(Jane Fox) = AIF 171 N
>
> so f^{-1}(AIF 171 N) = Jane Fox

The diagrams illustrating two mappings which are each other's inverses are the same except that the arrows are in opposite directions, as shown in Figure 2.1.

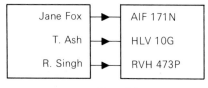

Figure 2.1

Example 1   **a** Give the inverse relation to 'begins with', with a domain set of words, and give the domain set of the inverse relation. State what kind of relation each is, and give the associated mappings.

b If f:$x \rightarrow \frac{3}{4}x$, give f^{-1}. State what kind of mapping each is, and give the associated relations.

Answer

a 'Apple', for example, begins with A. A *is the first letter of* Apple.

The inverse relation is 'is the first letter of', and its domain set is {letters}. 'Begins with' is a many-to-one relation: the associated mapping is $x \rightarrow$ first letter of x.

'Is the first letter of' is a one-to-many relation: the associated mapping is $x \rightarrow$ word beginning with x.

b As f:$x \rightarrow \frac{3}{4}x$, then $f(4) = 3$, $f(8) = 6$ and so on. f^{-1} must map 3 onto 4, 6 onto 8 and so on, so f^{-1}:$x \rightarrow \dfrac{4x}{3}$.

The associated relations are 'is $\frac{4}{3}$ of' and 'is $\frac{3}{4}$ of'.

Exercise 2.1

1 Give the inverse relation to each of the following relations, and give the domain of the inverse relation.

a 'Is the mother of a child named...'
b 'Is the nephew or niece of Uncle...'
c 'Sits in front of' (Domain set of pupils in a classroom, except those in the back row)
d 'Is taller than' (Domain set of people)

    e 'Is the capital of' (Domain set of capital cities)

    f 'Was the year after' (Domain set of years)

    g 'Contains a town named' (Domain set of countries).

2   For each of the relations in Question 1, state whether (i) the relation, and (ii) its inverse is one-to-one, one-to-many, many-to-one or many-to-many.

3   Give the inverse mapping to each of the following mappings, and give the domain of the inverse mapping.

    a $x \rightarrow$ mother of x **e** $x \rightarrow$ characters in play named 'x'

    b $x \rightarrow$ dog belonging to x **f** $x \rightarrow$ person older than x

    c $x \rightarrow$ person sitting on the left of x **g** $x \rightarrow$ wife of x

    d $x \rightarrow$ number of letters in word x

4   For each of the mappings in Question 3, state whether (i) the mapping, and (ii) the inverse mapping is one-to-one, one-to-many, many-to-one or many-to-many.

5   What kind of mapping is the inverse of

    a a one-to-one mapping   **c** a many-to-one mapping

    b a one-to-many mapping   **d** a many-to-many mapping?

6   With domain set {0, 1, 2, 3, 4, 5, 6}, draw mapping diagrams for each of the following mappings. Draw arrows (in a different colour) in the reverse directions, and find the inverse mappings.

    a $x \rightarrow 2x$ **c** $x \rightarrow \dfrac{x}{4}$ **e** $x \rightarrow x + \frac{1}{2}$

    b $x \rightarrow x + 1$ **d** $x \rightarrow x - 2$ **f** $x \rightarrow \frac{2}{3}x$

7   Find the inverses of the following mappings. Draw a diagram only if you find it necessary.

    a $x \rightarrow x + 7$ **c** $x \rightarrow \dfrac{x}{5}$ **e** $x \rightarrow \dfrac{4}{5}x$

    b $x \rightarrow 3x$ **d** $x \rightarrow x - 4$ **f** $x \rightarrow x^2$

8   For each of the following mappings, the domain set is {positive integers}. In each case give (in title or list form) the range set, (which is the domain set of the inverse mapping), and name the inverse mapping.

    a $x \rightarrow$ remainder when x is divided   **d** $x \rightarrow$ fraction whose numerator is x

    by 5   **e** $x \rightarrow x$ if x is odd, $x + 1$ if x is even

    b $x \rightarrow$ factor of x **f** $x \rightarrow x^2$

    c $x \rightarrow$ prime factor of x

In each case state the kind of mapping the given mapping is, and the kind that the inverse mapping is.

9 $f:x \rightarrow 3x$, $g:x \rightarrow x+2$. Find $f^{-1}(9)$, $g^{-1}(7)$, $fg(2)$, $f^{-1}g(4)$, $fg^{-1}(-2)$, $gf^{-1}(6)$, $ff^{-1}(12)$, $gg^{-1}(8)$, $f^{-1}g^{-1}(17)$, and $g^{-1}f^{-1}(1)$.

10 $h:x \rightarrow x-3$, $k:x \rightarrow \frac{1}{4}x$. Find $h^{-1}(1)$, $k^{-1}(7)$, $h^{-1}k(8)$, $hk^{-1}(3)$, $k^{-1}h(0)$, $h^{-1}k^{-1}(7)$, $hh^{-1}(4)$, $kh^{-1}(-1)$ and $k^{-1}h^{-1}(0)$.

11 $p:x \rightarrow \frac{3}{4}x$, $q:x \rightarrow x+\frac{1}{3}$. Find $pq(\frac{1}{2})$, $p^{-1}q(1)$, $p^{-1}q^{-1}(1)$, $pq^{-1}(1)$, $qp(4)$, $q^{-1}p(4)$, $q^{-1}p^{-1}(1)$ and $qp^{-1}(2)$.

12 If f and g have the same meanings as in Question 9, express as single expressions without brackets

   a $fg(x)$ **c** $f^{-1}g(x)$ **e** $ff^{-1}(x)$ **g** $g^{-1}f^{-1}(x)$
   b $gf(x)$ **d** $fg^{-1}(x)$ **f** $gf^{-1}(x)$ **h** $g^{-1}f(x)$

13 If h and k have the same meanings as in Question 10, express as single expressions without brackets

   a $h^{-1}(x)$ **c** $h^{-1}k(x)$ **e** $h^{-1}k^{-1}(x)$ **g** $hh^{-1}(x)$
   b $k^{-1}(x)$ **d** $k^{-1}h(x)$ **f** $k^{-1}h^{-1}(x)$ **h** $k^{-1}k(x)$

14 Mr Ash has a wife and two sons; he also has two brothers and a father. Draw mapping diagrams to illustrate your answers to these questions: which of the following *must* be Mr Ash himself?

   a His wife's husband   **c** His father's son
   b His son's father   **d** His brother's brother

15 Use your answers to Question 14 to answer this question. What kind of mapping is f, if

   a $ff^{-1}(x)$ can only be x **c** conditions **a** and **b** both apply?
   b $f^{-1}f(x)$ can only be x

Self-inverse mappings

What is the inverse of the relation 'is married to'? If Mr Ash is married to Mrs Ash, then Mrs Ash is married to Mr Ash – the inverse is 'is married to'. Such a relation is called a *self-inverse* or *symmetric* relation, and the associated mapping is also self-inverse. This is a one-to-one relation, but a self-inverse relation can be many-to-many, e.g. 'is in the same family as'. A self-inverse relation cannot be one-to-many or many-to-one.

An example of an algebraic mapping which is self-inverse is $x \rightarrow 5-x$. Here $1 \rightarrow 4$ and $4 \rightarrow 1$, $2 \rightarrow 3$ and $3 \rightarrow 2$, and so on. Again, if $f:x \rightarrow 5-x$, then

$$ff:x \rightarrow 5-(5-x)=x.$$

The symmetry of the mapping is illustrated by the symmetry of the mapping diagram.

It can be seen that $x \to a - x$ is self-inverse whatever number a is.

Apply the mapping $x \to \dfrac{12}{x}$ to various numbers, and show that it is a self-inverse mapping.

$x \to \dfrac{b}{x}$ is self-inverse whatever number b is.

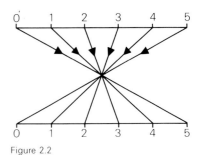

Figure 2.2

Exercise 2.2

1   If $f{:}x \to 6 - x$, $g{:}x \to x + 2$, find

   a $fg(4)$ **c** $fg^{-1}(4)$ **e** $gfg^{-1}(4)$ **g** $gfg(4)$
   b $gf(4)$ **d** $g^{-1}f(4)$ **f** $g^{-1}fg(4)$

2   If f and g have the same meanings as in Question 1, write as single expressions without brackets

   a $fg(x)$ **c** $fg^{-1}(x)$ **e** $gfg^{-1}(x)$ **g** $gfg(x)$
   b $gf(x)$ **d** $g^{-1}f(x)$ **f** $g^{-1}fg(x)$

3   If $h{:}x \to \dfrac{12}{x}$, $k{:}x \to 4x$, find

   a $hk(3)$ **c** $hk^{-1}(3)$ **e** $khk^{-1}(3)$ **g** $hkh(3)$
   b $kh(3)$ **d** $k^{-1}h(3)$ **f** $k^{-1}hk(3)$

4   If h and k have the same meanings as in Question 3, write as single expressions without brackets

   a $kh(x)$ **c** $hk^{-1}(x)$ **e** $khk^{-1}(x)$ **g** $k^{-1}hk^{-1}(x)$
   b $hk(x)$ **d** $k^{-1}h(x)$ **f** $k^{-1}hk(x)$

5   f is any mapping which is not self-inverse, g and h are self-inverse mappings. Which of the following mappings are self-inverse?

   gh, fgf, fgf^{-1}, $f^{-1}gf$, $fghf$

6   For the domain set {points of the compass} find
   a a one-to-one mapping which is self-inverse (not just 'is')
   b a one-to-one mapping which is not self-inverse.

7 For the domain set {months of the year} m:$x \rightarrow$ month n months after x. Find the smallest value of n (other than 0) for which m is self-inverse.

8 With domain set {0, 1, 2, 3, 4, 5}

$$f: \begin{cases} x \rightarrow x+3 \text{ if } x<3 \\ x \rightarrow x-3 \text{ if } x \geqslant 3 \end{cases}$$

Draw the mapping diagram for f and show that it is self-inverse. Make up a similar mapping, not necessarily with the same domain, which is also self-inverse.

9 Form the matrix **M** that represents the relation 'is a factor of' between the domain set {2, 3, 5} and the range set {4, 6, 10, 15}. Form also the matrix representing the inverse relation, and name this inverse relation. How is this second matrix related to **M**? What would be a characteristic of a matrix representing a self-inverse relation?

Inverse of a composite mapping

I think of a number, double it and add 7, and this gives 19. What was the number? A moment's thought shows that the answer is 6, but it is important to study the way in which this answer is obtained.

To find the answer, 19 is subjected to the mappings 'subtract 7' and 'divide by 2' *in that order*, which is the reverse of the order in which the mappings 'double' and 'add 7' were applied to the original number. In general the inverse of a composite mapping fg is $g^{-1}f^{-1}$. Similarly, that of fgh is $h^{-1}g^{-1}f^{-1}$, and so on.

Example 2   f:$x \rightarrow 3x$, g:$x \rightarrow x-8$. Express fg as a single mapping, and find its inverse as a single mapping.

Answer

fg:$x \rightarrow 3(x-8) = 3x-24$.

$f^{-1}:x \rightarrow \frac{1}{3}x$, $g^{-1}:x \rightarrow x+8$. The inverse of fg, i.e. $(fg)^{-1}$ is $g^{-1}f^{-1}:x \rightarrow \frac{1}{3}x+8$.

It is very often possible mentally to work out what is the inverse of a given composite mapping, especially when there are only two stages. When the working is to be written down, one way of setting it out is in four columns as shown in the following example.

Example 3   Find the inverse of $x \rightarrow \sqrt{\left(\frac{5-3x}{7} \right)}$

Answer

In the first of four columns, write the images of x after the various stages of the mapping, and in the second column write (in symbolic form for

the sake of brevity) the mapping at that stage. In the third column write
the inverse of each mapping.

x

$3x$	$\times 3$	$\div 3$
$5 - 3x$	Take from 5	Take from 5
$\dfrac{5 - 3x}{7}$	$\div 7$	$\times 7$
$\sqrt{\left(\dfrac{5 - 3x}{7}\right)}$	Sq. root	Square

In the fourth column, starting with x *at the bottom and working upwards*, carry out the mappings listed in the third column.

x

$3x$	$\times 3$	$\div 3$	$\dfrac{5 - 7x^2}{3}$
$5 - 3x$	Take from 5	Take from 5	$5 - 7x^2$
$\dfrac{5 - 3x}{7}$	$\div 7$	$\times 7$	$7x^2$
$\sqrt{\left(\dfrac{5 - 3x}{7}\right)}$	Sq. root	Square	x^2
			x

The inverse is $x \rightarrow \dfrac{5 - 7x^2}{3}$.

Exercise 2.3

1 Find the inverses of the mappings that map x onto

a $3x - 5$ **d** $\frac{1}{4}x + 7$ **f** $7 - 2x$ **h** $\dfrac{5}{2 - x}$

b $3(x - 5)$ **e** $\dfrac{6 - x}{3}$ **g** $\dfrac{2}{x + 4}$ **i** $5 - \dfrac{2}{x}$

c $\dfrac{x + 7}{4}$

2   If possible without any intermediate written working, write down the images of x under the inverses of the mappings that map x onto

a $2x+4$ **d** $5x-2$ **f** $\frac{2}{3}(x-1)$ **h** $\dfrac{4-x}{5}$

b $4(x+5)$ **e** $\dfrac{x}{5}+6$ **g** $7-3x$

c $\dfrac{x-3}{7}$ **i** $\dfrac{5}{4-x}$

3   Find the inverses of the following mappings.

a $x \rightarrow \dfrac{3x+2}{6}$ **e** $x \rightarrow \dfrac{1-\frac{1}{3}x}{4}$ **h** $x \rightarrow \frac{2}{3}(x^2-5)$

b $x \rightarrow 3(4-5x)$ **f** $x \rightarrow \sqrt{3-4x}$ **i** $x \rightarrow \dfrac{4-x^2}{3}$

c $x \rightarrow \dfrac{2}{4x+5}$ **g** $x \rightarrow \sqrt{\dfrac{2x+3}{7}}$ **j** $x \rightarrow \dfrac{3}{x^2+2}$

d $\dfrac{7-3x}{5}$

4   Find simple mappings f, g and h such that fgh:$x \rightarrow \dfrac{3x+2}{5}$, and find their inverses. Hence find the inverse of fgh.

Express hgf as a single mapping, and find its inverse.

5   Find simple mappings p, q and r such that pqr:$x \rightarrow \dfrac{6}{5-2x}$, and write down their inverses. Hence find the inverse of pqr.

Express rqp as a single mapping, and find its inverse.

6   Find simple mappings k, l and m such that klm:$x \rightarrow \sqrt{(1-x^2)}$, and write down their inverses. Hence find the inverse of klm.

Express mlk as a single mapping, and find its inverse.

Mappings and functions.   For brevity, the word 'function' is sometimes used to denote the *image* of a variable (frequently x) under a mapping which is a function: thus $3x-2$, for example, is said to be a function of x, and it is also a *composite function*; $5-x$ is said to be a *self-inverse function* and so on. This nomenclature will sometimes be used here.

Solving equations and transforming formulae

The method used for finding inverse mappings and functions can also be used for solving certain types of equation, and for transforming most formulae.

The equations that can be solved in this way are those in which the unknown quantity (frequently x) appears only once, e.g.

$$\sqrt{\left(\frac{12}{2-5x}\right)} = 3$$

The work is set out in four columns as before, but at the bottom of the fourth column, instead of x, 3 is written and is operated on by the mappings listed in the third column, working upwards as before. The working is shown here.

x			
$5x$	$\times 5$	$\div 5$	$\dfrac{2}{15}$
$2-5x$	Take from 2	Take from 2	$2-1\frac{1}{3}=\frac{2}{3}$
$\dfrac{12}{2-5x}$	Divide into 12	Divide into 12	$\dfrac{12}{9}=1\frac{1}{3}$
$\sqrt{\dfrac{12}{2-5x}}$	Sq. root	Square	9
			3

The answer is $x = \dfrac{2}{15}$.

This method cannot be used to solve equations in which x (or whatever the unknown quantity is) appears more than once, unless the equation can be rewritten in a form in which x appears only once. For example, the equation $x^2 - 6x = 10$ can be rewritten

$$(x-3)^2 - 9 = 10$$

and hence as

$$(x-3)^2 = 19$$

and then solved by the above method.

x			
$x-3$	-3	$+3$	$3+\sqrt{19}$ or $3-\sqrt{19}$
$(x-3)^2$	sq	sq. root	$\sqrt{19}$ or $-\sqrt{19}$
			19

This equation has two solutions, $3+\sqrt{19}$, i.e. 7.36, and $3-\sqrt{19}$, i.e. -1.36 (both to 3 significant figures).

Equations which cannot be rewritten in a form in which x appears only once, are solved (if at all) by a variety of methods, some of which are given in a later chapter.

Changing the subject of a formula

A is the **subject** of the formula $A=\pi r^2$, which is used to calculate the area A of a circle when the radius r is known (A and r being in suitable units). If we often need to calculate the radius of a circle whose area is known, it is convenient to **transform** the formula to make r the subject. In this case the transformed formula is

$$r = \sqrt{\frac{A}{\pi}}$$

Again, the work can be set out in four columns. The letter representing the quantity which is to be the **new** subject is written at the top of the first column, and that representing the **old** subject, at the bottom of the fourth column.

Example 4   Make g the subject of the formula

$$T = 2\pi \sqrt{\frac{l}{g}}$$

Answer: In four columns

g

$\dfrac{l}{g}$ Divide into l Divide into l $l \div \dfrac{T^2}{4\pi^2} = \dfrac{4\pi^2 l}{T^2}$

$\sqrt{\dfrac{l}{g}}$ Sq. root   Square $\dfrac{T^2}{4\pi^2}$

$2\pi\sqrt{\dfrac{l}{g}}$ $\times\, 2\pi$ $\div 2\pi$ $\dfrac{T}{2\pi}$

The transformed formula is $g = \dfrac{4\pi^2 l}{T^2}$. T

Exercise 2.4

1   Solve the following equations.

a $\dfrac{12}{2x+5} = 4$ **d** $\dfrac{7}{5-3x} = 1$ **g** $\dfrac{2}{\sqrt{(25-x^2)}} = \dfrac{1}{2}$

b $\sqrt{(7-4x)} = 2$ **e** $\sqrt{(3x-2)} = 7$ **h** $\dfrac{6}{1-x^2} = 8$

c $\dfrac{7-2x^2}{5} = -5$ **f** $\dfrac{5}{\sqrt{(1-2x)}} = 10$

2 Use the fact that $(x+3)^2 = x^2 + 6x + 9$
to solve the equation $x^2 + 6x = 4$.
Solve also the equation $x^2 + 6x = 1$.

3 Use the fact that $(x-5)^2 = x^2 - 10x + 25$
to solve the equation $x^2 - 10x = -23$.
Solve also the equation $x^2 - 10x = 5$.

4 Use the fact that $(x+\frac{1}{2})^2 = x^2 + x + \frac{1}{4}$
to solve the equation $x^2 + x = 1$.
Solve also the equation $x^2 + x = 3$.

5 Transform each of the following formulae to make the named quantity
the subject.

    a $v = u + at$; a **c** $P = 2(l+b)$; l **e** $y = mx + c$; m

    b $E = \frac{1}{2}mv^2$; v **d** $s = \frac{u+v}{2}t$; v **f** $S = 2\pi r(r+h)$; h

6 Transform the formula $d = \sqrt{(b^2 - 4ac)}$
    a to make a the subject,   **b** to make b the subject.

7 Transform the formula $r = \dfrac{D}{s-c}$
    a to make s the subject,   **b** to make c the subject.

8 Transform the formula $P = \dfrac{RT}{V}$
    a to make T the subject,   **b** to make V the subject.

9 Transform the formula $T = 2\sqrt{\left(\dfrac{h^2 + k^2}{hg}\right)}$
    a to make k the subject,   **b** to make g the subject.

10 Transform the formula $k = \dfrac{Y - y}{yt}$
    a to make Y the subject,   **b** to make t the subject.

11 Show that if A is the area of the shaded
region in Figure 2.3, then $A = \pi((r+t)^2 - r^2)$,
and transform this formula to make t the
subject.

Show also that $A = \pi(2rt + t^2)$, and transform
this formula to make r the subject.

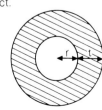

Figure 2.3

12 Figure 2.4 shows a cuboid which, like a match-box cover, has a top, bottom and sides but no ends. Find formulae for the following, and transform each formula to make l the subject.

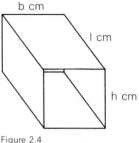

b cm

l cm

h cm

Figure 2.4

a V, the volume, in cm³,
b S, the total area of all four faces, in cm²,
c E, the total length of all twelve edges, in cm.

13 Make c the subject of the formula

$$x = \frac{-b + \sqrt{(b^2 - 4c)}}{2}$$

and simplify your answer so that it contains no brackets or fractions.

14 Figure 2.5 consists of two semi-circles of radius r cm, whose centres are d cm apart, and two straight lines which touch the semi-circles. Find, and transform to make d the subject, formulae for

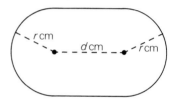

r cm d cm r cm

Figure 2.5

a P, the perimeter in cm,
b A, the area in cm².

15 A sum £P is invested for one year at r% simple interest, and the sum, together with the interest, then amounts to £A. Find a formula for A in terms of P and r, and transform it to make r the subject.

Further transformation of formulae

If the letter representing the quantity which is to be the new subject appears more than once in a formula, the formula cannot be transformed by the 'four column' method: a method like that used in solving simple equations has to be employed. The following example illustrates this method.

Example 5 Transform the formula $d = \dfrac{a+b}{a-b}$ to make a the subject.

Answer

Clear fractions by multiplying both sides of the equation by $a - b$.

$$d(a - b) = a + b$$

Remove brackets: $da - db = a + b$.

Rewrite the equation so that terms containing a appear on one side, and other terms on the other. This is done by adding db to both sides of the equation, and subtracting a from both sides, giving

$$da - a = b + db$$

Factorise the left-hand side: We will factorise the right-hand side as well, though this is not strictly necessary.

$$a(d - 1) = b(1 + d)$$

Divide both sides by the factor multiplying a, which is $d - 1$.

$$a = \frac{b(1 + d)}{d - 1}$$

The formula is now transformed as required.

Exercise 2.5

1   Transform the formula $t = \dfrac{\mu d}{\mu - 1}$ to make μ the subject.

2   Transform the formula $T = \dfrac{E}{l}(x - l)$ to make l the subject.

3   Transform the formula $T = \sqrt{\left(\dfrac{x}{x - y} \right)}$ to make x the subject.

4   Transform the formula $K = \dfrac{Y - y}{yt}$ to make y the subject.

5   Transform the formula $v = \dfrac{uf}{u - f}$

    a to make u the subject,   **b** to make f the subject.

6   Transform the formula $y = a(x + h) + b(x + k)$ to make x the subject.

7   A sector is enclosed by two radii of a circle of radius r, the angle between the radii being $x°$. Find a formula for the perimeter p of the sector, and transform it to make r the subject.

8   The length of the hypotenuse of a right-angled triangle is $a + b - h$, and the lengths of the other two sides are a and b. Show that $2ab - 2ah - 2bh + h^2 = 0$, and so obtain a formula for a in terms of b and h.

Chapter 3

Multiplication of matrices

The scalar product

The scorer is reckoning up the points for the teams in the athletics match. Aytown School athletes have gained 5 first places, 4 second places, 3 thirds, 2 fourths and 4 fifths. The numbers 5, 4, 3, 2, 4 can be regarded as a row matrix or as an *ordered set*. (Ordered because the order of the numbers matters: in other sets we have encountered the order did not matter).

In order to find how many points this team has scored, we need to know how many points are allocated for each place; in this match a first scores 7 points, a second 5, a third 3, a fourth 2 and a fifth 1. The numbers 7, 5, 3, 2, 1 form another ordered set. To find the total score we multiply

each member of the first set by the corresponding member of the second, giving $(5 \times 7) + (4 \times 5) + (3 \times 3) + (2 \times 2) + (4 \times 1) = 72$.

The result of carrying out this operation on two ordered sets is called the *scalar product* of the sets, so the scalar product of the ordered sets {5, 4, 3, 2, 4} and {7, 5, 3, 2, 1} is 72. We shall sometimes use the verb 'to scalar-multiply' to denote this operation.

Scalar multiplication — though not under that name — has been carried out before this chapter, for example in finding the mean of a frequency distribution (in Chapter 11 of Book 1). Again, scalar multiplication is used in finding the total cost of various numbers of articles at different prices.

Notice that we can find the scalar product of two ordered sets only if they have the same number of elements.

Exercise 3.1

1 The athletes of Beetown School took 4 first, 3 second, 5 third, 4 fourth and 7 fifth places. Calculate their total score, allocating the points on the same scheme as above.

2 In a certain street the numbers of houses in which 1, 2, 3, 4, 5 and 6 people live are respectively 10, 25, 30, 15, 10 and 6. No house holds more than 6 people. Find the total number of people living in all these houses.

3 Find the total cost of 6 large packets, 5 giant packets, 3 monster packets and 4 mammoth packets of chocolate if the cost of a large packet is 30p and those of a giant, a monster and a mammoth packet are respectively 50p, 80p and £1.20.

4 Find the total capacity of 10 bottles, 8 litre bottles, 6 magnums and 3 2-litre bottles, given that the capacity of a bottle is 0.75 l and that of a magnum is 1.5 l.

5 In a traffic census, 120 cars were observed to have 1 occupant each, 85 to have 2 each, 60 to have 3 each, 24 to have 4 each and 10 to have 5 each. None had more than 5. Write down two ordered sets to summarise this information, and find the total number of people in all the cars.

6 Find the scalar products of the following pairs of ordered sets.

   a {1, 3, 4, 7} and {2, 5, 0, 9}
   b {−2, 1, −3, 4} and {−6, 2, −1, 5}
   c {3, −4, 5, −6} and {−5, −2, 3, 5}
   d {5, 7, −5, −7} and {−7, 5, 7, −5}

7 A is the ordered set of the first 6 positive integers in ascending order; B is the ordered set of the same 6 integers in descending order. If $\times$ denotes scalar multiplication, find
    a $A \times A$,   **b** $A \times B$

8 Write down the scalar product of $\{a, b, c, d\}$ and $\{1, 1, 1, 1\}$.

9 Find x if the scalar product of $\{x, 2, 4\}$ and $\{1, 3, x\}$ is 36.

10 Find y if the scalar product of $\{y, 1, y\}$ and $\{3, 5, 7\}$ is 95.

11 Find t if the scalar product of $\{t, -3, t\}$ and $\{t, 2, -4\}$ is 15. (There are two possible answers.)

12 Write down all six of the ordered sets that can be made from the numbers 1, 2 and 3, used once each. What is the largest scalar product that can be formed by multiplying one of these ordered sets by itself or by another, and what is the smallest?

Multiplying two matrices

Returning to the athletics match, the points scheme may be written as a column matrix thus:

$$\begin{pmatrix} 7 \\ 5 \\ 3 \\ 2 \\ 1 \end{pmatrix}$$

The product of a row matrix and a column matrix with the same number of elements is defined as being the scalar product of the ordered sets of their elements, so

$$(5\ 4\ 3\ 2\ 4) \begin{pmatrix} 7 \\ 5 \\ 3 \\ 2 \\ 1 \end{pmatrix} = (72)$$

Here the product is regarded as a 1×1 matrix. It is convenient to use the matrix notation, because we can enlarge the first matrix to include the scores of the other two schools, Beetown and Ceetown: it becomes

$$\begin{pmatrix} 5 & 4 & 3 & 2 & 4 \\ 4 & 3 & 5 & 4 & 7 \\ 3 & 5 & 4 & 6 & 1 \end{pmatrix}$$

By scalar-multiplying each row in turn by the column matrix of points, we find the total points scored by each school.

$$
\begin{array}{c} \text{Aytown} \\ \text{Beetown} \\ \text{Ceetown} \end{array}
\begin{pmatrix} 5 & 4 & 3 & 2 & 4 \\ 4 & 3 & 5 & 4 & 7 \\ 3 & 5 & 4 & 6 & 1 \end{pmatrix}
\begin{pmatrix} 7 \\ 5 \\ 3 \\ 2 \\ 1 \end{pmatrix}
=
\begin{pmatrix} 72 \\ 73 \\ 71 \end{pmatrix}
$$

The column matrix $\begin{pmatrix} 72 \\ 73 \\ 71 \end{pmatrix}$, formed in this way, is defined as being the product of the two matrices on the left.

We can extend the process further. It is suggested that the points scheme should be replaced by one giving 4 for a first place, 3 for a second, 2 for a third, 1 for a fourth, and nothing for a fifth. By adding a second column to the matrix of points, and scalar-multiplying each row of the first matrix by it, we obtain the totals for both systems of scoring.

$$
\begin{array}{c} \text{Aytown} \\ \text{Beetown} \\ \text{Ceetown} \end{array}
\begin{pmatrix} 5 & 4 & 3 & 2 & 4 \\ 4 & 3 & 5 & 4 & 7 \\ 3 & 5 & 4 & 6 & 1 \end{pmatrix}
\begin{pmatrix} 7 & 4 \\ 5 & 3 \\ 3 & 2 \\ 2 & 1 \\ 1 & 0 \end{pmatrix}
=
\begin{pmatrix} 72 & 40 \\ 73 & 39 \\ 71 & 41 \end{pmatrix}
$$

(What difference does it make which system of scoring is used?)

This shows how matrices of various orders, not only row and column matrices, can be multiplied together, but note that each row of the first matrix must have the same number of elements as each column of the second matrix, or, to put it more conveniently, *the number of columns of the first matrix must be equal to the number of rows of the second matrix*. The product has the same number of rows as the first matrix, and the same number of columns as the second.

Note that it would not be possible to multiply the matrices the other way round, putting the matrix of points first. Matrix multiplication is said to be *non-commutative* – if **A** and **B** are two matrices and the product **AB** can be formed, **BA** cannot necessarily be formed; and even if **BA** can be formed, it is not usually equal to **AB**.

Example 1

$$
\mathbf{A} = \begin{pmatrix} 1 & 3 \\ 4 & 0 \\ -1 & 5 \end{pmatrix}, \quad
\mathbf{B} = \begin{pmatrix} 6 & 1 & 0 & 3 \\ 4 & -2 & 2 & -1 \end{pmatrix}
$$

Form, if possible, the product **AB**.

Answer

A has 2 columns and **B** has 2 rows, so the product **AB** can be formed. **AB** will have 3 rows (like **A**) and 4 columns (like **B**): draw brackets of the right size to hold **AB**.

The element in the first row and first column of **AB** is found by scalar-multiplying the first row of **A** by the first column of **B**: it is $(1 \times 6) + (3 \times 4) = 18$. (See the dotted lines below).

The element in the first row and second column of **AB** is found by scalar-multiplying the first row of **A** by the second column of **B**: it is $(1 \times 1) + (3 \times -2) = -5$. So far we have

$$\begin{pmatrix} 1 & 3 \\ 4 & 0 \\ -1 & 5 \end{pmatrix} \begin{pmatrix} 6 & 1 & 0 & 3 \\ 4 & -2 & 2 & -1 \end{pmatrix} = \begin{pmatrix} 18 & -5 & & \\ & & & \\ & & & \end{pmatrix}$$

Continue in the same way: the element in the *p*th row and *q*th column of **AB** is found by scalar-multiplying the *p*th row of **A** by the *q*th column of **B**. The final result is

$$\begin{pmatrix} 18 & -5 & 6 & 0 \\ 24 & 4 & 0 & 12 \\ 14 & -11 & 10 & -8 \end{pmatrix}$$

Exercise 3.2

1   **P** is a 3×2 matrix, **Q** is a 2×3 matrix and **R** is a 2×2 matrix. Which of the following products can be formed? **PQ, QP, QR, RQ, RP, PR**. Give the orders of those product matrices which can be formed.

2   Form the following matrix products.

a $\begin{pmatrix} 2 & 3 & 7 \\ 1 & 4 & 5 \end{pmatrix} \begin{pmatrix} 1 & 2 \\ 0 & 6 \\ 8 & 3 \end{pmatrix}$ **c** $\begin{pmatrix} 2 & 6 & 7 \\ 1 & 0 & -4 \\ 5 & -3 & 6 \end{pmatrix} \begin{pmatrix} 0 & 0 \\ 3 & -3 \\ -2 & 2 \end{pmatrix}$

b $\begin{pmatrix} 0 & -3 & 3 & 9 \\ 1 & 2 & 5 & -2 \\ 4 & 6 & -5 & 0 \end{pmatrix} \begin{pmatrix} 2 & 7 \\ 0 & -1 \\ 4 & 3 \\ -2 & 5 \end{pmatrix}$ **d** $\begin{pmatrix} 1 & 3 \\ 2 & -5 \\ -3 & 0 \end{pmatrix} \begin{pmatrix} 4 & 7 & -1 \\ 3 & -5 & 0 \end{pmatrix}$

3 $\mathbf{A} = \begin{pmatrix} 2 & 3 \\ 4 & -1 \end{pmatrix}$, $\mathbf{B} = \begin{pmatrix} 1 & -5 \\ 0 & 3 \end{pmatrix}$, $\mathbf{C} = \begin{pmatrix} 2 \\ -1 \end{pmatrix}$.

Form all that can be formed of the products **AB, BA, BC, CB, CA** and **AC**.

4 $X = \begin{pmatrix} 1 & 2 \\ 4 & -3 \\ 2 & 0 \end{pmatrix}$, $Y = \begin{pmatrix} 0 & 6 & -1 \\ 2 & 5 & 3 \end{pmatrix}$, $Z = \begin{pmatrix} 3 & 4 \\ 4 & -3 \end{pmatrix}$

Form all that can be formed of the products **XY**, **YX**, **YZ**, **ZY**, **ZX** and **XZ**.

5   L, **M** and **N** are matrices such that **LM** = **N**. What can be said about **M** if
  a   L and **N** are of the same order?
  b   **L** is a column matrix?
  c   **L** is a row matrix with 5 elements? What can then be said about **N**?

6   A has p rows and q columns, **B** has r rows and s columns. Write equations that connect p, q, r and s if
  a   **AB** and **BA** can both be formed,
  b   **AB** and **BA** can both be formed, and are of the same order.

7   Compile a 2-row matrix of your own choosing and multiply it, on the left, by $\begin{pmatrix} 1 & 0 \\ 0 & 1 \end{pmatrix}$.

What do you notice?

What 3×3 matrix will produce the same kind of result when multiplying a 3-row matrix?

8   Repeat Question 7 but with $\begin{pmatrix} 0 & 1 \\ 1 & 0 \end{pmatrix}$, instead of $\begin{pmatrix} 1 & 0 \\ 0 & 1 \end{pmatrix}$.

9   Find x and y if $\begin{pmatrix} 3 & x \\ x & 2 \end{pmatrix} \begin{pmatrix} 1 \\ 2 \end{pmatrix} = \begin{pmatrix} 11 \\ y \end{pmatrix}$.

10   Find a and b if $\begin{pmatrix} a & 1 & 2 \\ 2 & b & 3 \end{pmatrix} \begin{pmatrix} 2 \\ b \\ 3 \end{pmatrix} = \begin{pmatrix} 13 \\ 22 \end{pmatrix}$.

(There are two possible pairs of answers.)

11   The element of the first row and first column of the product

$\begin{pmatrix} p & 2 \\ 3 & 1 \end{pmatrix} \begin{pmatrix} p & 3 \\ p & 1 \end{pmatrix}$ is 15.

Find the two possible values of p and complete the product matrix in each case.

12   Find p, q, r and s if $\begin{pmatrix} p & q \\ r & s \end{pmatrix} \begin{pmatrix} 1 & -1 \\ 0 & 3 \end{pmatrix} = \begin{pmatrix} 4 & -10 \\ 3 & -3 \end{pmatrix}$.

13   Multiply the 3×5 matrix of places in the athletics match (see the beginning of this section) by (1 1 1) on the left. Explain the result.

What is the effect of multiplying any 3-row matrix by (1 1 1)?

14 In Book 1 we saw the following matrix, which conveys information about the pets belonging to various owners.

$$\begin{array}{c} \text{Mr Ash} \\ \text{Mrs Beech} \\ \text{Miss Fox} \end{array} \begin{array}{ccc} \text{Dogs} & \text{Cats} & \text{Budgerigars} \\ \begin{pmatrix} 1 & 2 & 4 \\ 2 & 1 & 0 \\ 0 & 4 & 7 \end{pmatrix} \end{array}$$

Multiply this matrix

a by (1 1 1) on the left,

b by $\begin{pmatrix} 1 \\ 1 \\ 1 \end{pmatrix}$ on the right.

What information does each of these products give?

15 The following matrix gives the numbers of faces, vertices and edges of certain polyhedra.

$$\begin{array}{c} \text{Cube} \\ \text{Square pyramid} \\ \text{Tetrahedron} \\ \text{Triangular prism} \\ \text{Octahedron} \end{array} \begin{array}{ccc} \text{Faces} & \text{Vertices} & \text{Edges} \\ \begin{pmatrix} 6 & 8 & 12 \\ 5 & 5 & 8 \\ 4 & 4 & 6 \\ 5 & 6 & 9 \\ 8 & 6 & 12 \end{pmatrix} \end{array}$$

Multiply this matrix by $\begin{pmatrix} 1 \\ 1 \\ -1 \end{pmatrix}$ on the right.

What relation does this result suggest, between the numbers of faces, vertices and edges of a polyhedron?

16 **M** is the matrix $\begin{pmatrix} 1 & -2 \\ 3 & 4 \\ 0 & -1 \end{pmatrix}$, and **M'** is the transpose of **M**, that is the matrix obtained by interchanging rows and columns.

Form **MM'** and **M'M**. What special feature do you notice about both these matrices? Form any other matrix and multiply it by its transpose, both ways, and see if both product matrices show this same feature. Can *any* matrix be multiplied by its transpose?

17 The Trans-Can Airline has 8 Viscounts, 6 Tridents and 2 Caravelles. East Atlantic Airways have 9 Viscounts, 1 Trident and 7 Caravelles, and the I1-Oil Company has 2 Viscounts, 11 Tridents and no Caravelles.

a Express this information as a 3×3 matrix **A**.

b The Viscount carries 50 passengers, the Trident carries 140 and the Caravelle 80. Write down a suitable product of two matrices which, when calculated, will determine the numbers of passengers that each airline is able to carry when all its aircraft are full.

c Evaluate this product.

d Describe what information would be given by pre-multiplying your matrix **A** by the row matrix (1 1 1). *(SMP)*

18 The matrix **M**, given below, shows the numbers (in thousands) of votes polled by each of the three parties who contested the three constituencies of Sometown in the last General Election:

$$
\begin{array}{cccc}
& \text{Sometown} & \text{Sometown} & \text{Sometown} \\
& \text{West} & \text{Central} & \text{East} \\
\text{Pink party} & 10 & 10 & 8 \\
\text{Green part} & 12 & 15 & 17 \\
\text{Mauve party} & 8 & 2 & 4
\end{array} = \mathbf{M}
$$

R is the matrix (1 1 1) and **C** is $\begin{pmatrix} 1 \\ 1 \\ 1 \end{pmatrix}$

Which of the matrices **RM**, **MR**, **CM** and **MC** can be formed? Form these, and state the significance of each.

Find a matrix **P** such that **PM** gives the 'majority' in each constituency, that is, the difference between the numbers of votes polled by the o most successful parties. Form **PM**.

19 a A toll bridge charges 8p for a motor-cycle, 12p for a car and 20p for a lorry. Express this information as a column matrix **C**.

b The numbers of these vehicles crossing one week-end are given by the matrix

$$
\mathbf{N} = \begin{array}{c} \\ \text{Sat} \\ \text{Sun} \end{array}
\begin{array}{c} \text{M/c} \quad \text{Cars} \quad \text{Lorries} \\ \begin{pmatrix} 134 & 209 & 21 \\ 65 & 95 & 28 \end{pmatrix} \end{array}
$$

Which of the products **CN** and **NC** can be evaluated? Denoting this product by **T**, evaluate **T** and state what information it gives.

c To obtain more revenue at week-ends three proposals are made:

I – double the charges on Saturdays only,

II – treble the charges on Sundays only,

III – increase the charges by half on both days.

The matrix **X** is such that the product **XT** gives the actual revenue for the weekend and what it would have been under each of the proposals I, II and III.

Write down **X**, evaluate **XT**, and state which proposal would have been the most profitable. *(SMP)*

20　A certain issue of commemorative stamps was printed in three denominations, 12p, 14p and 18p, and was on sale for two weeks. The following matrix gives the numbers of each kind of stamp that a certain small post office sold each week.

$$
\begin{array}{c}
 \\
\text{1st week} \\
\text{2nd week}
\end{array}
\begin{array}{ccc}
12p & 14p & 18p \\
\end{array}
\left(\begin{array}{ccc}
80 & 110 & 45 \\
60 & 120 & 50
\end{array}\right)
$$

Call this matrix **M**. Find matrices that will multiply **M** (stating whether the multiplication is on the left or on the right) to give the following information.

a　The total numbers of stamps sold in each separate week,
b　the total numbers of each kind of stamps sold in both weeks together,
c　the total value of the stamps sold in each separate week.

Identity matrix

The matrix $\begin{pmatrix} 1 & 0 \\ 0 & 1 \end{pmatrix}$ is called an *identity matrix* and is often denoted by the letter **I**. As will have been seen in answering Question 7 of Exercise 3.2, **I** has the property that if **A** is any other matrix such that the product **IA** can be formed, then **IA**=**A**, i.e. the matrix **A** is left unchanged by the multiplication. Also, if **B** is any matrix such that the product **BI** can be formed, then **BI**=**B**. Identity matrices of other orders can also be formed, which will have been done in answering Question 7.

Associativity

Compile any three matrices **A**, **B** and **C**, such that the products **AB** and **BC** can both be formed. Form **AB** and then (**AB**)**C**; again, form (**BC**) and then **A**(**BC**). You will find that these products are the same; this illustrates the fact that matrix multiplication is *associative*. We can simply write **ABC** as the product of the three matrices, and it will not matter which two of them are multiplied first.

Matrix multiplication resembles ordinary multiplication of numbers in being associative, though it differs from it in being non-commutative.

Multiplication of relation matrices

As has already been seen, the transpose of a relation matrix gives the inverse relation.

Multiplying two relation matrices may give a composite relation.

Example 2 Alice has two daughters, Betty and Clara. Betty has two daughters, Dorothy and Ethel.

a Draw a diagram to illustrate the relation 'is the mother of' among the set {Alice, Betty, Clara, Dorothy, Ethel}. Draw dotted arrows for the relation 'is the sister of'.

b Compile matrices for these relations; call them **M** and **S**.

c Form the products **M**^{2} and **SM**, and name the relations they give.

Answer

a

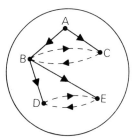

Figure 3.1

b

$$
\mathbf{M} = \begin{array}{c} \\ A \\ B \\ C \\ D \\ E \end{array}
\begin{array}{ccccc} A & B & C & D & E \\ \end{array}
\left(\begin{array}{ccccc}
0 & 1 & 1 & 0 & 0 \\
0 & 0 & 0 & 1 & 1 \\
0 & 0 & 0 & 0 & 0 \\
0 & 0 & 0 & 0 & 0 \\
0 & 0 & 0 & 0 & 0
\end{array}\right)
\qquad
\mathbf{S} =
\begin{array}{ccccc} A & B & C & D & E \\ \end{array}
\left(\begin{array}{ccccc}
0 & 0 & 0 & 0 & 0 \\
0 & 0 & 1 & 0 & 0 \\
0 & 1 & 0 & 0 & 0 \\
0 & 0 & 0 & 0 & 1 \\
0 & 0 & 0 & 1 & 0
\end{array}\right)
$$

c

$$
\mathbf{M}^2 = \begin{array}{c} \\ A \\ B \\ C \\ D \\ E \end{array}
\begin{array}{ccccc} A & B & C & D & E \\ \end{array}
\left(\begin{array}{ccccc}
0 & 0 & 0 & 1 & 1 \\
0 & 0 & 0 & 0 & 0 \\
0 & 0 & 0 & 0 & 0 \\
0 & 0 & 0 & 0 & 0 \\
0 & 0 & 0 & 0 & 0
\end{array}\right)
\qquad
\mathbf{SM} =
\begin{array}{ccccc} A & B & C & D & E \\ \end{array}
\left(\begin{array}{ccccc}
0 & 0 & 0 & 0 & 0 \\
0 & 0 & 0 & 0 & 0 \\
0 & 0 & 0 & 1 & 1 \\
0 & 0 & 0 & 0 & 0 \\
0 & 0 & 0 & 0 & 0
\end{array}\right)
$$

M^2 gives the relation 'is the mother of the mother of', i.e. 'is the grandmother of'.

SM gives the relation 'is the sister of the mother of', i.e. 'is the aunt of'.

Example 3 The map (Figure 3.2) shows the ferry services between Alport, Balport and Carport on one side of a channel and Downharbour and Eastharbour on the other, also the rail connections with the inland towns Northway, Outway and Pathway.

Form the matrices **F** and **R** which summarise the information about the ferry and rail connections. Form the product **FR**. What information does it give?

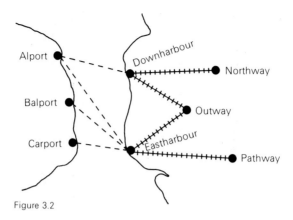

Figure 3.2

Answer

$$\mathbf{F} = \begin{array}{c} \\ A \\ B \\ C \end{array} \begin{array}{c} D \quad E \\ \begin{pmatrix} 1 & 1 \\ 0 & 1 \\ 0 & 1 \end{pmatrix} \end{array} \qquad \mathbf{R} = \begin{array}{c} \\ D \\ E \end{array} \begin{array}{c} N \quad O \quad P \\ \begin{pmatrix} 1 & 1 & 0 \\ 0 & 1 & 1 \end{pmatrix} \end{array}$$

$$\mathbf{FR} = \begin{array}{c} \\ A \\ B \\ C \end{array} \begin{array}{c} N \quad O \quad P \\ \begin{pmatrix} 1 & 2 & 1 \\ 0 & 1 & 1 \\ 0 & 1 & 1 \end{pmatrix} \end{array}$$

The matrix **FR** gives information about travel from Alport, Balport and Carport to Northway, Outway and Pathway. The element 2 shows that there are 2 routes from Alport to Outway – via Downharbour and via Eastharbour; the zero elements show that there are no routes to Northway from either Balport or Carport. The elements numbered 1 show that there is just one way of making each of the other journeys.

Exercise 3.3

1 Referring to Example 2 above, state what relations are given by the following matrices. (Do not actually form the matrices.)

  a M′,   b M′S,   c MM′,   d MS

2 Referring to Example 3 above: the ferry from Balport to Eastharbour is diverted to Downharbour, and a new rail link is built from Eastharbour to Northway. Form the matrices **F** and **R** and the product **FR** as they become after these changes, and describe the changes in the scheme of routes.

3 Ann, Bill, Chris and Don are sitting round a table. The matrix **M** gives the relation 'is sitting on the left of.'

$$\mathbf{M} = \begin{array}{c} \\ A \\ B \\ C \\ D \end{array} \begin{array}{cccc} A & B & C & D \\ \left(\begin{array}{cccc} 0 & 1 & 0 & 0 \\ 0 & 0 & 1 & 0 \\ 0 & 0 & 0 & 1 \\ 1 & 0 & 0 & 0 \end{array}\right) \end{array}$$

What relation is given by $\mathbf{M}'$?

Form the following matrix products, and state what relation each gives.
a MM',   b M², c M'²

Why are the last two answers the same?

4   Form the matrix **A**, which gives the relation 'is a factor of' between the domain set {2, 3, 5} and the range set {6, 10, 12, 15}; form also the matrix **B**, which gives the relation 'is a factor of' between the domain set {6, 10, 12, 15} and the range set {24, 30, 45, 48}. Form the product **AB**. What information does it give?

5   The map (Figure 3.3) shows the road and rail connections between three towns, A, B and C. Form the route matrices **W** for road and **R** for rail connections. Form the products **WR** and **RW**, and state what each represents. What would **W²** and **R²** represent?

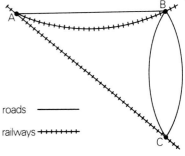

roads ———
railways +++++++

Figure 3.3

6   Form the matrices **X** and **Y**, giving the relations 'is opposite to' and 'is 90° clockwise from' between the members of the set {north, east, south, west}.

Form the products **X²** and **Y²**, and explain the results.

Form the products **XY** and **YX**, and explain why they are the same.

7   Form the matrix **T**, representing the relation 'is 1 more than' among the set {1, 2, 3, 4}. Form the matrices **T'** and **T²**, and state what relations they represent.

8   Form the matrix **U**, representing the relation 'is more than or equal to', among the set {1, 2, 3, 4}. What relation would be given by **U'**?

Defining **T** as in Question 7, form the matrices **TU** and **UT**. Why are they the same?

9 The matrix **R** represents the relation 'is at one end of' between the domain set of points {A, B, C} and the range set of lines {w, x, y, z} in Figure 3.4. Thus, the first row of **R** is (1 1 1 0), because A is at one end of w, x, and y, but not at one end of z. Complete the matrix **R**.

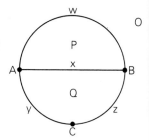

Figure 3.4

The matrix **S** represents the relation 'forms one boundary of' between the domain set {w, x, y, z} and the range set of regions {O, P, Q}. Thus, the first row of **S** is (1 1 0), because w forms a boundary of O and P but not of Q. Complete the matrix **S**.

Form the product **RS** and explain what it represents.

Form the product **RR'** and show that it contains the route matrix of the figure, regarded as a network.

10 Repeat Question 9 for Figure 3.5.

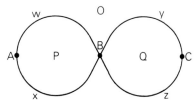

Figure 3.5

Chapter 4

Graphs

You have already done a considerable amount of work with graphs, perhaps including temperature graphs like those in the picture. A graph is a way of illustrating a mapping, usually a function: for example, the temperature graph illustrates the mapping $x \rightarrow$ temperature of patient x hours after midnight.

The temperature graph, and other graphs you have seen and drawn, serve a useful purpose: they give visual impressions of the effects of the mappings they illustrate. In this chapter we will study other uses of graphs.

Interpolation and extrapolation

The following information is to be illustrated by a graph.

A tank of liquid, A, is being heated while another tank, B, is allowed to cool. Their temperatures are recorded at ten-minute intervals and are as shown.

Time from starting, in minutes	0	10	20	30	40	50	60	70
Temperature of A, in °C		10	30	48	65	77	85	91	93
Temperature of B, in °C		100	75	58	44	35	29	24	20

The graphs are drawn by plotting the points corresponding to the given measurements, and joining them with smooth curves.

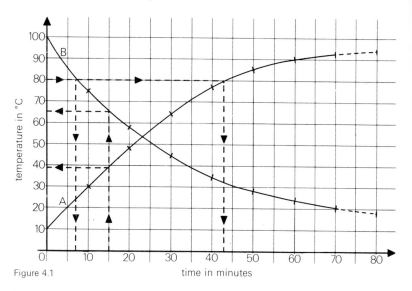

Figure 4.1   time in minutes

We can use the graphs to give tentative answers to certain questions.

1 What was the temperature of each tank 15 minutes after the start?

Draw a line vertically upwards from the 15 minute point on the time axis, to meet the graph of A. From the point where this line meets the curve, draw a horizontal line to the left to meet the temperature axis, and read off the temperature, which is 39°C. (See the dotted lines on the graph.) Continue the vertical line upwards to meet the graph of B, and proceed as before: this temperature is 65°C.

This process is called *interpolation*.

2 When was the temperature of tank A 80°C, and when was the temperature of tank B 80°C?

Draw a line horizontally to the right from the 80°C point on the temperature axis, to meet both graphs. From the points where this line meets the curves, draw lines vertically downwards to meet the time axis, and read off the times, which are 43 minutes and 7 minutes from the start.

This process is called *back-interpolation*.

3 When were the tanks at the same temperature?

This is shown by the point where the graphs cross: it can be seen that the tanks were at the same temperature after 23 minutes, when the temperature of each was 53°C.

Of course these questions cannot be answered with complete certainty, because we cannot be absolutely certain that the temperatures did change exactly as the graphs indicate; we only know their values at the instants when they were measured. However, we know that it is very probable that the temperatures did vary smoothly, in the way that the graphs suggest, and the answers are almost certainly correct to a useful degree of accuracy.

If we ask questions like

4 What will be the temperature of each body 80 minutes after the start?

we shall have to draw the graphs further (see the dotted curves) in the direction we think they will go, if they continue the same tendencies as before. This gives answers of 94°C and 18°C.

This process is called *extrapolation*. It is far more hazardous than interpolation, because it is far less certain how the temperature will vary after all the measurements have been completed, than it was how the temperature would vary in between readings. However, extrapolation is often more useful, because it may enable us to make some sort of prediction of how things will develop in the future.

Scales

Before you draw any of the graphs required in the next exercise, you will have to choose your scales. As a rule, the larger the scale of the graph, the more accurate the results obtained from it are likely to be, so choose the largest possible scale subject to the following conditions.

1 The graph must not be too large to fit onto the paper that is being used.

2 The scale should be simple, so that no awkward numerical calculations are needed. Ideally, each square should represent 1 unit, or 10 units, or some power of 10, but 1 square to 2, 5, 20, 50, 200 or 500 units are acceptable scales.

For example, if the quantity being plotted along one axis has a range of 0 to 30 units, and the width of the graph-paper is 18 cm (in centimetre squares), a scale of 1 cm to 2 units would probably be best, but if the range is 0 to 50, it may be best to reduce the scale to 1 cm to 5 units, even though this will use little more than half of the width of the paper.

Exercise 4.1

Keep the graphs you draw in answering questions marked †, as they will be needed later.

1† Two experiments are performed, in each of which a ball rolls in a groove in a sloping board. In the first experiment (A), the ball is released from a point 200 cm from P, the lowest point of the groove, and rolls down. In the second experiment (B), the ball is projected up the groove from P. In each case the distances of the ball above P are measured at intervals of 2 seconds, with results as shown.

Time in seconds	0	2	4	6	8	10
Distance in cm (A)	200	192	168	128	72	0
Distance in cm (B)	0	68	120	156	176	180

Draw graphs to illustrate these results (both on the same axes and with the same scales), and use them to answer these questions.

a In each experiment, where was the ball
(i) 3 s, (ii) 5 s, (iii) 7 s after the start?
b In each experiment, when was the ball
(i) 50 cm, (ii) 100 cm, (iii) 150 cm above P?
c If both experiments were performed at once, using two balls, where and when would the balls collide?

2 The following table, of a kind used by insurance companies, shows the expectation of life of males and females in the United Kingdom.

Age in years	0	10	20	30	40	50	60	70	80
Expectation (M)	69.4	61.0	51.3	41.7	32.2	23.3	15.6	9.6	5.6 years
Expectation (F)	75.6	66.9	57.1	47.3	37.7	28.6	20.2	12.8	7.1 years

Draw graphs to illustrate this information, and use them to estimate

a the expectation of life of each sex at 15, at 35 and at 55,
b for each sex, the age at which the expectation of life is 30 years,

c the age at which the expectation of life is 5 years longer for a woman than for a man,
d the expectation of life for each sex at 85.

3 The table gives the average weekly earnings of full-time manual workers in the U.K. for the years 1970 to 1977, 1974 being omitted.

Year	1970	1971	1972	1973	1975	1976	1977
Earnings males,	£28.05	30.93	35.82	40.92	59.58	66.97	72.89
Earnings females,	£13.99	15.80	18.30	21.16	34.19	40.61	44.31

Draw graphs to illustrate this information, and use them to make an estimate of

a the average weekly earnings of each sex in 1974,
b the average weekly earnings of each sex in 1978.
(Note that with this graph there can be no interpolation *between years*.)

4 Draw a graph of $x \to \tan x$, using the following values.

x, in degrees	0	20	40	60	80
$\tan x$	0	0.364	0.839	1.732	5.67

Use your graph to estimate the values of $\tan 30°$, $\tan 50°$ and $\tan 70°$, and compare the results with those obtained from tables.

Also use your graph to estimate the values of $\tan^{-1} 0.75$ (i.e. the angle whose tangent is 0.75), $\tan^{-1} 1.5$ and $\tan^{-1} 2$. Again compare your results with those from tables.

5† The table shows the population of the U.K. in certain years.

Year	1901	1911	1921	1931	1951	1961	1971
Population (millions) ·	38.2	42.1	44.0	46.0	50.2	52.7	55.5

Draw a graph to illustrate this information, and use it to estimate the population **a** in 1941, **b** in 1981.

6 The table shows the time of sunset in London on the first day of each month. (All times are G.M.T.)

Month	Jan.	Feb.	Mar.	Apr.	May	Jun.
Time of sunset	4.02	4.49	5.40	6.33	7.23	8.07 p.m.

Month	Jul.	Aug.	Sep.	Oct.	Nov.	Dec.
Time of sunset	8.21	7.49	6.48	5.39	4.34	3.55 p.m.

Draw a graph to illustrate this information, and use it to make an estimate of

a the times of sunset on 15 January, on 15 April and on 15 August,
b the days on which the sun sets at 5 p.m., and those on which it sets at 6 p.m.,
c the latest time at which the sun ever sets, and the day on which this occurs.

7 A reservoir has a gauge which measures the depth at a certain point, and the following table is supposed to give the volume of water in the reservoir (in millions of litres, MI) for various depths.

Depth in m	1	2	3	4	5	6	7	8	9	10
Vol. in MI	2	8	40	110	230	414	648	1010	1380	2020

Draw the graph of depth→volume, and use it to estimate

a the volume when the depth is 3.5 m, and the volume when the depth is 7.5 m,
b the depth when the volume is 200 MI, and the depth when it is 600 MI.

Later it was found that, as a result of changes in the bed of the reservoir, the table of volumes was inaccurate, and a fresh survey gave the following results.

Depth in m	1	2	3	4	5	6	7	8	9	10
Vol. in MI	2	40	120	220	360	500	672	904	1200	1560

Draw another graph on the same sheet, and find the effect the revised table has on the answers to a and b.

Find the depth for which the old and revised tables give the same volume, and find this volume.

8 The table shows the world records for running certain distances (as they were at the time of writing).

Distance in metres	100	200	400	800	1000	1500	2000
Time in seconds	9.9	19.5	43.8	104.3	136.2	213.1	296.2

Draw a graph to illustrate this information, and use it to estimate what the record might be if there were an event a of 600 m, b of 1200 m. By extrapolation, make an estimate of the possible record for 3000 m.

9 One of the graphs in Figure 4.2 is that of a self-inverse mapping, the others are (not in this order) of a one-to-one, a many-to-one, a one-to-many and a many-to-many mapping. State which is which.

Sketch the graph of the inverse of each of these mappings, assuming that the scale is the same on both axes. What transformation transforms the graph of a mapping onto that of its inverse?

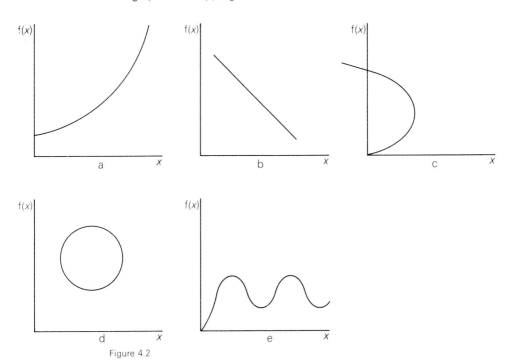

Figure 4.2

Straight-line graphs

The graph drawn to illustrate experimental or other observations may prove to be a straight line. If it is a straight line, the methods of Chapter 1 can be used to find its equation, and so to find the relation between the quantities involved. The relation is then said to be a *linear relation*, and the associated mapping is a *linear mapping*, though as a linear mapping is always one-to-one, it is more usually called a *linear function*.

If it is known beforehand that the relation is linear, it can be found by the methods of Chapter 1 without drawing the graph at all. The purpose of the graph may be to find out whether the relation is in fact linear. It may happen that the points plotted from the observations do not quite lie on a straight line, but are near enough so to make it seem likely that they would lie on a straight line but for small experimental errors. It may then be possible to draw, by estimation, the line on which they most nearly lie (called the *line of closest fit*), and to use this to find the relation.

Example 1   A spiral spring is suspended from one end, and to the other end is attached a scale-pan into which weights can be put. The length of the spring is measured after each additional load has been put into the scale-pan, with results as follows.

Total load (kg)	0.5	1	1.5	2	2.5	3	3.5
Length of spring (cm)	30.1	36.3	42.7	49.0	55.2	61.5	69.8

Draw a graph of load against length, and find for what range of values of the load the relation between the two is approximately linear. Draw

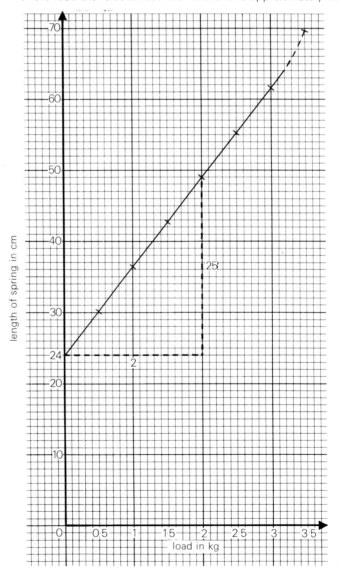

Figure 4.3

the line of closest fit, and find the relation between the load (W kg) and the length (X cm) for the range of values for which the relation is linear.

Answer

From the graph it can be seen that the relation is linear within the range $W \leqslant 3$, but not for a range including $W = 3.5$.

The gradient of the line is $\dfrac{25.0}{2} = 12.5$, and it cuts the X-axis at $(0, 24)$.

The equation of the line is therefore $X = 12.5W + 24$, and this is also the required relation.

Exercise 4.2

1 Plot on a graph the values of h and t given in the following table, and find for what range of values of t the relation between h and t is linear. Use the graph to find this relation.

t	3	4	5	6	7	8	9	10	11
h	0	7.2	9.0	10.8	12.6	14.4	16.2	18.5	21.3

2 In an experiment with a pulley system, the effort (E kg) required to lift a load of L kg was found for various values of L, with results as shown.

L	5	10	15	20	25	30
E	3.6	4.8	6.1	7.4	8.6	9.9

Draw the graph of $L{\rightarrow}E$, and show that there is, very nearly, a linear relation of the form $E = mL + c$, and find the values of m and c.

3 A person who frequently uses a certain taxi, notes the distance (d) in kilometres and the fare (£F) for each journey, the results being as shown.

d	1	1.5	2.5	3	4	6.5
F	1.20	1.50	2.10	2.80	3.00	4.50

Draw the graph of $d{\rightarrow}F$. On one journey the wrong fare was charged: which journey was it, and what should the fare have been? Use your graph to find the relation between d and F.

4 A clock can be regulated by turning a knob which has a pointer moving over a scale of numbers. The table shows the number of minutes (m) that the clock gains per week, for various settings (r) of the pointer.

r	1	3	4	6	7
m	-7	-2	$\frac{1}{2}$	$5\frac{1}{2}$	8

Plot the graph of $r{\rightarrow}m$, and show that the relation between the two quantities is linear. For what setting of the pointer is the clock exactly right? Find a formula giving m in terms of r.

5   A metal bar is heated, causing it to expand. Readings of length and temperature are taken at various times, with the following results.

Temperature in degrees C	10	60	100	140	200	250
Length in metres	2.100	2.102	2.1035	2.105	2.1075	2.110

If a graph is plotted of temperature against length, the changes in the length will hardly be observable. Suggest a quantity that could be plotted, instead of the length itself, to give a more satisfactory graph. Plot the points, draw the line of closest fit, and find a relation between temperature and length.

6   The table shows the ranges of weights of eggs of various grades.

Grade	7	6	5	4	3	2	1
Weight in g	Under 45	45–50	50–55	55–60	60–65	65–70	Over 70

On the same axes draw two graphs*

a   grade→minimum weight of egg,
b   grade→maximum weight of egg.

Find the two relations between the grade and the weight, and complete the statement, 'An egg of grade n must weigh more than ...g (if $2 \leqslant n \leqslant 7$) and less than ...g (if $1 \leqslant n \leqslant 6$).

7   A train is travelling at a steady speed when the brakes are applied and the train is brought to a stop. The speed is recorded at 10 second intervals, the recordings being as follows.

Time in seconds	0	10	20	30	40	50	60	70
Speed in km/h	102	102	94	71	48	25	2	0

Draw a graph of time→speed, assuming that this graph consists of three straight lines. Find the time that elapsed between the instant recording was started and the instant the brakes were applied. Find also the time that elapsed between the instant the brakes were applied and the instant the train stopped.

Find a relation between the speed (v km/h) of the train during the period when it was slowing down, and the time (t s) measured from the start of recording.

---

*   These graphs should, strictly, consist of numbers of separate points, since there can be no intermediate values, but it is permissible to draw a straight line through the points to show that the relation is linear.

8 A faulty weighing machine is checked by loading it with known weights and noting its readings. The results are as follows.

True weight in kgf (W)   0   1   2   3   4   5   6   7

Reading in kgf (x)   0   0.74 1.91 3.08 4.25 5.42 6.59 7.76
Draw a suitable graph and find

a the approximate range of values of W for which the relation between W and x is linear,
b the weight (apart from 0) which the machine gives correctly,
c a relation between W and x for values of W in the range found in **a**.

9 Make 4 dots on a sheet of paper, and join them with a number of lines; each line must begin and end on a dot, and no two lines must cross (see Figure 4.4).

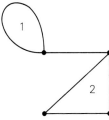

Note the number of lines (n), and the number of regions formed by the lines (in the figure there are 5 lines and 2 regions).

Figure 4.4

Repeat this several times and draw a graph of $n \rightarrow r$.* Find the relation between n and r.

Repeat the whole process with other numbers of dots (drawing all the graphs on the same sheet). Find a relation between n, r and the number of dots (d).

10 On squared paper draw a closed figure by joining 'lattice points', i.e. the vertices of the squares. The joining lines must not cross each other, and no lattice point must be inside the figure (see Figure 4.5). Repeat with other figures.

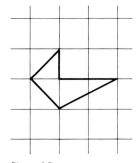

Figure 4.5

Find the area (A) of each figure, in terms of the squares of the paper, and plot a graph* of $n \rightarrow A$, where n is the number of lattice points on the perimeter of the figure. Find the relation between n and A.

Repeat the whole process but this time draw figures with just one lattice point inside each. Draw a fresh graph on the same sheet as the first one, and find the new relation. Repeat again with varying numbers of lattice points inside the figure, and find the relation between n, A and I, the number of lattice points inside the figure.

Algebraic graphs – solving equations and inequalities

If a graph of an algebraic function is drawn, interpolation, back-interpolation and the intersections of the graph with other graphs that can be drawn, can be used for many purposes, mainly for solving equations and inequalities.

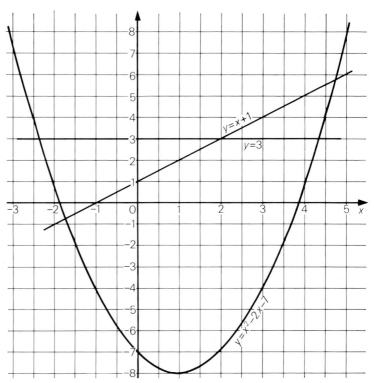

Figure 4.6

The graph in Figure 4.6 is that of $f: x \rightarrow x^2 - 2x - 7$, or $y = x^2 - 2x - 7$. The side of a square represents half a unit on the x-axis, and one unit on the y-axis.

Interpolation can be used to find values of $f(x)$ other than those which were calculated in order to plot the graph, e.g. $f(1.5) = -7.75$. Of course, these values could be found by calculation – more accurately, but less quickly.

Back-interpolation can be used to solve equations of the form $x^2 - 2x - 7 = k$, where k is a number. In the diagram the line $y = 3$ is drawn, so that the equation $x^2 - 2x - 7 = 3$ can be solved: the roots can be seen to be approximately $x=4.32$ and $x=-2.32$ (or it can be said that the solution set is $\{4.32, -2.32\}$). We can write $f^{-1}(3)=4.32$ or -2.32, as f^{-1} is a one-to-many mapping, and not a function.

It can be seen from the graph that $f^{-1}(k)$ has two values when $k>-8$, one value when $k=-8$, and no value at all when $k<-8$. In other words, the equation $x^2-2x-7=k$ has two roots when $k>-8$, one root when $k=-8$, and no roots (its solution set is $\emptyset$) when $k<-8$.

Intersections with straight-line graphs. By drawing straight-line graphs, the graph of x^2-2x-7 can be used to solve other equations, in fact, to solve any quadratic equation at all. In Figure 4.6 the line $y=x+1$ has been drawn, crossing the curve where $x+1=x^2-2x-7$. This is the equation whose roots are given by the intersections of the two graphs: they are seen to be $x=4.70$ and $x=-1.70$.

The equation $x+1=x^2-2x-7$ is the same as the equation $x^2-3x-8=0$. In order to use the graph of x^2-2x-7 to solve the equation $x^2-3x-8=0$, the equation has first to be rewritten in the form $x+1=x^2-2x-7$, and then the graphs can be used to solve it.

Inequalities. The graph of $f(x)$ crosses the line $y=3$ where $x=-2.32$ and $x=4.32$, as has already been noted. It can be seen that between these values of x, $f(x)<3$, whereas for other values of x, $f(x)>3$. Thus, the solution set of the inequality $f(x)<3$ is $\{x:-2.32<x<4.32\}$, and the solution set of $f(x)>3$ is

$$\{x:x<-2.32\}\cup\{x:x>4.32\}$$

In the same way it can be seen that the solution set of $f(x)<x+1$ (i.e. of $x^2-2x-7<x+1$, or $x^2-3x-8<0$) is $x:-1.70<x<4.70$.

Adapting equations to be solved by graphs

It has already been shown that the equation $x^2-3x-8=0$ has to be rewritten $x^2-2x-7=x+1$ in order that it may be solved by the graph that has been drawn. This is done by adding and subtracting terms to and from both sides of the equation in order to bring the left-hand side to x^2-2x-7, the function whose graph has been plotted.

Thus $x^2-3x-8=0$

Add x to both sides:

$$x^2-2x-8=x$$

Add 1 to both sides:

$$x^2-2x-7=x+1$$

The same treatment can be given to any quadratic equation: take for example $x^2+3x-2=0$. To make the left-hand side into x^2-2x-7, we must subtract $5x$ and subtract 5, giving

$$x^2 - 2x - 7 = -5x - 5$$

In order to solve this equation, the line $y = -5x - 5$ must be drawn: the intersections of this line with the graph of $f(x)$ will give the solution of $x^2 + 3x - 2 = 0$.

Exercise 4.3

1 Rewrite each of the following equations so that it can be solved by finding the intersections of a straight-line graph with the graph of $y = x^2 - 2x - 7$, and give the equation of the straight-line graph in each case.

a $x^2 - 2x = 0$ **c** $x^2 - 2x - 3 = 0$ **e** $x^2 + x - 5 = 0$
b $x^2 - 2x - 5 = 0$ **d** $x^2 - 3x - 2 = 0$ **f** $x^2 - 5x + 1 = 0$

2 **a** Write down the equation that would be solved by drawing the graphs of $y = x^2 - 2x$ and $y = 3x + 1$, and simplify your answer as much as possible.

b Repeat **a** but with the graphs of $y = 2x^2 + 3x$ and $y = x + 6$.

c Repeat **a** but with the graphs of $y = \dfrac{6}{x}$ and $y = x + 3$.

d Repeat **a** but with the graphs of $y = \dfrac{3}{x+1}$ and $y = 2x - 1$.

3 In each of the following cases, find the equation of the straight-line graph that would have to be drawn to solve the second equation, if the graph of the first equation were already drawn.

a $y = x^2$; $x^2 - 3x - 5 = 0$
b $y = x^2 + 2x - 3$; $x^2 + x - 5 = 0$
c $y = x^3 - 3x^2$; $x^3 - 3x^2 + 2x - 5 = 0$

d $y = \dfrac{3}{x-1}$, $x^2 - x - 3 = 0$

e $y = \dfrac{5}{x}$; $x^2 + 2x - 5 = 0$

Drawing the graph

Before the points for a graph can be plotted, the values of y have to be calculated, corresponding to the values of x that are to be used. It is often useful to draw up a table: for example, in calculating the values for $y = x^2 - 2x - 7$, the following table could be constructed.

$x=$	-3	-2	-1	0	1	2	3	4	5
$x^2=$	9	4	1	0	1	4	9	16	25
$-2x=$	6	4	2	0	-2	-4	-6	-8	-10
$-7=$	-7	-7	-7	-7	-7	-7	-7	-7	-7
$y=$	8	1	-4	-7	-8	-7	-4	1	8

Each row corresponds to one term of the function whose graph is to be plotted: it is easiest to work out, one row at a time, all the values of x^2 first and then all the values of $-2x$, while the -7's need no calculation. The three rows are then added to give the values of y. (Note that the **top** row, the row with values of x, is **not** added in.)

When you have calculated all the values of y, decide on the scale, and on how to place the axes so that all the points will go on your graph paper. Plot the points and join them up with the smoothest possible curve (**not** with a series of straight lines). If the shape of the curve between two points is uncertain, it may be advisable to plot another point between them.

Exercise 4.4

1 For the equation $y=g(x)=5+x-x^2$, calculate the values of y for

$$x=-3, -2, -1, 0, 1, 2, 3 \text{ and } 4.$$

Plot the points and draw the graph.

a Use the graph to solve the equations
(i) $g(x)=0$,   (ii) $g(x)=2$.
b What is the value of y for which $g^{-1}(y)$ has only one value?
c Draw the graph of $y=1-x$, and write down the values of x at the point where this graph cuts that of $g(x)$. Write down and simplify the equation whose roots are these values of x.
d Find what straight line must be drawn so that its intersections with the graph of $g(x)$ give the roots of $5-x-x^2=0$. Draw this line, and find the roots of this equation. Write down the range of values of x for which $5-x-x^2>0$.

2 For the equation $y=h(x)=\dfrac{6x}{5-x}$, calculate the values of y for integral values of x from -3 to $+3$ inclusive. Plot the points and draw the graph.

a Use the graph to solve the equations (i) $h(x)=2$, (ii) $h(x)=-2$.
b Draw the graph of $y=3-x$, and write down the value of x at the point where this graph cuts that of $h(x)$. Write down and simplify the

equation, one of whose roots is this value of x.

c Find the range of values of x for which $h(x) < 3 - x$, and $x < 3$.

3 Copy and complete the table of values for $y = \frac{1}{2}(x^2 - 2x - 4)$

x		-2	-1	0	1	2	3	4	5
x^2		4		0	1			16	25
$-2x$		4		0	-2			-8	-10
-4		-4		-4	-4			-4	-4
$x^2 - 2x - 4$		4		-4	-5			4	11
y		2		-2	-2.5			2	5.5

Using a scale of 2 cm to represent 1 unit on each axis, draw the graph of y for values of x between -2 and 5 inclusive.

Use your graph to find approximate solutions of the equation $x^2 - 2x - 4 = 0$.

On the same axes and using the same scales, draw the graph of $y = x - 1$. Write down and express in its simplest form the equation whose roots are given by the x-coordinates of the points of intersection of the two graphs. From your graph, determine the approximate value of each of these roots.

(*LD*)

4 Copy and complete the given table of values of the function

$$y = \frac{x^2}{2} + \frac{18}{x} - 10$$

for the values indicated. In the table, values have been corrected to one place of decimals.

x	1	1.5	2	3	4	4.5	5
$\dfrac{x^2}{2}$	0.5	1.1		4.5		10.1	
$\dfrac{18}{x}$	18	12		6		4	
-10	-10	-10		-10		-10	
y	8.5	3.1		0.5		4.1	

Draw the graph of the function for values of x from 1 to 5 using scales of 2 cm to 1 unit on both axes.

a From your graph, find the value of x giving the least value of y and this least value of y.

b By drawing a suitable straight-line graph, find the positive values of x which satisfy $\dfrac{x^2}{2}+\dfrac{18}{x}-10=x$. (LD)

5 If $y=x^2-6x+8$, find the values of y corresponding to $x=1$, 3 and 4. You are given the values $y=8$, 0, 3 and 8 when $x=0$, 2, 5 and 6 respectively.

Taking 2 cm to represent one unit on each axis, draw the graph of $y=x^2-6x+8$, for values of x from 0 to 6 inclusive.

Use your graph to find the range of values of x for which x^2-6x+8 is negative. By adding a suitable straight line to your graph, solve the equation

$$x^2-6x+8=\frac{3x}{5} \qquad\qquad (CB)$$

6 If $y=x^3-3x^2$, find the values of y corresponding to $x=-2$, 1, 2 and 3. You are given the values $y=-4$, 0 and 16 when $x=-1$, 0 and 4 respectively.

Using a scale of 2 cm to represent one unit on the x-axis and 2 cm to represent 4 units on the y-axis, draw the graph of $y=x^3-3x^2$ for values of x from -2 to $+4$ inclusive. Use your graph to solve the equation

$$x^3-3x^2=2 \qquad\qquad (CB)$$

7 Draw the graphs of $y=x(x-3)$ and $y=\dfrac{4}{x+4}$ for values of x from -1 to 4, using the same axes for both graphs, and taking 2 cm to represent one unit on both axes.

Use your graphs to estimate two values of x for which

$$x(x-3)(x+4)=4 \qquad\qquad (OC)$$

8 Taking 2 cm to represent 1 unit on each axis, draw the graph of

$$y=\frac{6x}{x+1}$$

plotting the points for which x is 0, $\frac{1}{2}$, 1, 2, 3, 4 and 5.

Using the same axes and scales, draw the graph of $y=x+1$.

From your graphs, find

a the range of positive values of x for which

$$\frac{6x}{x+1} < \tfrac{7}{2}$$

b the range of positive values of x for which

$$\frac{6x}{x+1} > x+1$$

c the solutions of the equation $6x = (x+1)^2$.   (OC)

9 Using a scale of 2 cm to 1 unit on both axes, draw the graph of
$y = \dfrac{x^2+8}{x+2}$ for values of x from -1 to 6.

Find from your graph

a the least value of y,
b the value of x which gives the least value of y,
c the set of values of x for which $y < 5$ (giving your answer in the form $a < x < b$, where a and b are numbers to be found).

10 Copy and complete the following table of values of the expression
$x - 4 + \dfrac{3}{x}$.

x	0.5	1	1.5	2	2.5	3	3.5	4
$x-4$		-3		-2			-0.5	
$\dfrac{3}{x}$		3		1.5			0.86	
$x-4+\dfrac{3}{x}$		0		-0.5			0.36	

Hence draw the graph of $y = x - 4 + \dfrac{3}{x}$ for values of x from 0.5 to 4, taking 4 cm as the unit on both axes.

Find, from your graph, the least value that y takes, and the corresponding value of x.

Find, in the form $a < x < b$, where a and b are numbers to be read off from your graph, the set of values of x for which y is less than 0.25.

                    (OC)

Gradient of a curve

In Chapter 1, we saw that if an object is moving with a steady speed, the graph of time against distance travelled by the object is a straight line whose gradient gives the speed with which the object is moving. If the speed is not steady, the graph will be a curve, whose gradient is different at every point. Figure 4.7 is a distance–time graph for an object moving in this way.

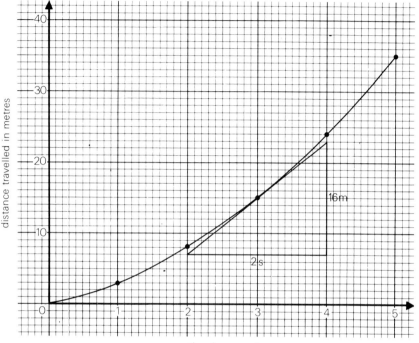

Figure 4.7   time in seconds

It can be seen that the speed is increasing, as a longer distance is travelled in any given second than in the previous second: for example, between $t=2$ and $t=3$, the distance travelled is 7 m, whereas between $t=3$ and $t=4$, the distance travelled is 9 m.

To find the speed *at a particular instant*, we have to find the gradient of the curve at the corresponding point, and this is done by drawing a *tangent* to the curve at that point, as is shown in the figure: a tangent has been drawn to the curve at the point where $t=3$. A tangent is a line that *touches* the curve, nearly always without crossing it.

The gradient of the tangent gives the gradient of the curve at the point where the tangent touches it. The tangent can be drawn any length. In finding the gradient, it is convenient to mark points on the tangent where the time-coordinates are whole numbers (usually points where the tangent crosses vertical lines of the graph-paper), so that the denominator of the gradient-fraction is a whole number. In the diagram the gradient of the tangent is $\dfrac{16}{2}=8$, so the speed at $t=3$ is 8 m/s.

Gradients of curves, like those of straight lines, may represent quantities other than speeds, according to the quantities being plotted on the graph. Or the gradient may be simply a number, if the graph does not represent any particular physical quantities.

Exercise 4.5

1 Draw the graph of time (t seconds)→distance (s metres) from the following table.

t	0	1	2	3	4	5	6
s	0	11	20	27	32	35	36

Draw tangents and find the speed when $t=2$ and the speed when $t=4$. What is the average speed for the whole 6 seconds?

2 Draw the graph of time (t seconds)→distance (s metres) from the following table.

t	0	1	2	3	4	5	6	7
s	0	7	10	12	12	10	7	0

Draw tangents and find the speeds when $t=2$ and when $t=5$. When is the object momentarily at rest, and how far has it travelled by then?

3 If a stone is allowed to fall freely, the distance, d metres, that it has fallen from its starting-point t seconds after it has been dropped, is given approximately by $d=5t^2$. Find the values of d for $t=0, 1, 2, \ldots 8$, and draw a graph. Find the speed with which the stone is falling when $t=2$, and its speeds when $t=4$ and when $t=6$.

4 In an experiment, a tank holds V litres of water t minutes after the start of the experiment, where $V=t(10-t)$ and $t<10$.

Draw the graph of $t \rightarrow V$ for values of t from 0 to 10. What quantity is represented by the gradient of this graph, and in what units is it measured? Find the values of this quantity when $t=2$ and when $t=7$.

When does the tank hold most water, and how much water is in it then? What is the gradient of the graph at the point corresponding to this instant?

5 A searchlight points vertically upwards and makes a patch of light on a horizontal cloud-base 500 m above. It is then tilted so that at time t seconds it makes an angle $t°$ with the vertical. Show that the patch of light has then moved through a distance d metres, where $d=500 \tan t°$. Draw the graph of $t \rightarrow d$ for $t=0, 10, 20, \ldots 60$. Find the speed with which the patch of light is moving when $t=20$, and the speed when $t=40$.

6 Use the graph you drew to answer Question 1 of Exercise 4.1 (page 48) to find the speed of each ball

   a 4 seconds, and **b** 6 seconds after the start.

7 Measure the gradient of the graph you drew to answer Question 5 of Exercise 4.1 (page 49), at the point corresponding to 1931. What information does this gradient give?

8 Draw the graph of $y = x^2 - 3x$ for values of x from -1 to 4. Find the gradients of the graph at the points where $x = 0$ and where $x = 2$. Give the coordinates of the point on the graph at which the gradient is zero.

9 Draw the graph of $y = x + \dfrac{6}{x}$ for values of x from 1 to 6. Find the gradients of the graph at the points where $y = 6$. Give the coordinates of the point on the graph at which the gradient is zero.

10 Use the graph you drew to answer Question 1 of Exercise 4.4 (page 59). Measure the gradient of this graph at the point where $x = -2$, and its gradient at the point where $x = +2$.

11 Use the graph you drew to answer Question 6 of Exercise 4.4 (page 61). Measure the gradients of this graph at the points where $x = -1$ and where $x = 3$. Give the coordinates of the point on the curve at which the gradient is zero.

12 Copy and complete the following table for $y = 2x^2 - 3x - 4$

x	-2	-1	0	1	2	3	4
$2x^2$	8				8		
$-3x$	6						-12
-4	-4	-4					
y		1			-2		

Draw a graph of $x \rightarrow y$, using a scale of 2 cm to 1 unit for x and 1 cm to 1 unit for y.

Using your graph, or otherwise,

   a solve the equation $2x^2 - 3x - 6 = 0$.

   b find the gradient of the graph at the points where $x = -1$ and $x = 3$,

   c find the value of x for which the gradient of the graph is zero.   *(LC)*

Chapter 5

Exponential Functions and Logarithms

The drawing illustrates the well-known story about the invention of chess. It is said that chess was invented to entertain a bored oriental monarch: so delighted was this monarch with the game that he told the inventor to name his own reward. The wily inventor asked only for one grain of wheat on the first square of the board, two on the second, four on the third, eight on the fourth, and so on for all the 64 squares of the board. The king thought this a modest request, but when his ministers came to calculate how much grain was needed, they found that all the wheat in the kingdom would not suffice.

Let us start a table:

No. of square	No. of grains
1	1
2	2
3	4
4	8
5	16
6	32
7	64
8	128
9	256
10	512
11	1024

This will do to go on with: although we have only reached the 11th square, the number of grains is already over a thousand. By the 21st square it will be over a million, by the 31st, over a thousand million, and we are still not half way through all the 64 squares. You can calculate the total number of grains is you wish, but it will take you quite a long time, even if you have a calculator.

The mapping 'number of square→number of grains' may be written $x{\rightarrow}2^{x-1}$, and is an example of an **exponential mapping**: as it is one-to-one, it may be called an **exponential function**.

Other examples of exponential mappings are

$$x{\rightarrow}2^x, \ x{\rightarrow}3^x, \ x{\rightarrow}3 \times 2^x, \ x{\rightarrow}2 \times 3^{x+2}, \ x{\rightarrow}(\tfrac{1}{2})^x.$$

So far, an exponential mapping has been defined only if the domain is a set of positive integers.

Example 1   f is an exponential mapping such that $f(1)=6$, $f(2)=18$, $f(3)=54$. Express f in the form $x{\rightarrow}\ldots$ and find $f(4)$ and (7).

Answer
Since $f(2)=3f(1)$, and $f(3)=3f(2)$, $f(x)$ must contain a factor 3^x. Since $f(1)=6$ whereas $3^1=3$, it must be that $f(x)=2 \times 3^x$, i.e. $f{:}x{\rightarrow}2 \times 3^x$.

$$f(4)=2 \times 3^4 = 2 \times 81 = 162$$

$$f(7)=2 \times 3^7 = 2 \times 2187 = 4374$$

Exercise 5.1

1   For the domain set {1, 2, 3, 4}, give the range sets of the following functions.

a $x{\rightarrow}2^x$ **c** $x{\rightarrow}3 \times 2^x$ **e** $x{\rightarrow}(\tfrac{1}{2})^x$

b $x{\rightarrow}3^x$ **d** $x{\rightarrow}2 \times 3^{x+2}$

2 Find the exponential functions that map the domain set {1, 2, 3, 4} onto each of the following range sets.

a {4, 16, 64, 256}   **d** {5, 10, 20, 40}   **f** $\{\frac{1}{3}, \frac{1}{9}, \frac{1}{27}, \frac{1}{81}\}$,

b {5, 25, 125, 625}   **e** {4, 2, 1, $\frac{1}{2}$}   **g** $\{\frac{1}{10}, \frac{1}{2}, 2\frac{1}{2}, 12\frac{1}{2}\}$

c {8, 16, 32, 64}

3 A large sheet of paper is 0.1 mm thick. It is folded repeatedly. Find the overall thickness of the folded paper after it has been folded

a 3 times   **b** 6 times   **c** 10 times

4 A forest fire burns in such a way that at the end of any hour the area destroyed is twice what it was at the beginning of that hour. At 12 noon, 1 ha has been burnt: if the fire rages unchecked, find the area that will have been destroyed

a by 2 p.m.   **b** by 6 p.m.   **c** by 8 p.m.

The area of the forest is 1000 ha; estimate the time by which the whole forest will have been burnt, if the fire is not controlled.

Find also the area that had been burnt

d by 11 a.m.   **e** by 10 a.m.

5 For the function $f(x) = 4 \times (1\frac{1}{2})^x$, find $f(1)$, $f(2)$ and $f(3)$.

6 If $g:x \rightarrow 100 \times 1.1^x$, find $g(1)$, $g(2)$ and $g(3)$.

7 A population of bacteria increases in such a way that at the end of every hour the number of bacteria is $1\frac{1}{2}$ times what it was at the beginning of that hour. At 8 a.m. there were 8×10^6 bacteria: find how many there were

a at 9 a.m.   **c** at 12 noon   **e** at 6 a.m.

b at 10 a.m.   **d** at 7 a.m.

Find the function that maps (number of hours, h, after 8 a.m.) onto (number of bacteria).

8 The amount for which a house is insured is 'index-linked' so that it increases by 10% each year. If this amount was £10 000 in 1976, find what it was in 1977, in 1978 and in 1979. Find in what year it first exceeds £15 000.

9 A mass of hot metal is cooling so that at the end of each hour its temperature (°C) is $\frac{1}{3}$ of what it was at the beginning of that hour. At midnight its temperature was 729°C: find its temperature at 1 a.m., 2 a.m. and 3 a.m. During what hour does its temperature first fall below 5°C?

Find the function that maps (number of hours after midnight$=t$) onto temperature in °C.

10 The mapping f:$x{\rightarrow}k^x$ is one-to-one for all non-negative values of k except two. What are these two values, and what kind of mapping is f if k has either of these values?

A problem with discs

Find some discs of different sizes, coins will do. Name them 1, 2, 3 ... starting with the smallest. Draw three circles, A, B and C, each larger than the largest disc.

To start with, use only discs 1 and 2. Put disc 2 in circle A, and disc 1 on disc 2. The first problem is to transfer the discs to circle C, subject to these conditions.

1 Only one disc at a time may be moved.

2 A disc can only be put on top of a larger disc, or into an empty circle.

With only the two discs, the problem is easy: move 1 to B, move 2 to C, put 1 on 2. This takes 3 moves.

Now use discs 1, 2 and 3: again start with them all in A, 1 on top and 3 at the bottom, and transfer them to C in as few moves as possible. Note the number of moves needed.

Now try it with four discs, and note the number of moves.

You can go on doing this with as many more discs as you have time for (and can find discs for), but you will find that the number of moves needed increases rapidly as the number of discs increases.

What is the function that maps number of discs (d) onto number of moves needed?

Negative indices

In Chapter 6 of Book 1 it was seen that, for example, 10^{-2} means 0.01 or $\dfrac{1}{10^2}$ and that, in general, 10^{-n} means $\dfrac{1}{10^n}$; also that $10^0=1$.

This interpretation of a negative index can be applied to powers of other numbers besides 10; for example 2^{-2} means $\dfrac{1}{2^2}=\tfrac{1}{4}$, so that an exponential mapping is defined for a domain of negative, as well as of positive, integers. In the question about the forest fire (page 69), if x denotes the number of hours after 12 noon, $x=-1$ refers to 11 a.m., when the area burnt was 2^{-1} ha, i.e. $\frac{1}{2}$ ha; similarly, $x = -2$ refers to 10 a.m. when the area burnt was 2^{-2} ha.

Fractional indices

For some examples of exponential mappings, e.g. that concerning the chess-board, no meaning can be attached to *fractional* members of the domain: we cannot speak of the $1\frac{1}{2}$th square of the chess-board, for example. In other cases, however, the situation is quite different: the forest fire has burnt a certain area after $1\frac{1}{2}$ hours, the hot metal had a certain temperature at 2.20 a.m., and so on. This suggests that we *can* give a meaning to fractional indices.

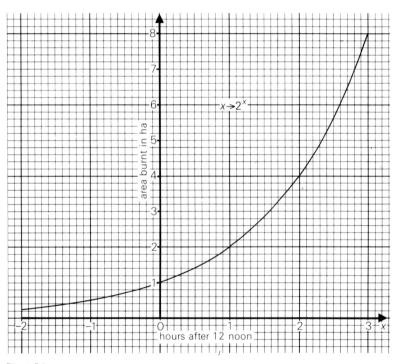

Figure 5.1

The graph (Figure 5.1) illustrates Question 4 of Exercise 5.1, and shows the spread of the forest fire until 3 p.m. and also the behaviour of the mapping $x \rightarrow 2^x$.

If we interpolate from the graph we find that the area burnt by 12.30 p.m. is about 1.4 ha, so that $\frac{1}{2} \rightarrow 1.4$ (approx.), i.e. $2^{\frac{1}{2}} = 1.4$. Again, at 1.30 the area burnt is about 2.8 ha, so that $2^{1\frac{1}{2}}$ is about 2.8. Similarly we can find approximate values for $2^{\frac{1}{3}}$, $2^{\frac{3}{4}}$, $2^{2\frac{1}{2}}$ and so on.

The laws of indices

While studying elementary algebra, and perhaps also in Chapter 6 of
Book 1, you probably encountered the three laws of indices, which are
here repeated in symbolic form as a reminder.

1   Multiplication: $a^x \times a^y = a^{x+y}$
2   Division: $a^x \div a^y = a^{x-y}$
3   Raising to a power: $(a^x)^y = a^{xy}$. (The process of raising to a power is
    sometimes called **exponentiation**.)

If fractional indices are to be used, they ought to obey these laws: we
should find, for example, that $2^{\frac{1}{2}} \times 2^{\frac{1}{2}} = 2^1 = 2$.

From Figure 5.1, $2^{\frac{1}{2}} = 1.4$. $1.4 \times 1.4 = 1.96$ which is nearly 2, suggesting
that $2^{\frac{1}{2}}$ is slightly more than 1.4. Clearly $2^{\frac{1}{2}}$ must be $\sqrt{2}$, which from
tables is about 1.414. Again, $2^{1\frac{1}{2}} = 2^1 \times 2^{\frac{1}{2}} = 2 \times \sqrt{2} = 2 \times 1.414 = 2.828$,
which agrees fairly well with the result from the graph.

Example 2   Find meanings for $2^{3\frac{1}{2}}$, $2^{\frac{1}{4}}$ and $2^{-\frac{1}{2}}$, and verify your results from the graph
where possible.

Answer
$2^{3\frac{1}{2}} = 2^3 \times 2^{\frac{1}{2}} = 8 \times 1.414 = 11.31$
$(2^{\frac{1}{4}})^2 = 2^{\frac{1}{2}} = 1.414$, so $2^{\frac{1}{4}} = \sqrt{1.414} = 1.189$

$2^{-\frac{1}{2}} = \dfrac{1}{2^{\frac{1}{2}}} = \dfrac{1}{1.414} = 0.707$

Exercise 5.2

1   Find meanings for the following, and verify your results from Figure 5.1.

   a $2^{2\frac{1}{2}}$ **b** $2^{\frac{3}{4}}$ **c** $2^{1\frac{1}{4}}$ **d** $2^{-1\frac{1}{2}}$ **e** $2^{-\frac{1}{4}}$

2   Give the range sets of the domain set $\{-2, -1, 0, 1, 2\}$ under the
    mappings

   a $x \to 2^x$ **b** $x \to 3^x$ **c** $x \to (\frac{1}{2})^x$ **d** $x \to (1\frac{1}{2})^x$ **e** $x \to 1^x$

3   Draw a graph of $x \to 3^x$ for values of x from -1 to 3.

   Find meanings for the following, and verify them from the graph you
   have drawn.

   a $3^{\frac{1}{2}}$ **b** $3^{1\frac{1}{2}}$ **c** $3^{2\frac{1}{2}}$ **d** $3^{-\frac{1}{2}}$ **e** $3^{\frac{1}{4}}$

4   Give the range sets of $\{1, 4, 9, 16\}$ under the mappings

   a $x \to x^{\frac{1}{2}}$ **c** $x \to x^{-\frac{1}{2}}$ **e** $x \to 3x^{\frac{1}{2}}$
   b $x \to x^{1\frac{1}{2}}$ **d** $x \to x^0$ **f** $x \to 30x^{-\frac{1}{2}}$

5 Give the values of

a 2^{-1} **d** 5^{-2} **g** $\left(\frac{3}{4}\right)^{-1}$ **j** 7^0

b 3^{-2} **e** $\left(\frac{1}{2}\right)^{-1}$ **h** $\left(1\frac{1}{2}\right)^{-2}$ **k** $\left(\frac{2}{3}\right)^{-2}$

c 10^{-3} **f** $\left(\frac{1}{3}\right)^{-3}$ **i** 1^{-5}

6 Give the values of the following (all are integers).

a $4^{\frac{1}{2}}$ **c** $9^{1\frac{1}{2}}$ **e** $81^{\frac{1}{4}}$ **g** $27^{1\frac{1}{3}}$

b $8^{\frac{2}{3}}$ **d** $16^{\frac{3}{4}}$ **f** $1^{3\frac{1}{2}}$ **h** $32^{\frac{2}{5}}$

7 Give the values of the following (all are rational).

a $4^{-\frac{1}{2}}$ **c** $9^{-2\frac{1}{2}}$ **e** $16^{-1\frac{1}{4}}$ **g** $81^{-\frac{3}{4}}$

b $8^{-\frac{1}{3}}$ **d** $27^{-\frac{2}{3}}$ **f** $1^{-\frac{3}{4}}$

8 Use tables to find the values of

a $5^{\frac{1}{2}}$ **c** $10^{1\frac{1}{2}}$ **e** $6^{-\frac{1}{2}}$ **g** $8^{\frac{1}{4}}$

b $7^{\frac{1}{2}}$ **d** $5^{-\frac{1}{2}}$ **f** $4^{\frac{1}{4}}$ **h** $3^{-\frac{1}{4}}$

9 Referring to Question 7 of Exercise 5.1, find the number of bacteria

a at 8.30 a.m.   **c** at 7.30 a.m.
b at 10.30 a.m.   **d** at 8.15 a.m.

10 Referring to question 9 of Exercise 5.1, find the temperature of the metal

a at 12.30 a.m.   **c** at 12.15 a.m.
b at 1.30 a.m.   **d** at 1.45 a.m.

11 The 'half-life' of a certain radio-active substance is 10 hours: this means that in 10 hours the substance decays so that the mass of a given amount falls to half its previous value. A mass of 100 g at noon, for example becomes 50 g by 10 p.m. Find the mass

a at 5 p.m.   **c** at 2.30 p.m.
b at 3 a.m.   **d** at 7.30 p.m.

Logarithms

If f is an exponential function such that $x \rightarrow a^x$, where a is a positive number, then f^{-1} is said to be a *logarithmic function*, and $f^{-1}(x)$ is called the *logarithm* of x to base a.

For example, if $f:x \rightarrow 2^x$, then $f(3) = 8$ so $f^{-1}(8) = 3$. So 3 is the logarithm of 8 to base 2, written $\log_2 8$. Again, $\log_2 32 = 5$ (since $2^5 = 32$), $\log_2 1 = 0$, $\log_2 \frac{1}{2} = -1$. The following table gives the logarithms of some numbers to base 2.

Number	Logarithm
$\frac{1}{4}$	-2
$\frac{1}{2}$	-1
1	0
2	1
4	2
8	3
16	4
32	5
64	6
128	7
256	8
512	9
1024	10

We can use these logarithms to carry out certain calculations, but of course only with numbers which appear in the table.

To find 16×32: log 16=4, log 32=5.
(The suffix 2 is omitted in this section, as all logarithms are to base 2.)

This means

$16 = 2^4,\ 32 = 2^5$

and $\qquad\qquad 16 \times 32 = 2^{4+5} = 2^9,$

From the table, $\qquad 2^9 = 512$ (as log 512=9),

so $\qquad\qquad\qquad 16 \times 32 = 512$

This is an example of the *first law of logarithms*:

log $ab = $ log $a + $ log b

To find $1024 \div 64$: log 1024=10, log 64=6.

So $\qquad\qquad\qquad 1024 = 2^{10},\ 64 = 2^6$

and $\qquad\qquad 1024 \div 64 = 2^{10-6} = 2^4$

and from the table, $\qquad 2^4 = 16$

This is an example of the *second law of logarithms*:

$$\log \frac{a}{b} = \log a - \log b$$

To find 32^2: log 32=5 so $32 = 2^5$,

and $32^2 = (2^5)^2 = 2^{10} = 1024$

To find $\sqrt[3]{512}$: $512 = 2^9$, so $\sqrt[3]{512}$, i.e. $512^{\frac{1}{3}}$, is

$$(2^9)^{\frac{1}{3}} = 2^3 = 8$$

These are examples of the *third law of logarithms*:

$$\log (a^n) = n \log a$$

Of course these laws apply to logarithms to any base: it can be seen that they correspond to the three laws of indices.

Needless to say, all the above calculations could be done quite easily without the use of logarithms, but they illustrate the **principles** of logarithmic calculation.

A simple nomogram

This is a calculating device, on the same principle as the slide-rule. To multiply two numbers, find them on the A and C lines, and place a ruler across the points corresponding to them. The point where the ruler crosses the B line corresponds to the product. Try this out with various pairs of numbers.

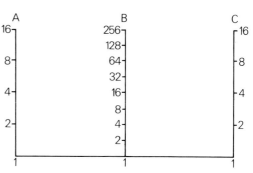

Figure 5.2

Find out how to use the nomogram for division.

Logarithms of other numbers

Obviously logarithms would be of little use if they could be used to multiply no numbers except powers of 2. We can find approximately the logarithms (to base 2) of other numbers by back-interpolation, using Figure 5.1.

From this graph we can see that $\log_2 3 = 1.58$. From this we can deduce that

$$\log_2 6 = \log_2 2 + \log_2 3 = 1 + 1.58 = 2.58,$$

$$\log_2 12 = 3.58, \ \log_2 24 = 4.58, \text{ and so on.}$$

$$\text{Also } \log_2 9 = 2 \times \log_2 3 = 2 \times 1.58 = 3.16,$$

hence $\log_2 18$, $\log_2 27$ etc.

By using the graph to find an approximate value for $\log_2 5$ we could also obtain approximate values for $\log_2 10$, $\log_2 20$, $\log_2 25$ etc.

Exercise 5.3

1 Use the table of logarithms to base 2 to find

a 8×128 **c** $64 \div 256$ **e** $\sqrt{256}$ **g** $128 \div \frac{1}{4}$

b $512 \div 32$ **d** 8^3 **f** $1024 \times \frac{1}{4}$

2 Draw a larger nomogram like that in Figure 5.2, taking the A and C scales as far as 64 and the B scale as far as 4096. Use it to calculate

a 16×64 **c** $\frac{1}{4} \times 512$ **e** $1024 \div 32$ **g** $256 \div \frac{1}{4}$

b 32×128 **d** $2048 \div 32$ **f** $512 \div 64$ **h** $(64)^2$

3 Use the information given in the paragraph headed 'Logarithms of other numbers' to mark the points on your nomogram lines corresponding to 3, 6, 12, 9, 18, and as many other numbers as possible. Use your nomogram to find

a 12×27 **c** 54×36 **e** $(36)^2$ **g** $576 \div 24$

b 18×24 **d** $324 \div 54$ **f** $162 \div 27$ **h** $27 \div 108$

4 Use the graph to find the logarithms to base 2 of

a 5 **b** 7 **c** 1.5 **d** $\frac{1}{3}$ **e** $\frac{2}{5}$

5 Given that $\log_2 3 = 1.58$ and $\log_2 5 = 2.32$, find the approximate values of the logarithms to base 2 of

a 15 **c** 25 **e** 30 **g** $\frac{3}{5}$ **i** $\frac{1}{15}$

b 9 **d** 10 **f** $\sqrt{5}$ **h** $1\frac{2}{3}$

6 Make a copy (possibly by tracing) of the graph on page 70. Measure the gradient of the graph at the points where $x = -1, 0, 1$ and 2. For each point calculate the value of the fraction $\dfrac{\text{gradient}}{2^x}$. What do your results suggest?

Logarithms to base 10

In the previous section, logarithms to base 2 have been used for the sake of simplicity: the most frequently used logarithms are those to base 10. These are the 'common logarithms' given in tables, or found by pressing the 'LOG' keys on many calculators. If the base of a logarithm is not given, it means it is a common logarithm.

The advantage of common logarithms is that the tables need only give logarithms of numbers between 1 and 10: from these, the logarithms of

all other numbers can easily be found. For example, from the tables, log
$2.34 = 0.3692$. So log $23.4 = \log(2.34 \times 10) = \log 2.34 + \log 10$
$$= 1.3692$$
$$\log 2340 = \log(2.34 \times 1000) = 3.3692$$
$$\log 0.234 = \log(2.34 \times 0.1) = \log 2.34 + \log 0.1$$
$$= 0.3692 - 1$$

The last logarithm is written $\overline{1}.3692$, the $-$ sign over the 1 indicating
that the 1 is negative although the .3692 is positive. It is usually
pronounced 'bar one point three six nine two'. The number in front of
the decimal point is called the **characteristic** of the logarithm. It is the
same as the power of ten when the number is put into standard form.
The part of the logarithm after the decimal point is sometimes called the
mantissa.

Since a small error in the work with logarithms (or any other calculating
aid) can cause a very large error in the answer obtained, it is advisable
always to work out a rough answer **before** beginning to use the
logarithms.

The method of carrying out calculations by logarithms is best learnt by
studying examples.

Example 3   Multiply 834 by 0.0753.

Answer
This is about 800×0.1, so a rough answer is 80.
$834 = 8.34 \times 10^2$
from tables, log $8.34 = 0.9212$

so log $834 = 2.9212$

$0.0753 = 7.53 \times 10^{-2}$

from tables, log $7.53 = 0.8768$

so log $0.0753 = \overline{2}.8768$

$$\begin{array}{r} \text{Adding} \quad 2.9212 \\ \overline{2}.8768 \\ \hline 1.7980 \end{array}$$

(The first digit is 1 because $2 + \overline{2} + 1$ (carried) $= 1$.)

To find the answer we use 'antilogarithm' tables if these are available: if
not, we use the logarithm tables 'backwards'. Either way, we look up the
.7980 only, ignoring the characteristic 1 for the time being. We find
6281 (in most tables the decimal point is omitted) and as the
characteristic is 1, the answer is 62.81 which agrees reasonably with the
rough answer. The last digit is always unreliable: in fact a more accurate
answer would be 62.80.

Example 4   Divide 29.7 by 0.0642.

Answer

This is about $30 \div 0.06$, so a rough answer is $3000 \div 6 = 500$.

Using tables as before, $\log 29.7 = 1.4728$
$$\log 0.0642 = \overline{2}.8075$$
Subtract: 2.6653

$(1 - \overline{2} = 3$ but the 'borrowed' 1 reduces the first digit to 2.)

From antilogarithm or logarithm tables, the answer is 462.7, which again agrees reasonably with the rough answer. Again the last figure is slightly out: the answer should be 462.6.

Example 5   Find the cube root of 0.525.

Answer

This is about $\sqrt[3]{\frac{1}{2}}$. As $(\frac{3}{4})^3 = \frac{27}{64}$, which is nearly $\frac{1}{2}$, the answer will be somewhere near $\frac{3}{4}$.

To find the cube root of a number we must divide its logarithm by 3, but as dividing a negative characteristic is a rather complicated process, it is best to write 0.525 as $525 \div 1000$ (1000 is chosen because it has an exact cube root).

$$\log 525 = 2.7202$$

dividing by 3 gives 0.9067 (to 4 decimal places).

$$\text{Antilog } 0.9067 = 8.067$$

$$\text{Also } \sqrt[3]{1000} = 10,$$

so the answer is $8.067 \div 10 = 0.8067$, which is not far from $\frac{3}{4}$.

Here, in the course of finding a cube root, we divided by 1000; if the number had been very much smaller we might have had to divide by 1 000 000, e.g. $0.00012 = 120 \div 1\,000\,000$. In finding a *fifth* root it might be necessary to divide by 10^5 or 10^{10}.

Exercise 5.4

1   (Positive characteristics) Find the values, correct to 3 significant figures, of

a 3.56×2.13	**d** 839×22.5	**g** 7.07×3450	**i** 31.4×836
b 4.29×8.17	**e** 66.3×702	**h** 2370×9840	**j** $(25.9)^2$
c 12.9×31.8	**f** 297×529		

2 (Positive characteristics) Find the values, correct to 3 significant figures, of

    a $79 \div 2.56$ **d** $90.6 \div 24.5$ **g** $34.8 \div 7.93$ **i** $1890 \div 456$

    b $9.34 \div 4.39$ **e** $2395 \div 37.2$ **h** $98\,700 \div 3.49$ **j** $79.7 \div 61.3$

    c $827 \div 34.8$ **f** $729 \div 8.1$

3 Find the values, correct to 3 significant figures, of

    a 0.23×67.2 **e** 0.0458×967 **h** 0.00567×0.0805

    b 572×0.56 **f** 0.0629×0.0392 **i** 0.679×0.0079

    c 0.345×0.217 **g** 35.2×0.0073 **j** $198 \times 0.000\,963$

    d 0.567×0.729

4 Find the values, correct to 3 significant figures, of

    a $2.54 \div 7.26$ **e** $6.22 \div 833$ **h** $0.0399 \div 651$

    b $0.789 \div 34.6$ **f** $0.0567 \div 0.353$ **i** $2.22 \div 0.00041$

    c $0.652 \div 4.71$ **g** $0.394 \div 0.0082$ **j** $0.000\,321 \div 0.0883$

    d $9.46 \div 417$

5 Find, correct to 3 significant figures, the cube roots of

    a 19   **b** 358   **c** 4.89   **d** 524   **e** 2750

    and the fifth roots of

    f 7   **g** 83   **h** 481   **i** 385

6 Find, correct to 3 significant figures, the cube roots of

    a 0.6   **b** 0.245   **c** 0.37   **d** 0.0518   **e** 0.00433

    and the fifth roots of

    f 0.338   **g** 0.569   **h** 0.072   **i** 0.009

Logarithmic scales

Figure 5.3 shows a logarithmic scale, in this case giving the wavelength of various kinds of rays. It is calibrated in the same way as the lines of the nomogram in Figure 5.2, except that powers of 10 are used instead of powers of 2. Only by using a logarithmic scale can such a wide range of lengths be shown on one diagram: if an ordinary linear scale were used, and if the shortest wavelengths were represented by 0.1 mm, the longest would need a line of length about 10^{14} km to represent them – such a line would be long enough to reach some of the nearest stars.

Note that on a logarithmic scale, as on one of the nomogram lines, a *point* half-way between two given points does not represent eh *number* half-way between those represented by the given points. For example, the point half-way between A (representing 1) and B (representing 10) represents, not 5 or 5.5, but $10^{\frac{1}{2}}$, that is $\sqrt{10}$ or about 3.16.

Example 6

Find the numbers represented by the points C and D on the wavelength scale (Figure 5.3). Also, give the correct positions for the points representing 5×10^{-2} and 3×10^{2}.

Answer

C is half-way between the points representing 10^4 and 10^5, and so represents $10^{4\frac{1}{2}} = 31\ 600$, approximately.

D is about one quarter of the way from 10^{-3} to 10^{-2}, so represents about $10^{-2.75}$. This is the antilogarithm of -2.75. Now $-2.75 = \bar{3}.25$, whose antilogarithm, from the tables, is about 1.78×10^{-3}, or $0.001\ 78$.

To find the correct position for 5×10^{-2}, find its logarithm, which is $\bar{2}.7$ approximately. So the point should be about 0.7 of the way from the 10^{-2} point to the 10^{-1} point.

Similarly, $\log (3 \times 10^2) = 2.48$ approximately. This point should therefore be 0.48 (nearly half) of the way from the 10^2 point to the 10^3 point.

Exercise 5.5

1 Draw a line 10 cm long and calibrate it as a logarithmic scale, making one end 1 and the other 10^{10}, and making intermediate points as 10, 10^2, 10^3 and so on. Mark points to represent the following numbers, writing each number by the corresponding point.

5, 70, 400, 3000, 2×10^5, 6×10^6, 8×10^7, 5×10^8, 9×10^9

2 Make a logarithmic scale 21 cm long, and mark points on it at intervals of 1 cm, labelling them 1, 10, 10^2, 10^3 etc., up to 10^{21}. Use it to represent the distances from London of the following places. (If you do not live in London, and if you prefer, replace the first few distances by distances of some places from where you live.)

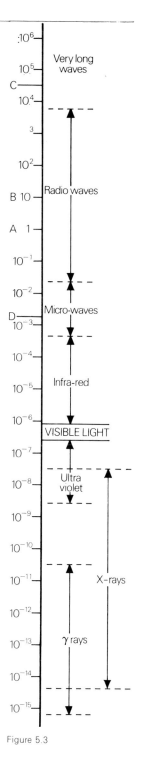

Figure 5.3

Distances in km

Cambridge	80
Manchester	300
Thurso	1000
New York	8500
Sydney	17000
The moon	4×10^5
The sun	1.5×10^8
Pluto (Planet)	6×10^9
Nearest star	4×10^{12}
Nearest nebula	1.4×10^{20}

3   Make a logarithmic scale to represent numbers from 1 to 1.5×10^9, marking points to represent 10, 10^2, 10^3 etc. This is to be a time-scale, to represent the numbers of years that have passed since various events. Put in whatever historical events you consider important, at the correct places. For prehistoric events, you could put in the following very rough dates which have been suggested.

First human beings 2×10^5 years ago

Age of dinosaurs, 6.5×10^6 to 1.2×10^7 years ago

Oldest fossils are 5×10^8 years old

Earth formed, 1.5×10^9 years ago

Chapter 6

Calculations and calculators

Many branches of mathematics do not involve numbers at all, and even in those branches that do involve them, the numbers used are often quite simple so no long calculations are needed. Up to this stage, there has been very little need for long calculations, but from now on they will occasionally be required. Such calculations can be made easier by using logarithms, as shown in the previous chapter, but in recent years the use of electronic calculators has become very widespread, and it is now permitted by most examining authorities. The first part of this chapter is concerned with the use of electronic calculators, but all the questions in the chapter can be worked by logarithms.

Types of calculator

Calculators vary so widely that it is impossible to give any general instructions for their use; you will have to study the instructions that apply to your own instrument.

The simplest calculators will carry out only the four basic operations of addition, subtraction, multiplication and division, and although much can be done with these, a few extra facilities can be useful. If you are about to buy a calculator, it may well be worth the relatively small extra cost to obtain one which has a memory (key usually marked M or STO) or brackets (keys marked ()) or both: also very useful are a square root ($\sqrt{\ }$), a reciprocal key ($\frac{y}{x}$ or $\frac{x}{y}$), an exponential key (y^x or x^y), and what is usually described as 'scientific notation', which in fact means standard form. Keys for sine, cosine and tangent are useful, but are perhaps something of a luxury, and a logarithm key even more so. A calculator which has many more keys than these is probably a specialist instrument intended for scientists, engineers or accountants.

Simple calculations

The calculators in most common use, and available at the most reasonable prices, act exactly as might be expected: if you wish to add 713 and 184.2, you simply press the keys in the order

$$7\ 1\ 3\ +\ 1\ 8\ 4\ .\ 2\ =$$

and the answer, 897.2, appears on the display. However, even for this simple calculation some instruments require a different procedure, so even at this stage it is best to check your calculator to see if it works as expected.

Accuracy

As nearly all calculators work with decimals, they cannot be completely accurate with all calculations. For a simple example, try $2 \div 3$: as the answer is a recurring decimal, $0.\dot{6}$, the calculator cannot display it all but will show a row of 6's ending in a 6 or, more accurately, in a 7. Now press the keys $\times 3 =$. The result should of course be 2 but it is much more likely to be given as 1.99...9 or as 1.99...8 or as 2.00...1. However, as most calculators give answers to far more figures than are usually needed at this stage, this slight inaccuracy matters very little: there is more danger of answers being given to *more* figures than are justified by the accuracy of the information fed into the instrument.

Overflow

This is a rather more serious matter. Set some calculation such as
32 000 × 26 000 into your instrument. If it deals in 'scientific notation', it
will probably display 8.3200 ... 08. This is simply standard form, the 08
meaning '× 10^8'. If the calculator does not work in scientific notation, it
will probably give some kind of distress signal, such as displaying E for
error. However, the difficulty is easily overcome by putting the numbers
into standard form **before** the calculator is used, thus:

$$32\,000 \times 26\,000 = 3.2 \times 10^4 \times 2.6 \times 10^4$$
$$= 3.2 \times 2.6 \times 10^8 = 8.32 \times 10^8$$

(By calculator 3.2 × 2.6 = 8.32)

The same applies when small numbers are involved. Some calculators
put all numbers less than 1 into standard form automatically, but one
without scientific notation may give 0 as the answer when set to divide,
say, 2.1 by 300 000. Here, again, standard form is the remedy.

Negative numbers

Try your calculator with 5 − 9: if it gives the answer −4, this means it
can deal with negative numbers, which is a great advantage, as will be
seen later. Some calculators have a key marked +/−, for changing the
signs of numbers, but many of those without this key can nevertheless
deal with negative numbers.

At this stage you could use Questions 1, 2, 3 and 4 of Exercise 5.4
(page 77) as practice, if you have not already worked them by
logarithms (or even if you have!).

Sequence of operations

Take a very simple calculation such as 2 + 3 × 5. Since the convention is
to perform multiplication before addition, the result should be
2 + 15 = 17, but if it is fed into a calculator in the order given, the result
is far more likely to be 25: the instrument adds 3 to 2, and then
multiplies by 5. To obtain the answer 17, it is necessary to press the keys
in the order 3 × 5 + 2: even then, with some instruments it is necessary to
press the = key after the 5, or the answer 21(3 × (5 + 2)) will be
obtained. It is worth while to find out whether your own calculator
needs the = key here or not: it is a waste of time to be repeatedly
pressing the = key when it is not needed.

As a rule, it is best to deal first with any numbers in brackets, then with
multiplication and division, and lastly with addition and subtraction.

(You may have learned the mnemonic BODMAS to remind you of this – the O means 'of' as in '$\frac{2}{3}$ of 39'.)

A calculation such as $5.2 - \dfrac{3.6}{2.4}$ may be performed as follows, if the calculator will deal with negative numbers:

$$3 \ . \ 6 \div 2 \ . \ 4 - 5 \ . \ 2$$

(with = after 4, if necessary).

The answer will appear as -3.7, but this does not matter as we know the answer is positive, and can ignore the $-$ sign.

A calculation like $\dfrac{117 \times 0.047}{21 \times 3.468}$ is treated as

$$1 \ 1 \ 7 \ \times \ . \ 0 \ 4 \ 7 \div 2 \ 1 \div 3 \ . \ 4 \ 6 \ 8,$$

giving 0.0755.

The multiplications and divisions can be taken in any order: in some calculations a good choice of order can avoid overflow.

Rough answers

As with logarithms, a small error in using the calculator (pressing the key next to the right one, for example) can lead to a large error in the answer. It is therefore always advisable to make a rough estimate of the answer before using the calculator at all.

Example 1   Find the value of $1.45 + 0.237 - \dfrac{0.432}{53 \times 0.0089}$

Answer
This is approximately

$$1.4 + 0.2 - \frac{0.4}{50 \times 0.01} = 1.6 - \frac{0.4}{0.5} = 1.6 - 0.8 = 0.8$$

Dealing with the fraction first, the sequence is
$$0 \ . \ 4 \ 3 \ 2 \div 5 \ 3 \div \ . \ 0 \ 0 \ 8 \ 9 - \ . \ 2 \ 3 \ 7 - 1 \ . \ 4 \ 5$$

This gives -0.7712. (With some calculators it will be necessary to press the = key at one or more stages.) As we know the answer is positive, it is 0.7712, which agrees well with the rough answer.

Example 2   Find the value of $17.3 \times 8.49 + 0.031 \times 5124$.

Answer
This is approximately

$$20 \times 10 + 0.03 \times 5000 = 200 + 150 = 350$$

A calculator with brackets or memory can deal with this as it stands: for one without these facilities the problem could be rewritten as follows: find

$$\left(\frac{17.3 \times 8.49}{0.031} + 5124 \right) \times 0.031$$

The sequence of multiplication, division, addition and multiplication gives 305.7, which agrees reasonably with the rough answer.

Otherwise, of course, the first product, i.e. 17.3×8.49 ($=146.9$) could be noted on paper and added to the second after that has been found.

Example 3   Find the *total* surface area of a cylinder of length 14.7 cm and radius 5.8 cm.

Answer
The total surface area of a cylinder is given by $S = 2\pi rh + 2\pi r^2$.

In this case, this is about $6 \times 6 \times 15 + 6 \times 6^2$, i.e. about $36 \times 15 + 36 \times 6$, or 36×20 which is 720. It is best to rewrite the expression as $2\pi r(h+r)$ which here is $2 \times \pi \times 5.8 \times (14.7 + 5.8)$. The sequence is

$$1\ 4\ .\ 7\ +\ 5\ .\ 8\ \times\ 5\ .\ 8\ \times\ 2\ \times\ 3\ .\ 1\ 4\ 2$$

Some calculators have a special key for π, which would of course be used instead of 3.142.

The answer is 747 cm^2.

Each of the questions in Exercise 6.1 can be answered in a single sequence (i.e. without writing down any intermediate results), using a calculator with only the basic operations $+$, $-$, $\times$ and $\div$.

Those who use logarithms and not calculators can use all the exercises in this chapter as practice in logarithmic calculations. It must be remembered that logarithms help with division and multiplication but not with addition and subtraction: if Example 2, above, were to be worked by logarithms, the antilogarithm would have to be found after the first multiplication, and added later to that found after the second multiplication.

Rough estimates of the answers should be made before using the calculator (or logarithms) to answer any of the questions in Exercise 6.1, except Question 1.

Exercise 6.1

1   Use your calculator to perform the following simple calculations, and check your results mentally.

a $(3+5) \times 4$ h $(5 \times 4) + 3$ o $12 \div (2 \times 3)$ u $11 - 3^2$

b $3 + (5 \times 4)$ i $7 \times (6 - 2)$ p $(12 \div 2) \times 3$ v $(11 - 3)^2$

c $(7 - 2) \times 3$ j $(7 \times 6) - 2$ q $7 \times (6 \div 2)$ w $(4 \times 3) + (5 \times 2)$

d $7 - (2 \times 3)$ k $(6 + 9) \div 3$ r $(7 \times 6) \div 2$ x $4 \times (3 + 5) \times 2$

e $(9 - 3) - 2$ l $6 + (9 \div 3)$ s $7^2 + 5$ y $(6 \times 9) - (7 \times 3)$

f $9 - (3 - 2)$ m $(9 - 8) \div 4$ t $(7 + 5)^2$ z $6 \times (9 - 7) \times 3$

g $5 \times (4 + 3)$ n $9 - (8 \div 4)$

2 Find the values of the following, giving all answers correct to three significant figures.

a $47.39 + (3.295 \times 7.68)$

g $17.43 \times \left(1.346 + \dfrac{3.147}{0.892}\right)$

b $0.0574 \times \dfrac{1.468}{0.973}$

h $\dfrac{359.4 + 98.6}{50.7 \times 0.843}$

c $(2349 + 1587) \times 0.0852$

i $\dfrac{1057 - 578}{3.96 \times 4.2}$

d $84.29 - \dfrac{5}{0.158}$

j $2.3 \times \left(4.97 - \dfrac{3.78}{0.95}\right)$

e $\dfrac{23.7 \times 0.6494}{1895 \times 0.00522}$

k $0.78 \times \left(\dfrac{47.05 - 29.23}{627 \times 0.01862}\right)$

f $\dfrac{37.04 - 18.59}{2670}$

l $\dfrac{3.97 \times 2.08 \times 0.75}{24.87 \times 3.7 \times 1.83}$

3 Calculate the volume of a cylinder whose radius is 23.8 cm and whose height is 34.7 cm, giving the answer correct to 3 significant figures.

4 An article cost £23.60 originally, but VAT at 15% was added to this price, and later, in a sale, the price (including the VAT) was reduced by 12%. Find the sale price.

5 A block of wood is 23.8 cm long, 14.6 cm wide, and 9.7 mm thick. Its mass is 723 g. Find correct to 3 significant figures

a the mass of 1 cm³ of the wood,
b the mass of 1 m³ of the wood,
c the mass of a block of the same kind of wood whose dimensions are 17.6 cm × 11.5 cm × 7.7 cm,
d the length that must be cut off the first block to reduce its mass to 500 g.

6 A car travels 35 miles (to the nearest mile) on one gallon of petrol. Given that 1 mile = 1.609 km and that 1 gallon = 4.546 litres, find (to the nearest kilometre) how many km the car travels on 1 litre of petrol.

7 Using the formula $P = m\dfrac{v - u}{t}$, calculate P

    a when $m=0.46$, $v=29$, $u=13.4$, $t=0.07$

    b when $m=25.8$, $v=136$, $u=83$, $t=0.53$

8   Using the formula $F=\dfrac{mv^2}{r}$, calculate F

    a when $m=0.075$, $v=23.2$, $r=1.8$ **b** when $m=27$, $v=85$, $r=184$

9   The formula $s=ut+\frac{1}{2}at^2$ may be rewritten $s=t(u+\frac{1}{2}at)$. Use it in this form to find s

    a when $t=24.7$, $u=33$, $a=9.8$ **b** when $t=0.76$, $u=894$, $a=256$

10 By rewriting the expression $3x^2-5x+4$ in the form $x(3x-5)+4$, find its value

    a when $x=2.17$ **b** when $x=14.4$.

11 Rewrite the expression $2x^2+3x-7$ in a form similar to that shown in Question 10. Hence find its value

    a when $x=1.26$ **b** when $x=1.27$.

    What information do your results give, about a root of the equation $2x^2+3x-7=0$?

12 Find the gradients of the lines joining the following pairs of points.

    a (0, 2.73) and (3.96, 8.07)   **c** (1, 2.68) and (5, -7.92)

    b (1.59, 7.52) and (4.59, 1.38)

13 Solve the equations (answers to 3 sig. fig.)

    a $3.74x+12.98=23.07$ **c** $19.56-0.0064x=19.39$

    b $762x-283=1042$

Brackets

The bracket keys on a calculator are used when they might be expected to be used, i.e. in calculations such as $(2.6+3.7) \times (3.9-1.5)$. They must also be used in cases where brackets are implied but not actually printed: for example, in an expression such as $6.8+3.4 \times 5.7$, it is the convention that the multiplication is performed first, whereas the sequence

$$6 \;.\; 8 \;+\; 3 \;.\; 4 \;\times\; 5 \;.\; 7 \;=$$

will give $(6.8+3.4) \times 5.7 = 58.14$. As was seen in the previous section, the difficulty can be overcome by performing the multiplication first; otherwise the sequence

$$6 \cdot 8 + (3 \cdot 4 \times 5 \cdot 7) =$$

will give the same result, namely 26.18.

Again, the calculation of $\dfrac{349}{233+1059}$ must be carried out as

$$3\ 4\ 9 \div (\ 2\ 3\ 3\ +\ 1\ 0\ 5\ 9\ )\ =$$

the result being 0.2701.

Some calculators have several sets of brackets, so that a calculation like

$$\frac{1.23 \times 3.6 + 4.67 \times 9.56}{23.8 + 19.5}$$

can be performed in one sequence.

Square root

The square root key, if one is available, normally gives the square root of whatever number is on the display. For example, if $\sqrt{(27^2 + 33^2)}$ is to be calculated, the value of $27^2 + 33^2$ is found in the usual way, and then the $=$ key must be pressed before the $\sqrt{}$ key, giving the result 42.64. An inversion key, if available (usually marked INV) can be used in combination with the square root key to give the squares of numbers.

Memory

A calculator with a memory usually has a key marked M or STO ('store'); pressing this puts into a memory store whatever number is on display at the time. Another key, which may be marked MR or RCL ('recall') will produce on the display whatever is in the memory store, or will add it to, subtract it from, multiply it by or divide it into, whatever is on the display, according to the instruction given. For example

$$1.5 \text{ M } 2.3 + 5.4 \times \text{MR}$$

will give

$$(2.3 + 5.4) \times 1.5, \text{ i.e. } 11.55$$

Some calculators have several memory stores; some have keys marked M+, M−, M× to enabie whatever number is in the memory to be added to, subtracted from, or multiplied.

If a calculator has a memory but no brackets, the memory can often be used in place of brackets, though not in the same place in the sequence.

For example, to find $\dfrac{349}{233+1059}$ the sequence is

$$2\ 3\ 3\ +\ 1\ 0\ 5\ 9\ =\ M\ 3\ 4\ 9\ \div\ MR\ =$$

To find $(2.6+3.7) \times (3.9-1.5)$, the sequence is

$$2\ .\ 6\ +\ 3\ .\ 7\ =\ M\ 3\ .\ 9\ -\ 1\ .\ 5\ \times\ MR\ =$$

The memory is useful when a whole succession of numbers have to be multiplied by the same number: for example, if an examination is marked so that the maximum is 143, and the marks have to be converted to percentages, this means that each mark must be multiplied by $\frac{100}{143}$. If we perform the sequence $1\ 0\ 0\ \div\ 1\ 4\ 3\ =\ M$, and the first mark is, say, 83, we set in $8\ 3\ \times\ MR$ and read off the first mark as a percentage, and then continue with all the other marks.

There are, of course, many other uses for the memory.

The M+ key is particularly useful in finding scalar products: for example, to find the total value of 23 stamps at 11p, 35 at 14p, 41 at 16p and 17 at 18p, the sequence could be
$23 \times 11 = M35 \times 14 = M+41 \times 16 = M+17 \times 18 = M+MR$

Some calculators have a 'constant' key, usually marked K; this gives some of the facilities of a memory, but not all.

The questions in Exercise 6.2 are intended to give practice in the use of bracket, memory and square root keys, but calculators without these keys can be used if intermediate answers are written down and square root tables are used. As with Exercise 6.1, the questions are suitable for practice with logarithms.

Also as with Exercise 6.1, rough estimates of the answers should be made, except to Question 1.

Exercise 6.2

1 Use your calculator to find the answers to the following simple calculations, and check your results mentally.

a $(3 \times 7)+(5 \times 8)$

f $\dfrac{9}{8-5}$

b $(4 \times 3)+(5 \times 7)+(6 \times 2)$

g $\dfrac{6 \times 9}{4+2}$

c $(4+5) \times (7+3)$

h $\dfrac{7+9}{7-3}$

d $(19-7) \times (11-4)$

i $\dfrac{12}{(4 \times 7)-8}$

e $\dfrac{4}{3+5}$

j $(5 \times 9)+\dfrac{18}{6}$

k $\dfrac{(2 \times 8) + (3 \times 4)}{9 - 2}$ **m** $[(3 \times 4) + 7] \times [(5 \times 2) + 1]$

l $\dfrac{(2 \times 9) + (3 \times 8) + (4 \times 7)}{1 + 2 + 3 + 4}$

2   Find the values of the following, giving all answers correct to three significant figures.

  a $(34.67 \times 1.097) + (392 \times 0.8765)$

  b $(1987 - 768) \times (0.396 + 1.063)$

  c $[(347 - 96) \times (187 + 32)] \times 0.0738$

  d $\dfrac{476.6}{2.456 + 9.072}$

  e $\dfrac{34.97 \times 23.08}{986 - 234.48}$

  f $\dfrac{27.9 + (25.6 \times 9.03)}{(8290 \times 0.076) + 23.7}$

  g $\dfrac{(91.2 \times 43.8) - (316 \times 0.885)}{347 - 282}$

  h $(3.45 \times 5) + (6.78 \times 6) + (9.12 \times 7)$

  i $(2.3 + 7.9)^2 - (1.7 + 6.8)^2$

  j $\dfrac{3.34 + (5.69 \times 0.858)}{(3.34 + 5.69) \times 0.858}$

  k $9.45 + [3.56 \times (67 - 54.72)]$

3   Find the total surface area of a cuboid whose length, breadth and height are respectively 23.6 cm, 17.7 cm and 11.4 cm.

4   Find the total cost of 13 articles at £2.78 each, 17 at £1.35 each, and 23 at 88p each.

5   A moving object travels at 23 m/s for 17 seconds, then at 35 m/s for 27 seconds, then at 11 m/s for 33 seconds. Find its average speed in metres per second, correct to 2 sig. fig.

6   A train travels for 33 miles at an average speed of 65 m.p.h., then for 27 miles at an average speed of 77 m.p.h., then for 11 miles at an average speed of 51 m.p.h. Find its average speed for the whole journey, to the nearest m.p.h.

7   The numbers of votes received by each candidate in an election were as follows.

Green	14 572
Grey	9 479
Pink	4 860
Purple	453

Find **a** what percentage of the total votes each candidate received, **b** the angles of a pie-chart which could be drawn to illustrate this information.

8 Find the length of the side BC of a triangle in which $\angle A$ is a right-angle

    a if AB=23.5 cm, AC=31.7 cm   **b** if AB=0.46 cm, AC=0.58 cm

(Give each answer to the same number of significant figures as that to which the information is given.)

9 Use the formula $f=\dfrac{uv}{u+v}$ to find f, correct to the nearest millimetre

    a when $u=23.5$ cm, $v=17.3$ cm   **b** when $u=12.8$ cm, $v=-9.4$ cm

10 Use the formula $T=2\pi\sqrt{\left(\dfrac{L}{g}\right)}$ to find T correct to 3 sig. fig.

    a when $L=1.35$, $g=9.81$ **b** when $L=0.816$, $g=32.2$

11 Use the formula $T=2\pi\left(\dfrac{h^2+k^2}{hg}\right)$ to find T correct to 3 sig. fig.

    a when $h=23.6$, $k=17.8$, $g=981$ **b** when $h=1.34$, $k=1.87$, $g=32.2$

12 Find the gradients of the lines joining the points

    a (2.95, 4.12) and (1.08, 6.73)   **b** $(-3.74, 5.67)$ and $(8.49, -7.06)$

13 Solve the equations

    a $3.76x+2.75=6.82x$ **c** $183x+392=576-127x$
    b $5.92x-18.4=3.71x+4.97$

giving all answers to 3 sig. fig.

Reciprocals

The reciprocal key (when there is one on a calculator) is normally marked $\dfrac{1}{x}$ and, of course, gives the reciprocal of whatever number is set in: for example the sequence 2 5 $\dfrac{1}{x}$ gives 0.04. It can be used in such calculations as: 'Given that 1 mile=1.609 km, express 1 km as a fraction of a mile'. The answer is $\dfrac{1}{1.609}$ mile, which is given by the calculator as 0.62150403, but as the information, namely 1.609, was given to only 4 sig. fig., it is likely that the answer is also only correct to this degree of accuracy, and should be given as 0.6215.

The reciprocal key can be used to shorten calculations such as $\dfrac{2.7}{3.2+\sqrt{(1.4\times9.8)}}$. Here the sequence is

$$1.4 \times 9.8 = \sqrt{} + 3.2 = \frac{1}{x} \times 2.7 =$$

the answer being 0.3911.

Exponential key

This key, when present, is usually marked x^y or y^x. It saves repeated multiplication when high powers are to be found, and can be used for *fractional* indices, including cube and other roots. For example, to find 3^9 the sequence is 3 y^x 9 =, giving the answer 19 683.

To find the cube root of 3, or $3^{\frac{1}{3}}$, we could use the sequence

3 y^x . 3 3 3 3 3 = or, better, 3 y^x 3 $\dfrac{1}{x}$ =, the answer being 1.44225

to 6 sig. fig. Some calculators have a separate key for roots, which may be marked $\sqrt[x]{y}$, and with some, roots are found by using the inversion key in combination with the exponential key.

'Scientific notation'

It has already been mentioned that some calculators will automatically put numbers into standard form under certain conditions. Numbers can usually be set into such calculators in standard form, normally by pressing a key marked EE. Thus, to set in 3.76×10^7 the sequence is 3 . 7 6 EE 7. For 3.76×10^{-7}, the 7 is followed by $+/-$.

Exercise 6.3

1 Evaluate correct to 3 sig. fig.

a $\dfrac{41.7}{(732\times0.46)+(516\times0.39)}$ **b** $\dfrac{23.6}{\sqrt{(23.6^2+38.9^2)}}$

2 If $\dfrac{1}{u}+\dfrac{1}{v}=\dfrac{1}{f}$, find f,

  a when $u=15.8$, $v=11.7$ **b** when $u=23.1$, $v=-18.6$

3 Find to 4 sig. fig. the sum of

a $1 + \frac{1}{2} + \frac{1}{3} + \frac{1}{4} + \ldots \frac{1}{10}$ **b** $\frac{1}{1^2} + \frac{1}{2^2} + \frac{1}{3^2} + \frac{1}{4^2} + \ldots + \frac{1}{10^2}$

4 If two electrical resistors, one of R_1 ohms and the other of R_2 ohms, are placed in a circuit in parallel, their effective combined resistance is R ohms, where

$$\frac{1}{R} = \frac{1}{R_1} + \frac{1}{R_2}$$

Find the effective combined resistance, when placed in parallel, of resistors of

a 2.6 ohms and 3.7 ohms **b** 1.4 megohms and 5.2 megohms

5 Given that 1 mm = 0.394 of an inch, find

a the number of millimetres in an inch,
b the number of square millimetres in a square inch.

6 Evaluate, correct to 4 sig. fig.

a 2.4^6 **b** 1.1^{10} **c** 0.987^{12}

7 Evaluate, correct to 4 sig. fig.

a $5^{\frac{2}{3}}$ **b** $8^{0.8}$ **c** 3.8^{-4} **d** $17^{-\frac{3}{4}}$

8 Find the cube root of

a 2 **b** 0.6 **c** 185

9 Find the fifth roots of the numbers in Question 8.

10 A car was valued at £11 500 at the beginning of one year, and at £9200 at the end of the same year. Find the depreciation factor, i.e. the number by which the value at the beginning of the year must be multiplied to give the value at the end of the year.

If the depreciation factor is the same for each year, find the value of the car after another 7 years.

11 Find to 5 sig. fig. and in standard form, the number of grains of wheat on the 30th square of the chess-board, in the story told at the beginning of Chapter 5 (page **00**).

12 Find the number of moves needed for the disc problem described in Chapter 5 (page **00**), if 20 discs were used. What is the largest number of discs with which the transfer can be carried out in fewer than ten million moves?

13   The price of a 200 g packet of a certain kind of butter was 35p in 1980 and 40p in 1981. If it has continued, and will continue, to increase by the same factor each year, what will be its price in the year 2000?

14   If $p=3.76 \times 10^7$, $q=4.89 \times 10^{11}$, $r=8.42 \times 10^{-9}$, find the values of

a pq **c** qr **e** $\dfrac{q}{r}$ **g** $pq+\dfrac{100}{r^2}$

b rp **d** $\dfrac{p}{q}$ **f** $\dfrac{r}{p}$

giving all answers to 3 sig. fig. and in standard form.

15   Given that the velocity of light is 3×10^5 km/s find

a the number of kilometres in a light-year, i.e. the distance travelled by light in a year,
b the time taken by light from the sun to reach the planet Pluto, 5.95×10^9 km away.

The last exercise in the chapter consists of questions on various topics, all giving scope for the use of the calculator.

Exercise 6.4

Give the answer to each of these questions to whatever you consider is a reasonable degree of accuracy.

Change of units, speeds etc.

1   Given that 1 mile=1.609 km, express 70 m.p.h. in metres per second.

2   On a day when £1 was worth 2.205 dollars or 11.14 francs, find how many francs a dollar was worth.

3   Given that 1 yard=0.9144 m, find which is the faster runner, one who runs 400 m in 50.1 seconds, or one who runs 440 yards in 50.6 seconds.

5   Find which is the better buy, a 500 g packet for £2.15, or a 454 g packet for £1.95.

5   1 tonne=1000 kg, 1 ton=2240 lb, and 1 lb=0.4536 kg. Find by how many lb 1 ton exceeds 1 tonne.

Ratio, proportion, percentage

6   Find 16.75% of £548.76.

7   Express £34.68 as a percentage of £672.

8   Find what sum must be invested at a rate of interest of $11\frac{1}{2}$% per year in order to produce interest of £340 per *month*.

9   Find the simple interest on £3675 for 115 days at a rate of interest of 12% per year.

10   Find the simple interest on £273 for 214 days at a rate of interest of $13\frac{1}{2}$% per year.

11   A put £3600 into a business, B put £2900 and C £1750. The amount of the profit that was to be shared between them, in proportion to the amounts they put in, was £1245. Find how much each received.

12   An article costs £209.30 including VAT at 15% (i.e. 15% of the price before tax). Find what it would cost if VAT were reduced to 8%.

13   A car dealer is holding a sale. In the sale, a car whose list price is £10 500 is offered for £9600. Find what percentage discount is being offered. With the same percentage discount, find

  a the sale price of a car whose list price is £8600,
  b the list price of a car whose sale price is £6034.

14   A prize of £20 is to be divided between three pupils, as nearly as possible in proportion to the marks they scored in an examination. The marks are 92, 83 and 71: find the amounts of the prizes.

Area, volume, mensuration

15   Find the radius of a circle whose area is 100 cm².

16   Find the volume of a cylinder whose length is 7.8 cm and whose radius is 3.9 cm.

  If the mass of the cylinder is 3.32 kg, find the mass of 1 m³ of the metal of which it is made.

17   A cylindrical container is to hold exactly 1 litre. Find its height if the radius of its base is to be 5.6 cm.

18   The diameter of a wheel of a bicycle is 26 inches: find how many times it turns when the bicycle is ridden from Lands End to John o' Groat's, a distance of 876 miles (1 mile = 63 360 inches).

19   The dimensions of a rectangular roof are 5.8 m by 2.7 m. All the rain which falls on the roof is collected in a cylindrical tank of diameter

1.2 m. Find

a the volume of water which falls on the roof when '1 cm of rain' falls, that is, enough rain to cover any horizontal surface to depth of 1 cm, if it did not run away.

b the amount by which the depth of water in the tank increases, when 1 cm of rain falls.

c the number of cm of rain that must have fallen in a storm after which the depth of water in the tank has increased by 30 cm.

Averages

20 A car is driven for 20 minutes at 72 km/h and then for 42 minutes at 63 km/h. Find the average speed for the whole 62 minutes.

21 A train, on a journey of 220 miles, is scheduled to run at an average speed of 82 m.p.h. For the first 65 miles its average speed is only 64 m.p.h. Find the average speed which it must maintain for the rest of the journey, if it is to arrive on time.

22 Find the mean of these numbers: 23.7, 25.4, 22.8, 27.0, 21.9, 26.6, 24.5.

The mean of these seven numbers, together with an eighth number, is 26.0 cm. Find this eighth number.

23 In a school the mean height of the 85 sixth-formers is 176 cm, and the mean height of the 643 other members of the school is 136 cm. Find the mean height of all the members of the school.

24 In an investigation of the numbers of eggs in blue-tits' nests, the following observations were made.

Number of eggs	4	5	6	7	8	9	10	11
Number of nests	3	16	28	31	17	8	6	1

Find the mean number of eggs per nest.

Formulae

25 Use the formula $V = \dfrac{\pi h^2}{3}(3r - h)$ to find V

a when $r = 14.2$, $h = 2.6$ **b** when $r = 7.8$, $h = 6.9$

26 Use the formula $v^2 = h^2 + 2as$ to find v

a when $u = 27$, $a = 5.6$, $s = 132$ **b** when $u = 31$, $a = -3.5$, $s = 56$

27 Use the formula $d = t\dfrac{\mu - 1}{\mu}$, to find d

    a when $t = 1.23$, $\mu = 1.44$ **b** when $t = 0.0046$, $\mathbf{u} = 1.078$

28 Use the formula $F = \dfrac{E}{L}(x - L)$ to find F

    a when $E = 23.5$, $L = 1.64$, $x = 1.89$
    b when $E = 7393$, $L = 0.348$, $x = 0.392$

29 Use the formula $x = \dfrac{-b + \sqrt{(b^2 - 4ac)}}{2a}$ to find x

    a when $a = 248$, $b = 807$, $c = 159$
    b when $a = 0.063$, $b = 0.052$, $c = -0.036$

30 The formula $S = \frac{1}{2}n(n + 1)$ gives the sum, S, of the first n natural numbers (positive integers). Verify this statement by adding the numbers up to 20, and then substituting 20 for n in the formula. Use the formula to find the sum of the first hundred natural numbers, and that of the first thousand natural numbers. Find (by successive trials) the smallest value of n for which S is more than a million.

Miscellaneous

31 A block of wood 26 cm long is cut down to 23 cm long, and the other dimensions are also reduced, so that the block now has the same shape as it had before. Find the percentage reduction in

    a the width of the block,
    b the total surface area of the block,
    c the volume of the block.

32 A leaden sphere of diameter 11 cm is melted down and then recast into 1253 smaller spheres, all of the same size. Find the diameter of each of these smaller spheres.

Find also how many times the total surface area of all the small spheres is larger than that of the original sphere.

33 In Figure 6.1

    a use trigonometry to calculate BC and BD
    b use Pythagoras' theorem to calculate AC and CD
    c find the areas of the three triangles.

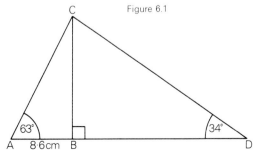

Figure 6.1

34   The lengths of the diagonals of a rhombus are 8.6 cm and 6.3 cm. Calculate

a the area of the rhombus   **b** the sizes of its angles

35   The table shows the distances in miles between six cities.

	Derby	Glouc.	Leic.	Not.	Oxford
Cambridge	96	123	68	83	83
Derby	—	93	28	16	90
Gloucester	—	—	85	110	52
Leicester	—	—	—	25	73
Nottingham	—	—	—	—	98

a Find the length of the shortest circular tour, starting and finishing at Cambridge and visiting all the other five cities, giving the order in which they are visited.

b A conference is to be held in one of the cities, with delegates from each of them. Find in which of the cities the conference should be held, so as to make the total distance travelled by the delegates as small as possible.

36   Write down, or set into the memory of your calculator, a number of three digits, of which the first exceeds the last by at least 2 (e.g. 341). From this number subtract the number which has the same digits but in reverse order (e.g. 143). Take the number which results, and *add* it to the number which has the same digits but in reverse order. Note the 4-digit number which results. Repeat the process several times, beginning with a different number each time, and comment on the result.

37   Repeat Question 36, but this time with a number of *five* digits. You will find that now the final result is not always the same number, but is always one of three different numbers. Find what these numbers are, and under what conditions each of them is produced.

38   Show that 371 431 is a multiple of 173. Find the remainder when 371 431 is divided

a by 174   **b** by 175

Chapter 7

Trigonometry, the sine and cosine

In Chapter 15 of Book 1 we saw how to make use of the *tangent* of an angle: in Figure 7.1 the tangent of angle A is the fraction $\dfrac{BC}{AB}$ and has the same value whatever the size of the triangle, provided angle A is kept constant. We saw that we could use the tangent

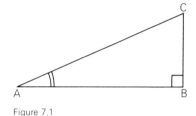

Figure 7.1

1 to find the length of either AB or BC if we know the length of the other, and if we know the size of angle A,

2 to find the size of angle A if we know the lengths of both AB and BC.

None of these calculations involves AC, the *hypotenuse* of the triangle. Calculations involving the hypotenuse can be done using the tangent, together with Pythagoras' theorem, but it is far simpler to use either or both of two other quantities, the *sine* and the *cosine*.

We will begin with the sine. In Figure 7.1, the sine of A is the fraction $\frac{BC}{AC}$: so the sine is the quantity obtained by dividing the length of the opposite side (that is, the side opposite to the angle involved) by the length of the hypotenuse. We can write briefly,

$$\text{sine} = \frac{\text{opposite}}{\text{hypotenuse}}$$

and therefore

$$\text{opposite} = \text{hypotenuse} \times \text{sine}$$

It is helpful to remember 'O.H.M.S.' which can mean, not only 'On Her Majesty's Service' but also

Opposite over **H**ypotenuse **M**akes **S**ine
and
Opposite equals **H**ypotenuse **M**ultiplied by **S**ine

Example 1   In Figure 7.1, if AC = 5.2 cm and angle A = 23°, calculate BC.

Answer
BC is the opposite side and AC is the hypotenuse, so

$$BC = 5.2 \times \text{sine } 23°$$
$$= 5.2 \times 0.3907 \text{ (from tables)}$$
$$= 2.032$$

Since the data are only given to 2 sig. fig., the answer should be given as 2.0 cm.

Example 2   A ladder 6 metres long leans at an angle of 74°. Calculate the height of its upper end above the (horizontal) ground.

Figure 7.2

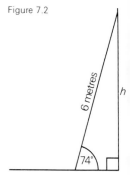

Answer
In Figure 7.2 it can be seen that the height (marked *h*) forms the 'opposite' side of a right-angled triangle whose other two sides are the ladder and the ground. The hypotenuse is formed by the ladder, and so is 6 m long. We therefore have

$$h = 6 \times \sin 74°$$

(In calculations it is customary to shorten

'sine' to 'sin')

$$= 6 \times 0.9613$$

$$= 5.768$$

Answer $= 5.8$ m, approximately

Example 3   The triangle XYZ is right-angled at Y, XZ$=8$ cm, YZ$=3.2$ cm. Calculate the size of angle X.

Answer
YZ is the 'opposite' side, and XZ is the hypotenuse, so

$$\sin X = \frac{3.2}{8} = 0.4$$

Using the tables 'backwards', we find that angle X is 24°.

Example 4   A door which is 90 cm wide can be opened until the edge of it furthest from the hinge is 48 cm from the doorway. Find the angle through which it can be turned.

Answer
Figure 7.3 is a plan view of the door. The door, 90 cm wide, forms the hypotenuse of a right-angled triangle, while the line 48 cm long forms the side opposite to the angle X which is needed. So we have

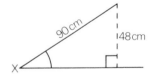

Figure 7.3

$$\sin X = \frac{48}{90} = 0.5333$$

giving X$=32.2°$: in this case 32° is probably the best answer.

Answers to the questions in Exercises 7.1, 7.2, 7.3 and 7.4 should be given to 2 significant figures or the nearest millimetre (angles to the nearest degree) except where there are other instructions.

Exercise 7.1

1   In each of the triangles in Figure 7.4 find the length of the side marked with a letter.

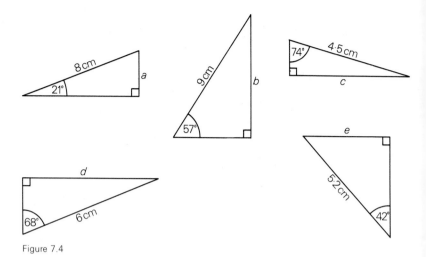

Figure 7.4

2   **a** In triangle PQR, $\angle R = 90°$, $\angle P = 34°$, PQ = 7.1 cm; find the length of QR.

b In triangle UVW, $\angle V = 90°$, $\angle W = 56°$, UW = 11.2 cm; find the length of UV.

c In triangle DEF, $\angle D = 90°$, $\angle E = 71°$, EF = 4.2 cm; find the length of DF.

3   The diagonals of a rectangle are each 9 cm long, and make angles of 42° with the longer sides. Find the length of the shorter sides.

4   Find the height, and hence the area, of an equilateral triangle of which each side is 4.4 cm long.

5   Find the height of an isoceles triangle if each of the equal sides is 11 cm long and each of the equal angles is 71°.

6   A vector whose length is 7 units makes an angle of 37° with the x-axis. Find its y component.

7   The string of a kite is 43 m long, and makes an angle of 23° with the ground. Assuming that the string is straight and the ground horizontal, find the height of the kite above the ground.

8   An aeroplane takes off and flies a distance of 2400 m in a straight line making an angle 18° with the ground. Find its height above ground at this moment.

9   A boat sails across a river (whose banks may be regarded as straight) in a direction making an angle of 64° with the direction of the current. Find the width of the river, if the boat has to sail 77 m to get across.

10   A boat sails from a harbour H on a bearing of 213. There is a small island 17 km from H, on a bearing of 230. Find the distance of the boat from the island when the boat is at its nearest point to the island.

11   In each of the triangles in Figure 7.5, find the size of the marked angle.

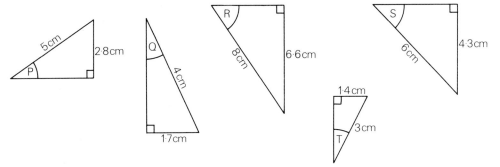

Figure 7.5

12   **a** In triangle ABC, $\angle A = 90°$, BC = 8 cm, AC = 4.8 cm. Find the size of $\angle B$.
      b in Triangle PQR, $\angle Q = 90°$, PR = 11 cm, QR = 3.7 cm. Find the size of $\angle P$.
      c In triangle, XYZ, $\angle Z = 90°$, XY = 7.2 cm, YZ = 1.2 cm. Find the size of $\angle X$.

13   One side of a rectangle is 4.7 cm long, and each diagonal is 8.3 cm long. Find the angles between the diagonals and the sides.

14   An isosceles triangle is 6.4 cm high (i.e. the perpendicular distance from the vertex where the equal sides meet, onto the opposite side, is 6.4 cm), and the equal sides are each 8.9 cm long. Find all the angles of the triangle.

15   AD is the perpendicular from the vertex A to the side BC of the triangle ABC. AB = 9 cm, AD = 8 cm, and AC = 15 cm. Find all the angles of triangle ABC.

16   One end of a pole 3.2 m long is raised to a height of 1.3 m above the (horizontal) ground. Find the angle which the pole makes with the ground.

17   Two straight roads cross. A point on one road is 250 m from the cross-roads, and is 115 m from the nearest point on the other road. Find the angle at which the roads cross.

18   After flying in a straight line for 2200 m from taking off, an aeroplane is 870 m above the ground. Find the angle its flight-path made with the ground.

19 A and B are points on the 107 and 137 metre contours. There is a straight road between A and B, and the distance from A to B, measured along this road, is 165 m. Find the angle between the road and the horizontal.

20 The banks of a certain stretch of a river are parallel and 22 m apart. A swimmer swims across the river in a straight line, but is so carried down by the current that he actually swims 35 m in crossing. Find the angle between the swimmer's line of travel and the banks of the river.

Finding the hypotenuse

In some problems it is necessary to calculate the hypotenuse of a right-angled triangle (AC in Figure 7.1) when an angle and the side opposite to it are known (i.e. $\angle A$ and BC in Figure 7.1).

Suppose for example, BC = 3 cm, $\angle A = 20°$. Then

$$AC \sin 20° = 3,$$

so
$$AC = \frac{3}{\sin 20°} = \frac{3}{0.342} = 8.77 \text{ cm}$$

In all calculations of this kind, it is necessary to divide by the sine of an angle, and as this is nearly always an awkward number, calculators or logarithms are almost essential.

Example 5   What length of ladder will be needed to reach to height of 52 m, if the ladder must make an angle of at most 75° with the horizontal?

Answer
Taking the angle as 75° and x m as the length of the ladder, we have

$$x \sin 75° = 52$$

$$x = \frac{52}{\sin 75°} = \frac{52}{0.966} = 53.8$$

The length is 54 m (to the nearest metre).

Figure 7.6

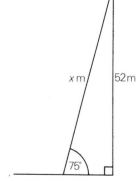

Exercise 7.2

1   In each of the triangles in Figure 7.7, find the length of the side marked with a letter.

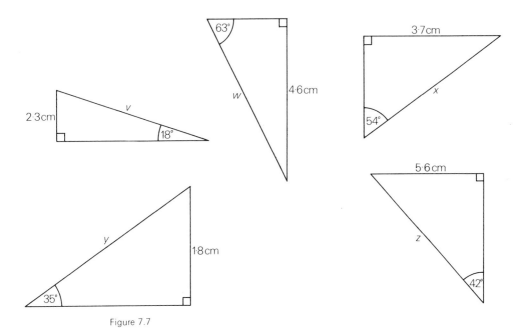

Figure 7.7

2 **a** In triangle DEF, $\angle D = 90°$, $\angle E = 43°$, DF = 37 cm; find the length of EF.
   b In triangle QRS, $\angle R = 90°$, $\angle Q = 27°$, RS = 8.6 cm; find the length of QS.
   c In triangle UVW, $\angle W = 90°$, $\angle V = 76°$, UW = 12.5 cm; find the length of UV.

3 ABC is a triangle in which AB = AC. $\angle ABC = \angle ACB = 67°$, and the perpendicular distance of A from BC is 7.4 cm. Find the lengths of AB and AC.

4 O is the foot of the perpendicular from X to the side YZ of the triangle XYZ. XO = 5.2 cm, $\angle Y = 54°$, $\angle Z = 39°$. Find the lengths of XY and XZ.

5 The longer diagonal of a rhombus makes angles of 22° with the sides. The length of the shorter diagonal is 6.8 cm. Find the length of each side.

6 In the parallelogram ABCD, AB = 11 cm, $\angle A = 71°$ and the area of the parallelogram is 50 cm². Find the length of BC.

7 Find the length of a vector which makes an angle of 57° with the *x*-axis and whose *y* component is 2.

8 A mast is supported by a guy-line running from its top to a point on the ground 17 m from its foot, and making an angle of 24° with the vertical. Find the length of this guy-line.

9   A road runs north and south across open country. A party of walkers are at a point 950 m west of the road, and start to walk on a bearing 035. How far must they walk before they reach the road?

10   Find the length of string needed for a kite to fly at a height of 50 m above ground, when the string (taken as being straight) makes an angle of 25° with the ground.

The cosine

We could manage very well, as regards right-angled triangle calculations, with only the tangent and the sine, but it is convenient also to use another quantity, the **cosine**, when dealing with certain problems.

In Figure 7.1 the cosine of $\angle A$ is the fraction $\dfrac{AB}{AC}$. AB is usually called the **adjacent** side, as it is adjacent to (i.e. next to) the angle involved. We can write

$$\text{cosine} = \frac{\text{adjacent side}}{\text{hypotenuse}}$$

and

$$\text{adjacent side} = \text{hypotenuse} \times \text{cosine}$$

Unfortunately there is no very obvious way to remember the sequence AHMC: perhaps the student can devise one.

We have

Adjacent over **H**ypotenuse **M**akes **C**osine
and
Adjacent equals **H**ypotenuse **M**ultiplied by **C**osine

The abbreviation 'cos' is normally used for cosine.

Vectors

It can be seen in Figure 7.8 that if a vector has length **r**, and makes an angle θ with the positive direction of the **x**-axis, then the components of the vector are

$$\begin{pmatrix} r \cos \theta \\ r \sin \theta \end{pmatrix}.$$

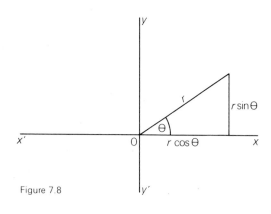

Figure 7.8

This is an important result in later work.

Example 6

In triangle PQR, (Figure 7.9),
$\angle P = 90°$, $\angle Q = 32°$, $QR = 4.8$ cm.
Find the length of PQ.

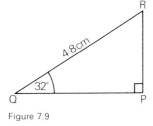

Figure 7.9

Answer

PQ is the adjacent side, so

$PQ = QR \cos \angle Q = 4.8 \cos 32°$

$\qquad = 4.8 \times 0.848$ (from tables)

$\qquad = 4.07$ so the length is 4.07 cm

Example 7

In triangle XYZ (Figure 7.10),
$\angle Y = 90°$, $YZ = 3.8$ cm, $XZ = 7$ cm.
Find the size of angle $\angle Z$.

Answer

YZ is the adjacent side, so

$\cos \angle Z = \dfrac{YZ}{XZ} = \dfrac{3.8}{7} = 0.543$

Using the tables 'backwards',

$\qquad \angle Z = 57°$

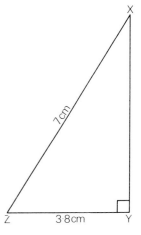

Figure 7.10

Example 8

The roof of a shelter is a rectangular sheet, 3.5 m long and 2.4 m wide. It slopes at an angle of 20° to the horizontal, with the longer edges horizontal. Find what area of the ground it protects from vertical rain.

Answer

The sheltered area is a rectangle whose length is 3.5 m, and whose width is shown in the figure as OP. In the triangle OPQ, OP is the adjacent side, so

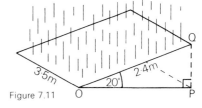

Figure 7.11

$OP = 2.4 \cos 20°$
$\quad = 2.4 \times 0.94 = 2.256$ cm

Sheltered area
$\quad = 3.5 \times 2.256 = 7.9$ m²

Example 9   A Christmas tree is to be erected in a hall 4 m high, but when the foot of the tree is on the floor, the top touches the ceiling when the tree is still at angle of 13° with the vertical. Find the height of the tree.

Answer

The tree forms the hypotenuse of a right-angled triangle of which the 'adjacent' side is the height of the hall (see Figure 7.12).

If the height of the tree is *h* metres, we have

$$h \cos 13° = 4, \text{ so}$$

$$h = \frac{4}{\cos 13°} = \frac{4}{0.974} = 4.11$$

The tree is 4.1 metres high.

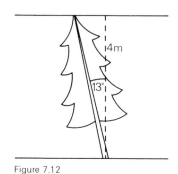

Figure 7.12

Exercise 7.3

1   In each of the triangles in Figure 7.13, find the side or angle marked with a letter.

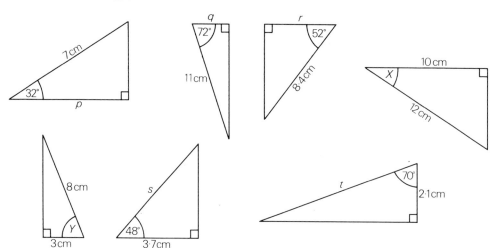

Figure 7.13

2   **a** In triangle LMN, $\angle L = 90°$, $\angle N = 32°$, MN = 42 cm. Find the length of LN.
        b In triangle OPQ, $\angle O = 90°$, OQ = 7.4 cm, PQ = 9 cm. Find the size of $\angle Q$.
        c In triangle TUV, $\angle T = 60°$, $\angle U = 90°$, TU = 3.8 cm. Find the length of TV.

3   The diagonals of a rectangle are each 11 cm long, and make angles of 27° with the longer sides. Find the lengths of the longer sides.

4   In the parallelogram PQRS, PQ = RS = 3.2 cm, $\angle P = \angle R = 63°$, and the diagonal QS is perpendicular to PQ and to RS. Calculate the length of PS and RQ.

5   Find the angles of a rhombus whose sides are all 6.4 cm long and of which one diagonal is 10.2 cm long.

6   A stretch of coast-line may be regarded as straight, running due east and west. From an inland point P the coast-line could be reached by travelling 3.2 km due north. What distance must be travelled from P in order to reach the coast-line, if one travels on a bearing of 328?

7   A helicopter rises from a point X on the ground and flies a distance of 260 m in a straight line: it is then directly over a point 78 m from X. What angle did its line of flight make with the horizontal?

8   A pole is supported by guy-lines running from its top to points on the (horizontal) ground. One guy-line is 7.2 m long and makes an angle of 35° with the vertical; how high is the pole? Another line is 8.5 m long; what angle does this line make with the vertical?

9   What is the smallest angle that a pole 4 m long can make with the vertical, if it is in a room whose height is 3.4 m?

10 A swing is attached by ropes 2.6 m long. A girl swings herself so that when she is at here highest point, she is 0.8 m below the point where the ropes are attached. Through what total angle does she swing?

11 On a map whose scale is 1:50 000, two points at different levels are shown by dots 1.2 cm apart. The distance in a striaght line between the points is 660 m. Find the angle made with the horizontal by the line joining the points.

12 From a point A, a church spire is observed in a due northerly direction. From a point B, which is 220 m due west of A, the bearing of the same spire is 036. Find the distance of the spire from B.

13 Two ships sail from the same harbour at the same time. One ship, A, sails due east at 12 km/h and the other, B, sails on a bearing of 062. It is observed that B is always due north of A. Calculate the speed of B.

14 A rod AB which is 15 cm long can just be fitted inside a cylindrical can of radius 4 cm. Find the angle between the rod and that diameter of one end of the can which passes through A.

Further problems on the sine and cosine

To be able to use the sine or cosine (or the tangent) at this stage, it is necessary to work with a right-angled triangle. In all the problems encountered so far, the figure has consisted of a right-angled triangle, but to deal with other problems it is sometimes necessary to draw one or more additional lines, to form a right-angled triangle. For example, if the figure is an isosceles triangle, drawing the line of symmetry will divide it into two congruent right-angled triangles, and this may be helpful.

Example 10   In the triangle ABC, AB=AC=6 cm, and $\angle A=56°$. Calculate the length of the side BC, and the area of the triangle.

Answer

Draw the line AX where X is the mid-point of BC: this line bisects $\angle A$ and is perpendicular to BC. In the triangle AXB,

$$BX=AB \sin BAX$$

$$=6 \sin 28°$$

$$=6 \times 0.469=2.82 \text{ cm}$$

$$BC=2BX=2 \times 2.82=5.64 \text{ cm}$$

To find the area, we need to know AX, the height of the triangle.

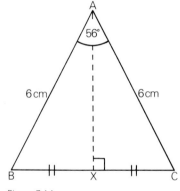

Figure 7.14

$$AX=AB \cos BAX=6 \cos 28°$$

$$=6 \times 0.883=5.30 \text{ cm}$$

The area is

$$\frac{1}{2} \times 5.64 \times 5.30=14.9 \text{ cm}^2$$

Example 11   The doors of a garage are each 1.6 m wide, and each will turn from the closed position only through an angle of 70°. Find

a the width of the opening between the doors, when they are open as wide as they will go,

b through what additional angle the doors must be made to turn in order to increase the width of the opening to 3 m.

Answer

In Figure 7.15, BC represents the doorway, and AB and CD represent the doors, open to their fullest extent. The dotted lines AX and DY are drawn at right-angles to BC.

a In the triangle ABX,

BX = AB cos ABX

$= 1.6 \times \cos 70°$

$= 1.6 \times 0.342 = 0.547$ m

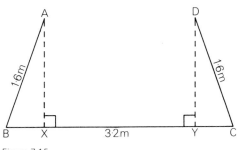

Figure 7.15

Now   AD = XY = BC − BX − CY = 3.2 − 0.547 − 0.547

$= 2.11$ m

b If AD is to be increased to 3 m, then XY must also be 3 m, and the new values of BX and CY must be 0.1 m each.

So the new value of ∠ABX is given by

$$\cos BX = \frac{0.1}{1.6}$$

$$= 0.0625$$

and   ∠ABX = 86.4°

So each door must be made to turn through an additional angle of 16.4°. (If the answer is to be given to the nearest degree, 17° is the best answer: the opening should be too wide rather than too narrow.)

Exercise 7.4

1 In the triangle XYZ, XY = XZ = 4.4 cm, and ∠X = 126°. Find the length of YZ, and the area of the triangle.

2 In the triangle OPQ, OP = OQ, ∠O = 72°, and PQ = 9.4 cm. Find the lengths of OP and OQ, and the area of the triangle.

3 Find the lengths of the diagonals of a rhombus, if each side is 8.2 cm long, and the angles are 52° and 128°.

4 Each side of a rhombus is 5.8 cm long, and one diagonal is 3.6 cm long. Find the length of the other diagonal, and the sizes of all the angles.

5 A regular pentagon, each side of which is 4 cm long, is inscribed in a circle. Find the radius of the circle.

6 A regular octagon is inscribed in a circle of radius 6.5 cm. Find the length of each side of the octagon.

7 A regular polygon is inscribed in a circle of radius 6 cm. Each side of the polygon is about 1.25 cm long: how many sides has it?

8 Each of two of the sides of a kite is 9 cm long, and the angle between them is 38°. The angle between the other two sides is 156°. Find the lengths of these two sides, and the lengths of the diagonals.

9 Figure 7.16 shows the trapezium WXYZ in which WX is parallel to YZ. WX= XY=4 cm, YZ=8 cm, LY=52°. Find the length of WZ and the sizes of all the other angles.

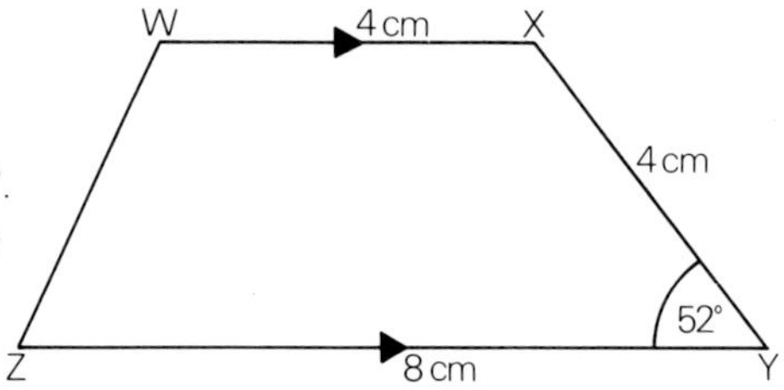

Figure 7.16

10 Two towers, T and U, are 20 m apart. From the top of T the angle of elevation of the top of U is 23° and the angle of depression of the bottom of U is 65°. Find the distances from the top of T to the top and to the bottom of U.

11 Each arm of a pair of dividers is 5 cm long. Find the angle between the arms when the points are 4 cm apart.

12 A boat sails 3 km on bearing 052 and then 2 km on bearing 123. Find how far north and how far east it then is from its starting point.

13 A step ladder 2.2 m long is hinged at its upper end to a strut 1.8 m long. When the step-ladder and strut are erected, the hinge is 1.6 m above the floor. Find the angles the ladder and the strut then make with the floor.

14 A lean-to shed is 2 m high at one side, and 1.5 m high at the other. The width of the roof, measured down the slope, is 1.8 m. Find the angle of slope of the roof, and find the width of the shed, measured horizontally.

15 A box is 2.4 m long, 1.8 m wide and 1.2 m high. It is lying on a horizontal floor, on one of its largest faces. It is then tilted through 22° about one of its longer edges, which remains on the floor. Find the height above the floor of each of the other long edges.

16 A party of explorers are travelling due northward, when they come to a lake. In order to avoid it, they travel for 4 km on bearing 040. Find how far they now are from the line of their original route. They then change direction to bearing 330, and continue in this direction until they return to the line of their original route. Find the additional distance they had to travel as a result of having to make the detour round the lake. (In this question, work to 3 significant figures.)

17 A surveyor stands at a point A and measures the angle of elevation of the top, T, of a building (see Figure 7.17) and finds it to be 28°. He then walks a (horizontal) distance of 14 m towards the building,

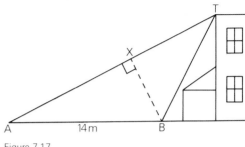

Figure 7.17

to a point B, and finds that the angle of elevation of T is now 65°. If X is the point on AT such that $\angle AXB = 90°$, calculate

a the length of BX   **c** the length of BT
b the size of $\angle$ATB   **d** the height of the building

18 The radius of a bicycle-wheel is 66 cm. At a certain instant a point P of the tyre is in contact with the road. Find the height of P above the road when the wheel has turned through

a 63°   **b** 163°   **c** 263°

19 Two observation posts, A and B, are on the same level and 800 m apart. When an aeroplane is at a point O, vertically above the line AB, its angle of elevation from A is 63° and from B, 27°. Find

a the distance OA   **c** the height of O above ground level.
b the distance OB,

20 With the same axes and on the same scale, draw the graphs of $x \rightarrow \sin x$ and $x \rightarrow \cos x$ for the domain set $x: 0 \leqslant x \leqslant 90°$. What symmetry have

a each separate graph,   **b** the two graphs taken together?

Problems on sine, cosine and tangent, and Pythagoras' theorem

Example 12   A lighthouse A is 6 km due north of a lighthouse B. A ship C has bearings of 150 and 060 from A and B respectively. Calculate the distance BC. The ship now sails due north to a point D which is on bearing 060 from A. Calculate the distances AD and BD and the bearing of D from B.   *(SA)*

Answer

Since ABC is a triangle right-angled at C

BC = 6 cos 60°,
    = 6 × 0.500 = 3.0 km

Since CD and AD are parallel to RA and BC respectively, ABCD is a parallelogram, and

AD = BC = 3.0 km

X is the point due north of A and due west of D.

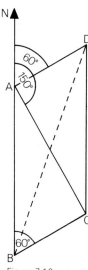

Figuer 7.18

$$DX = 3 \sin 60° = 3 \times 0.866 = 2.60 \text{ km}$$

$$AX = 3 \cos 60° = 1.5, \text{ so } BX = 6.0 + 1.5 \text{ km} = 7.5 \text{ km}$$

$$BD^2 = BX^2 + DX^2 = 7.5^2 + 2.6^2 = 56.25 + 6.76 = 63.01$$

so   BD = 7.9 km

Also $\tan \angle ABD = \dfrac{DX}{BX} = \dfrac{2.60}{7.5} = 0.347$, so $\angle ABD = 19.1°$, and the

bearing is 019.

Exercise 7.5

1   In Figure 7.19, the angles QPS and PRQ are right angles, the angle QPR is 27° and PQ = 20 cm. Calculate the lengths of QR, PS and QS.

(*OC*)

Figure 7.19

2   ABCD is a trapezium with AB parallel to DC. The sides DA, AB, and BC are each of length 8 cm and the angles at C and D are each 50°. Calculate

   a the length of CD,   **b** the area of the trapezium   (*OC*)

3   In Figure 7.20, ABCD is a
rectangle in which AB = 8 cm and
BC = 6 cm. The side BC is
produced to the point E such that
the angle CDE = 20°. Calculate

   a   the length of EC
   b   the length of DE
   c   the size of the angle EAB

(OC)

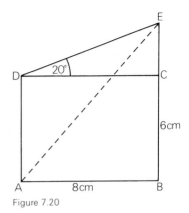

Figure 7.20

4   In Figure 7.21, the angles DAB,
ABC and ACD are all right angles;
AC = 10 cm and the angle
CAB = 53°. Calculate

   a   the length of AB
   b   the length of AD
   c   the size of the angle ABD

(OC)

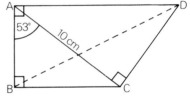

Figure 7.21

5   AXYZ is a rectangle in which AX = 8 cm. D is a point on YZ such that
AD = 10 cm and YD = 5 cm. B and C are points on XY such that
XB = 2 cm and ∠BCD = 139°. Calculate

   a   ∠ABX   **b**   ∠ADZ   **c**   DC   (CB)

6   D is the foot of the perpendicular from A to the side BC of the triangle
ABC. AB = 20 cm, AC = 13 cm, BD = 16 cm. Find

   a   AD   **b**   DC   **c**   the area of triangle ABC.   (CD)

7   Figure 7.22 shows part of a simple
mechanism. The rod OA is 22 cm
long, and rotates about O, while B
moves backwards and forwards
along the line OX. The rod AB is
38 cm long. Find the size of ∠OBA

   a   when OAB is a right angle,
   b   when AOB is a right angle,
   c   when angles OAB and AOB are
equal.

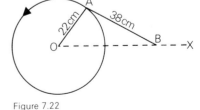

Figure 7.22

8   Figure 7.23, not drawn to scale, shows a coastguard station C and
three positions, P. Q and R of a ship which is steaming due south
at 32 km/h.

At 09.00 the ship is at P, which is 10 km from C. The bearing of C from P is 242 and Q is south-east of C. Calculate

a the distance PQ,
b the time, to the nearest minute, when the ship will be at Q.
c the distance CR, where R represents the position of the ship at 09.30.

(*CB*)

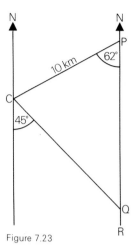

Figure 7.23

9 ABCD is a trapezium in which AD is parallel to BC. AB=5 cm, BC=12 cm, $\angle DAB=40°$ and $\angle CDA=32°$. Calculate

a the perpendicular distance between the parallel sides,
b the length of AD,
c the area of the trapezium.

10 A regular pentagon ABCDE is inscribed in a circle with centre O and radius 10 cm. Find

a angle AOB,   **c** the length of one of its sides.
b the area of the pentagon,

The mid-points of the sides of the pentagon are now joined to form a smaller regular pentagon. If M is one of these mid-points, find the length OM. Hence find the ratio of the area of the smaller pentagon to that of the larger. (*SA*)

11 In a triangle PQR, $\angle P=45°$, $\angle Q=30°$ and QR=6 cm. The perpendicular QS from Q to PR produced is itself produced to T so that $ST=\frac{1}{3}QS$. Calculate QS, SR, SP and angle TPS. Find also the area of triangle TQP. (*SA*)

12 Starting from a harbour H, a ship sails for 10 km on bearing 325 and then for 12 km on bearing 085. Find

a its distance north of H,
b its distance east of H,
c the bearing on which it should sail in order to return to H by as short a route as possible,
d the distance it will have to sail to reach H by this shortest route.

13 A tower TA is 55 m high: on top of it there is a flagstaff AF. From a point on the ground, on the same level as T, the angles of elevation of A and F are respectively 38° and 42°. Find the height of the flagstaff.

Chapter 8

More statistics

In Chapter 11 of Book 1 we saw how to draw the frequency graph and to find the mode, median and mean of a number of quantities which are all positive integers. By way of revision, the following example is given.

Example 1   Draw the frequency diagram and find the mode, median and mean of the following distribution, which relates to the numbers of eggs in the nests of blue-tits (as given in Question 24, page 96).

Number of eggs	4	5	6	7	8	9	10	11
Number of nests (frequency)	3	16	28	31	17	8	6	1

Answer
The *frequency diagram* is as shown in Figure 8.1.

The **mode** is 7 (the number with the highest frequency).

Since there are 110 nests altogether, the **median** is half-way between the numbers for the 55th and 56th nests, but as both these are 7, the median is 7.

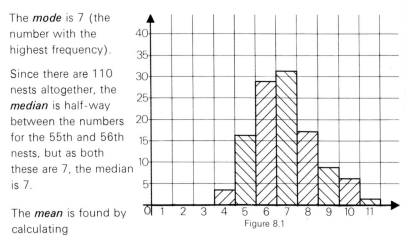

Figure 8.1

The **mean** is found by calculating $(4 \times 3) + (5 \times 16) + (6 \times 28) + \ldots$ and so on: this gives 756, the total number of eggs; dividing 756 by 110 gives the mean which is 6.87.

Grouped frequency

In many cases the quantities involved are **not** positive integers. Consider, for example, the heights of a set of lupin plants, some of which are illustrated at the head of this chapter. The height of each plant may have any value between about 40 cm and 160 cm, and it would be far too laborious to classify each plant according to its own individual height.

The method adopted is to classify the values of the quantity concerned (in this case, the heights of the plants) into groups, which may be of any size. The heights can be classified into those between 40 cm and 50 cm, those between 50 cm and 60 cm, and so on, as shown by the table.

Height in cm	40–50	50–60	60–70	70–80	80–90	90–100
Frequency	3	7	19	25	31	57

Height in cm	100–110	110–120	120–130	130–140	140–150	150–160
Frequency	73	45	29	18	11	7

Frequency diagram. A frequency diagram can be drawn, but since each column represents a whole range of values, the width of the column is not a matter of arbitrary choice: the column must fill the whole range, as shown in Figure 8.2. This kind of frequency graph is also called a **histogram**.

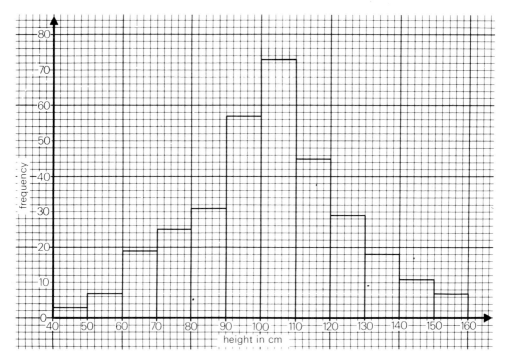

Figure 8.2

Mode. We cannot state which individual height is the most frequent, but we can identify the **modal group**, the group with the highest frequency: this is the 100–110 cm group.

Median. Since there are 325 plants altogether, the median (the one in the middle when they are arranged in order of size, as in the drawing) is the height of the 163rd plant. There are 142 plants less than 100 cm high, and 215 with heights up to 110 cm. The median must therefore be in the range 100 to 110 cm. At present we can say no more than this about the median, but later in this chapter we will see how to make a closer estimate of it.

Mean. As we do not know the heights of the individual plants in each group, we assume that the mean height of the plants in any group is the height which is in the middle of the range for that group: for example, that the mean height of the plants in the first group is 45 cm, that of those in the second group is 55 cm, and so on. To find the mean of the entire set of heights we therefore calculate $(45 \times 3) + (55 \times 7) + (65 \times 19) + (75 \times 25)$... and so on, finishing with $... + (155 + 7)$. This gives 33 255: dividing 33 255 by 325, the number of plants, gives 102.3 cm for the mean.

Borderline cases

The student may well ask, 'What about plants which are *exactly* 50 cm or 60 cm or 70 cm or 150 cm high? Into which group are they put?

This is an important question and will be dealt with later, but for the present we will assume that there is no plant whose height in centimetres is an exact multiple of 10, and that all heights can be put into one group or another. The corresponding assumption should be made when answering the questions in Exercise 8.1.

Grouping integral values

The group treatment can be applied when the quantities recorded, although positive integers, take so many different values that it would be impracticable to deal with them individually. Examples of cases where this treatment would be appropriate are an analysis of the numbers of words in sentences of a passage of writing, and of the numbers of runs scored at cricket by a large number of batsmen.

Exercise 8.1

In each case

a draw a frequency graph to illustrate the information given
b state which is the modal group
c state which group contains the median
d calculate the mean.

1 The heights of a number of children are measured and classified as follows.

Height (cm)	145–150	150–155	155–160	160–165	165–170	170–175	175–180
Frequency	10	25	36	66	17	8	2

2 The table shows the weights of eggs laid by two breeds of hens under certain conditions.

Weight in grams	40–45	45–50	50–55	55–60	60–65	65–70	70–75
Frequency (breed A)	2	9	22	38	20	8	1
Frequency (breed B)	6	20	31	25	15	3	0

3 Estimates were made of the ages of the first 400 people to use a certain public library on a certain day.

Estimated age in years	0–10	10–20	20–30	30–40	40–50	50–60	60–70	70–80
Frequency	7	84	56	50	34	34	72	63

4 The girths of 100 young trees in a plantation were measured, with results as shown.

Girth in cm	25–30	30–35	35–40	40–45	45–50	50–55	55–60
Frequency	7	28	32	21	8	2	2

5 The scores of the batsmen of the Much Slogging cricket club were analysed at the end of one season, with the following result.

Number of runs	0–4	5–9	10–14	15–19	20–24
Frequency	35	27	16	18	13

Number of runs	25–29	30–34	35–39	40–44	45–49
Frequency	11	3	6	10	2

(This time there are no borderline cases. Make the columns of your frequency graph extend from 0 to $4\frac{1}{2}$, $4\frac{1}{2}$ to $9\frac{1}{2}$, $9\frac{1}{2}$ to $14\frac{1}{2}$ and so on.)

Correct treatment of borderline cases

In order to deal properly with borderline cases, it is necessary to know how accurately the measurements were made. To return to the lupin plants, suppose they were measured to the nearest centimetre. This means that, for example, all heights in the range h: $39.5 \leqslant h < 40.5$ would be classified as 40. It is a matter of convention that these are included in the '40 to 50' range. The '40 to 50' range therefore includes all heights in the range h: $39.5 \leqslant h < 49.5$, and the boundaries between the groups are not 40, 50, 60, 70 etc., but 39.5, 49.5, 59.5, 69.5 etc.

Effect on the frequency diagram. In order to take account of the above result, the columns of the frequency diagram should correctly extend from 39.5 to 49.5, 49.5 to 59.5 and so on.

Effect on the calculation of the mean. Since the '40 to 50' range is in fact the 39.5 to 49.5 range, the middle of this range is not 45 but 44.5, and this is the number that should be multiplied by 3 in the course of calculating the mean. Similarly the 'mid-interval values' for the other ranges are 54.5, 64.5 and so on. Fortunately we do not have to calculate the mean all over again: it can be shown that the effect of reducing every value by 0.5 is simply to reduce the mean by 0.5, so that it should be 101.8 instead of 102.3.

Estimated mean

In Chapter 11 of Book 1 we saw how the calculation of the mean can be simplified by the use of an estimated mean. This device can also be used when grouped frequencies are involved. We might have estimated the mean height of the lupin plants to be 104.5 cm. (This is a more useful estimate than if a 'round' number had been chosen, as it makes the deviations simple numbers.) The table would be as follows.

Height in cm	40–50	50–60	60–70	70–80	80–90	90–100
Mid-interval value	44.5	54.5	64.5	74.5	84.5	94.5
Deviation	-60	-50	-40	-30	-20	-10
Frequency	3	7	19	25	31	57
Deviation × frequency	-180	-350	-760	-750	-620	-570

Height in cm	100–110	110–120	120–130	130–140	140–150	150–160
Mid-interval value	104.5	114.5	124.5	134.5	144.5	154.5
Deviation	0	$+10$	$+20$	$+30$	$+40$	$+50$
Frequency	73	45	20	18	11	7
Deviation × frequency	0	$+450$	$+580$	$+540$	$+440$	$+350$

The sum of the bottom row is -870; dividing this by 325 (the total number of plants) gives -2.7. Subtracting 2.7 from our estimate of 104.5 gives 101.8, and this is the mean.

Exercise 8.2

1 Correct the answer you obtained for the mean in Question 1 of Exercise 8.1, if the heights of the children were measured **a** to the nearest centimetre, **b** to the nearest 5 mm.

How, if at all, is the modal group affected?

2 Correct the answers you obtained for the means in Question 2 of Exercise 8.1 if the weights of the eggs were given **a** to the nearest gram, **b** the nearest half-gram.

3 Correct the answer you obtained for the mean in Question 4 of Exercise 8.1 if the girths of the trees were measured **a** to the nearest cm, **b** to the

nearest 5 cm (so that the '25–30' group, for example, includes only the values given as 25 cm).

For each of the remaining examples, carry out the instructions given at the head of Exercise 8.1 (page 120).

4 A number of children were timed running round their school playing-field. The times were measured to the nearest second, and were grouped as follows.

Time in seconds	100–110	110–120	120–130	130–140
Frequency	5	12	23	15

Time in seconds	140–150	150–160	160–170	170–180
Frequency	38	21	9	6

5 After an examination the marks of the candidates were classified as follows.

Marks	0–9	10–19	20–29	30–39	40–49
Frequency	2	7	33	84	122

Marks	50–59	60–69	70–79	80–89	90–99
Frequency	133	78	30	8	3

6 The birth-weights of 300 babies born in a certain hospital were recorded to the nearest 50 g and classified as follows.

Weight (kg)	1.5–2	2–2.5	2.5–3	3–3.5	3.5–4	4–4.5	4.5–5
Frequency	5	28	72	99	68	25	3

7 A record was made of the amounts spent by the first 300 customers at a supermarket one day. (The amounts were recorded to the nearest 10p.)

Amount in £	under 2	2–4	4–6	6–8	8–10
Frequency	70	78	48	32	17

Amount in £	10–12	12–14	14–16	16–18	18–20
Frequency	24	14	8	5	4

8 A doctor kept a note of the number of visits each patient on his list has made to his surgery during the course of a year. The numbers were classified as follows.

Number of visits	0–4	5–9	10–14	15–19
Frequency	1250	1134	510	356

Number of visits	20–24	25–29	30–34	35 and over
Frequency	184	120	87	32

(For the '35 and over' group, take the mid-interval value as 42.)

9 Another doctor noted the length of time each patient spent in her surgery during one week. The times were noted to the nearest minute, and were classified as follows.

	1–3	4–6	7–9	10–12	13–15	16–18	19–21
Frequency	8	18	42	55	38	36	27

Statistical projects

Carry out some of these statistical projects, possibly as one of a team. For each project, you should proceed as follows.

1 Decide exactly what you are going to measure, and to what degree of accuracy you can measure it.

2 Decide on the probable range of values you will encounter, and into what groups you are going to arrange the values. (It is sometimes useful to carry out a small 'pilot' project first, to help you with these decisions.)

3 Make a 'tally-sheet' on which to enter your readings.

4 Carry out the project, entering your readings on the tally-sheet.

5 Draw a frequency graph.

6 State the modal group.

7 State which group contains the median.

8 Calculate the mean.

If you are carrying out any of the projects *after* working through the last section of this chapter, also

9 Make a cumulative frequency table and draw a cumulative frequency graph.

10 Find the median, the quartiles and the interquartile range.

As with the statistical projects in Book 1, it is more interesting to obtain two sets of readings and to compare the results. For example, in carrying out a project which involves members of your school, you could compare the results from older and younger pupils, or from boys and girls if yours is a mixed school.

1   Lengths of sentences. Count the numbers of words in the first 100 or 200 sentences in a book; then compare your results with those from another book, preferably of a different kind.

2   Cricket scores. Analyse the scores of individual batsmen recorded in one day's newspaper (in the season). Compare home with away teams, county cricket with club cricket (as recorded in a local newspaper) or make any comparison that appeals to you.

3   Football goals. If it is the football season (or if you can obtain records of past seasons) analyse the *total* numbers of goals scored by teams to date. Perhaps compare higher with lower division teams.

4   Use a stop-watch to find the time it takes each of a number of people to carry out some simple task, such as working through a very simple sum or reassembling a dismantled spring clothes-peg.

5   Put someone in a position where no clock or watch is visible, and ask him or her to tell you when a minute has passed, starting from a given signal. Record the time that actually has passed. In projects of this kind you can analyse the times themselves, or the *errors*.

6   Ask a number of people to estimate the length of a given line, or the weight of a given object, or the number of small objects in a glass jar. Here, again, an analysis of the *errors* may be even more interesting.

7   If the school keeps records of the heights and weights of pupils, and you can be allowed to use these, make an analysis of them.

8   Find the distances that pupils travel to school (you will probably need a local map to enable you to measure them accurately enough).

9   Record the amounts spent in a supermarket. Compare one supermarket with another, or one time of day with another, or the amounts spent by men with those spent by women.

You will probably be able to think of other ideas for yourself, but remember that the quantity you are to measure should be one that either varies continuously or can take a *large* number of integral values.

Cumulative frequency

It is sometimes useful to compile a *cumulative frequency* table.

For the heights of the lupin plants, the following table gives the ordinary frequencies and the cumulative frequencies. (It will be seen that the group boundaries have been corrected as shown in the paragraph after Exercise 8.1.)

Heigh in cm	39.5–49.5	49.5–59.5	59.5–69.5	69.5–79.5	79.5–89.5
Frequency	3	7	19	25	31
Cumulative frequency	3	10	29	54	85

Height in cm	89.5–99.5	99.5–109.5	109.5–119.5	119.5–129.5
Frequency	57	73	45	29
Cumulative frequency	142	215	260	289

Height in cm	129.5–139.5	139.5–149.5	149.5–159.5
Frequency	18	11	7
Cumulative frequency	307	318	325

You can see that the cumulative frequency for any group of values is obtained by adding all the frequencies for all the groups up to and including that group: for example, the cumulative frequency for the third group (59.5–69.5) is $3+10+19=29$, that for the next group is 25 more, i.e. 54, and so on.

The *cumulative frequency graph* is drawn by plotting the cumulative frequencies (vertically) against the readings, in this case the heights (horizontally), as shown in Figure 8.3. The points are joined to form a smooth curve.

The shape of this graph is typical of the cumulative frequency graphs of many distributions. Where can you see something like it in the picture at the head of this chapter?

Finding the median. One use of the cumulative frequency graph is in finding a better approximation to the median. In the picture, the plant with median height is the one in the middle of the row when the plants are arranged in order of height, and as has already been seen, this is the 163rd plant. On the graph a line is drawn horizontally from the point representing 163 (the point 'half-way up the curve') to meet the curve: another line is drawn down to the horizontal axis, to meet it at the point representing the median (or at least, a good approximation to it): here, the median is seen to be about 102 cm.

Exercise 8.3

Draw cumulative frequency graphs for the distributions given in Questions 4, 5, 6, 7, 8 and 9 of Exercise 8.2 (pages 123 to 124), and use

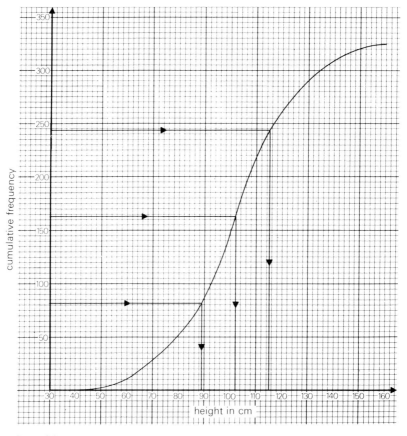

Figure 8.3

them to find the approximate medians of these distributions. Keep the graphs to use later.

Range

The mean, the median and the mode give information about a set of numbers, but this information is very far from complete. The frequency diagrams shown in Figure 8.4 relate to distributions with the same mean, median and mode, but otherwise with very different characteristics. In the first, the numbers of the set are all close to the mean, whereas in the second they are spread over a much wider range. If the two distributions represent, for example, the marks gained by the members of two classes in an examination, we can see that the first were consistent and all scored a moderate mark, whereas the performances of members of the second class differed widely, some doing very well and others very badly. If the two distributions represent the scores of two batsmen, the first can be relied on for a score but never makes a very large one, while

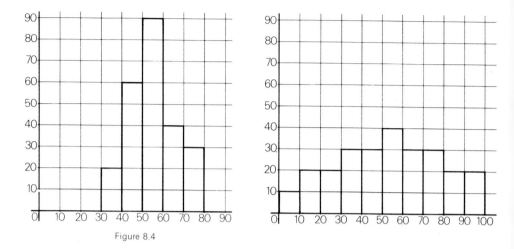

Figure 8.4

the second may score anything from a 'duck' to a century. It is useful to have a number which will give a measure of this spread or dispersion.

One such number is the *range* itself, the difference between the largest and smallest values. The shortest lupin plant may be 40 cm high (we cannot tell exactly, from the available information) and the tallest, perhaps 159 cm; if so, the range is 119 cm.

Interquartile range

The range is an unsatisfactory measure of dispersion, as it can easily be affected by one or two 'freak' values. Just one plant that was a failure and grew only 3 cm high would greatly affect the range of heights; one exceptional candidate who scored 100 (and perhaps one who was ill and scored 0) in the examination would distort the range of marks out of all recognition.

We therefore sometimes use the *interquartile range*, which might be described as the 'range of the middle half'. It is the difference between the *quartiles*, the values which are one quarter and three quarters of the way from the smallest to the largest (just as the median is half way). They can be found from the cumulative frequency graph, as may be seen in Figure 8.3. The lower quartile is the height of the 82nd plant, which can be seen to be about 89 cm, while the upper quartile is the height of the 244th plant, which is about 115 cm. This gives for the interquartile range $115 - 89 = 26$ cm.

Projects

Draw the cumulative frequency graphs relating to the statistical projects you have carried out, and use these graphs to find the median and the interquartile range in each case.

Other uses of the cumulative frequency graph

Figure 8.5 is a cumulative frequency graph relating to the scores of 2000 candidates in an examination. This graph can be used to answer questions such as the following.

If the pass mark is 40%, how many candidates will pass?

Find 40 on the horizontal axis, draw a line up to meet the curve, and then a line across to the vertical axis: this comes to 680, so that 680 *failed* and 1320 passed.

If 60% of the candidates are to pass, what will the pass mark have to be?

60% of 2000 is 1200; if 1200 pass, then 800 fail. Find 800 on the vertical axis, draw a line across to meet the curve, and then a line down to the horizontal axis: this meets it at 46, showing that the pass-mark will have to be 46.

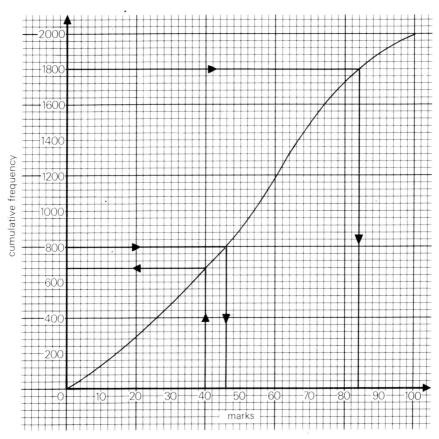

Figure 8.5

The best 10% are to be awarded a 'distinction': what is the qualifying mark for a 'distinction'?

This means that 1800 will *not* achieve distinction: find 1800 on the vertical axis and proceed as before. The distinction mark is 84.

Exercise 8.4

Use the cumulative frequency graphs you drew in answering the questions in Exercise 8.3 to find the quartiles and the interquartile range for each distribution.

The questions in Exercise 8.5 are taken from the O-level examinations of various boards, and cover the work of the whole chapter.

Exercise 8.5

1 In an examination, the marks scored by 200 candidates are listed below.

Mark	0–10	11–20	21–30	31–40	41–50
Frequency	3	5	12	17	23

Mark	51–60	61–70	71–80	81–90	91–100
Frequency	27	45	44	20	4

Make up a cumulative frequency table for these data.

a Draw the *cumulative* frequency curve for this distribution and estimate the median mark.
b Given that the pass mark was 40, estimate how many candidates failed.
c Those scoring 76 or more were awarded a 'distinction'. Estimate the number of candidates who received this award.
d Those scoring between 65 and 76 were awarded a 'merit'. Estimate what percentage of the candidates received a merit.
e Estimate the mean mark of those candidates scoring not more than 50 marks.

(LC)

2 A train is due to leave a certain station at 10.00 each day. A record is kept of the number of minutes late the train leaves on 50 days, with the results shown below.

	less than 2	less than 4	less than 6	less than 8	less than 10	less than 12
Number of minutes late	2	4	6	8	10	12
Number of days	20	35	43	46	49	50

a By drawing a cumulative frequency graph, or otherwise, estimate the median time of lateness of the trains. (If you draw a graph, use a scale of 1 cm to 1 minute on the time axis, and a scale of 2 cm to 10 units on the cumulative frequency axis.)
b Estimate the mean time of lateness of the trains.
c A man who wants to catch the train arrives on the platform at 10.04. Calculate the probability that he will catch the train.   *(LC)*

3 Each of sixty people was asked to draw freehand a line of length 20 cm. The measured lengths of the resulting lines were tabulated as follows.

Length | > in cm | ⩽	11 13	13 15	15 17	17 19	19 21	21 23	23 25
Frequency	3	6	11	15	13	10	2

Draw the cumulative frequency curve and hence, or otherwise, estimate

a the median length of the lines,
b what percentage of the lines were too short.   *(LC)*

4 The table shows the frequency distribution of the best throws of a group of students throwing the javelin for the first time.

Distance in metres	Number of students	Distance in metres	Number of students
16–	3	26–	9
18–	5	28–	5
20–	6	30–	3
22–	8	32 and over	2
24–	9		

a Make the cumulative frequency table.
b Construct the cumulative frequency graph.
c The median best throw is to be read from the graph. What point on the frequency scale should be chosen to do this? Determine the median.
d Find the semi-interquartile range.   *(SB)*

5 The table shows the frequency distribution of the marks in an examination. Construct the cumulative frequency table and draw the cumulative frequency curve. Use the graph to find the median and determine the interquartile range.

Marks	Number of candidates	Marks	Number of candidates
1–10	9	31–40	57
11–20	15	41–50	69
21–30	41	51–60	78

61–70	63	81–90	43
71–80	55	91–100	13

(SB)

6 The marks gained by 500 candidates in an examination are grouped in the following table.

Marks	20–29	30–39	40–49	50–59	60–69	70–79	80–89
Frequency	40	120	200	100	20	16	4

Calculate a mean mark of the grouped frequencies.

Make a table of cumulative frequencies for marks below $29\frac{1}{2}$, $39\frac{1}{2}$ etc.

Draw a cumulative frequency graph and use it to find

a a median mark,
b the approximate number of candidates who obtained a mark of at least 55%.

(LC)

7 A year group of 428 children is divided into two equal 'bands' R and S. The teacher for band R has examination marks already shown as a cumulative frequency curve, whilst those for band S are not yet graphed.

a From the graph shown here, estimate the upper and lower quartiles for band R. The median mark is given as 68.
b Marks for band S

Mark	0–9	10–19	20–29	30–39	40–49	50–59	60–69	70–79	80–89	90–99
No. of children	0	6	32	51	48	34	19	11	8	5
Mark less than	10	20	30	40	50	60	70	80	90	100
No. of children	0	6	38							

(i) Copy and complete the third and fourth rows of the table for band S marks.
(ii) Using scales of 1 cm to 10 marks and 1 cm to 25 children, draw the cumulative frequency curve for band S marks.
(iii) From your graph for band S, read off, and write down, the median and upper and lower quartile marks.
c (i) Write down a reasonable deduction you can make about the performances of the two bands of children by comparing the median marks only.
(ii) Make a further comparison between the marks of the two bands of children.

(SMP)

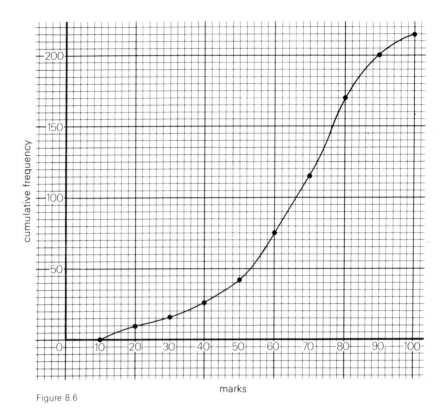

Figure 8.6

8   Figure 8.7 shows a cumulative frequency curve for the heights of 100 specimens of a certain species of plant.

   a Find the median and the inter-quartile range.
   b State the probability that a plant chosen at random from this sample will be shorter than (i) the median, (ii) 30 cm.   (*SMP*)

9   The cumulative distribution of marks gained by a group of 60 pupils in an examination is given in the table below.

Mark	10	20	30	35	40	45	50	65
Number of candidates gaining this mark or less	0	4	12	23	38	48	53	60

Using a vertical scale of 2 cm to represent 10 candidates and a horizontal scale of 2 cm to represent 10 marks, plot these values and draw a smooth curve through your points.

   a Use your graph to estimate the median mark and the inter-quartile range.
Grade E was awarded to pupils scoring 30 marks or less and grade A to those scoring more than 50 marks.

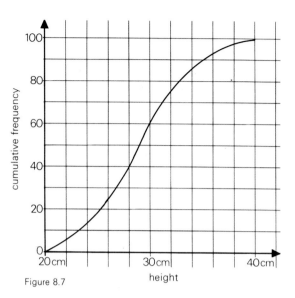

Figure 8.7

b A pupil was selected at random from the 60. Find the probability that
(i) the pupil was awarded grade E,
(ii) the pupil was awarded either grade E or grade A.   (*CD*)

10 A sample of 100 tea bags from an automatic packing machine has the following distribution.

Weight of tea bag (nearest 0.1 g)	3.0	3.1	3.2	3.3	3.4	3.5	3.6
Number of tea bags	1	6	34	42	14	2	1

a Calculate the mean weight of a tea bag in this sample.
b From this sample, estimate the weight of the tea bags in a carton of 72.
c Explain why you would expect the weight of the 72 tea bags in a carton to be more than 220 g.
d It says on the side of the carton that the average weight is 250 g. How much extra tea, on the average, will be needed in each bag to achieve this?   (*SMP*)

11 Wild service trees in two woods were measured and their diameters, correct to the nearest centimetre, are summarised in the table below.

Diameter (cm)	1–5	6–10	11–15	16–20
Crookhorn Shaw	6	4	5	4
Netherwood	1	5	8	20

Diameter (cm)	21–25	26–30	31–35	Total
Crookhorn Shaw	7	3	1	30
Netherwood	4	1	1	40

(Trees less than $\frac{1}{2}$ cm in diameter are not included.)

a (i) Draw two separate frequency diagrams to illustrate this information.
(ii) What percentage of trees in each wood has recorded diameters from 11 cm to 25 cm inclusive?
b Comment on your results in **a**
c Calculate the mean diameter of the trees in Crookhorn Shaw.
d (i) State the modal class in Netherwood.
(ii) It is estimated that the average increase in diameter is about 0.5 cm per year. Use this fact to estimate the greatest and least possible ages of the trees in this class in Netherwood.   (*SMP*)

12 Some bamboo canes are tied in bundles of equal lengths, measured to the nearest 10 cm. The number in each bundle is shown in the table.

Length	60	70	80	90	100	110	120
Number	21	35	15	29	32	43	25

a What are the shortest and longest possible lengths of cane in the 70 cm bundle?
b Construct a histogram.
c Calculate the arithmetic mean.   (*SB*)

13 The table shows the masses, to the nearest kg, of the men in eight rowing crews at a regatta. Form a frequency distribution using the intervals 50–54, 55–59, 60–64, ... Construct a histogram and comment on any special features it may possess. Calculate the arithmetic mean from the frequency distribution.

72	77	79	83	74	76	75	71	62
69	70	72	77	78	72	68	68	58
78	77	79	76	85	81	72	77	58
79	77	75	82	77	77	70	70	53
73	70	77	72	85	81	73	75	50
69	77	79	77	85	80	77	85	52
78	76	79	83	102	86	83	75	50
77	84	74	81	86	85	81	78	55

14   These are the heights of 50 pupils, measured to the nearest 2 cm.   (*SB*)

144	142	148	150	154	154	152	154	154	152
152	154	152	156	158	158	158	152	158	158
156	152	148	148	156	150	150	156	158	150
156	154	154	152	154	152	154	150	156	160
158	154	152	164	148	152	154	154	150	154

   a Make a frequency table.
   b Construct a histogram.
   c What is the modal height?
   d Calculate the arithmetic mean.   (*SB*)

15   An examination, taken by 100 candidates, was marked out of 100, and separate analyses were made of the tens and units digits of the marks. The analysis of the tens digits was as follows.

Tens digit:	0	1	2	3	4	5	6	7	8	9
Frequency:	0	0	6	14	27	30	16	5	2	0

Draw a frequency graph of this distribution, using a scale of 2 cm to 1 unit on the 'digits' axis (have this the long way of your paper) and 4 cm to 10 units on the frequency axis. Calculate the mean of the distribution, and from it deduce the best estimate you can of the mean mark of the 100 candidates, supposing that no other information were available.

The analysis of the units digits was as follows.

Units digit:	0	1	2	3	4	5	6	7	8	9
Frequency:	6	6	11	8	12	14	15	7	8	13

Using the same scales as you used for your first frequency graph, but on a different sheet of graph paper, draw a frequency graph of this distribution. State briefly why you would expect your two graphs to be different in shape. Given that the mean of the second distribution is 4.9, make a more accurate estimate of the mean mark of the 100 candidates.   (*LC*)

Chapter 9

Set language and set numbers

The children may well look puzzled – the gamekeeper has written his notice in set language but has forgotten to add the information that

T = {trespassers}
P = {people who will be prosecuted}

Set language, like other languages, has parts of speech but it has fewer than most languages. There are:

1 Nouns, which are the names of sets, usually denoted by capital letters, but including the universal set $\mathscr{E}$ and the empty set ϕ; also the names of members of sets, usually denoted by small letters;

2 Verbs – if the subject is the name of a set, the verb can be $=$, $\neq$, $\subset$, $\not\subset$, $\supset$ or $\not\supset$. If the subject is a member of a set (i.e. an element), the verb can be $\in$ or $\notin$;

3   Conjunctions, $\cap$ and $\cup$;

4   The adjective '.

The meanings of all the above symbols should be familiar to you, as they appear in Chapters 1 and 12 of Book 1.

Translation into and out of set language is easier than it is with most languages.

Example 1   If $\mathscr{E}=\{$animals$\}$, $C=\{$cats$\}$, $B=\{$black animals$\}$, $m=$my pet, $y=$your pet, translate into ordinary English:

a $C\subset B$ **b** $B\subset C'$ **c** $m\in C\cap B$ **d** $y\in C'\cap B'$ **e** $B'\cap C\neq\emptyset$

Answer

a   Cats are a subset of black animals, i.e. all cats are black. This of course is untrue, but that is not the point, we are merely concerned to find the *meaning* of the sentence.

b   Black animals are a subset of non-cats, i.e. no cats are black.

c $C\cap B$ means 'black cats', so this sentence means 'my pet is a black cat'.

d $C'\cap B'$ is the set of animals which are not cats and are not black, so this means 'your pet is not a cat and is not black'.

e $B'\cap C$ is the set of cats which are not black, and the statement that this set is not empty is equivalent to saying, 'there are some cats which are not black' or 'not all cats are black'.

Example 2   With the same sets as in Example 1, write in symbols the sentences:

a   Some cats are black,

b   No cats are black,

c   My pet is a cat but is not black,

d   Your pet either is a cat or is black (or is both).

Answer

a $\{$black cats$\}$ is denoted by $B\cap C$: here this set is said to exist, i.e. not to be empty, so the statement is $B\cap C\neq\emptyset$.

b   The statement is the opposite of the previous one, so can be expressed $B\cap C=\emptyset$, but it can be put in many other ways, e.g. $B\subset C'$ ('all black animals are non-cats'), $C\subset B'$ ('all cats are non-black animals'), $B\cap C'=B$, $B\cup C'=C'$.

c $\{$cats which are not black$\}=C\cap B'$, so this statement is $m\in C\cap B'$.

d $\{$all cats and all black animals$\}=B\cup C$, so this statement is $y\in B\cup C$.

Note that many statements can be expressed symbolically in several different ways: thus $A\subset B$ is equivalent to $B'\subset A'$, $A\cap B=A$, $A\cup B=B$, and $A\cap B'=\emptyset$.

Exercise 9.1

1   If $\mathscr{E}=\{$books$\}$, $F=\{$books of fiction$\}$, $R=\{$books I have read$\}$, write sentences equivalent to these symbolic statements:

a $R \subset F$ **c** $R \cap F = \phi$ **e** $R \subset F'$

b $F \subset R$ **d** $R \cap F \neq \phi$ **f** $R' \cap F' \neq \phi$

2   If $\mathscr{E}=\{$edible things$\}$, $F=\{$fruit$\}$, $A=\{$apples$\}$, $L=\{$foods I like$\}$, write in symbolic form:

    a Apples are fruit   **d** I like all fruit except apples

    b I like apples   **e** I like some sorts of fruit

    c I dislike apples   **f** I dislike some sorts of fruit

3   If $\mathscr{E}=\{$people$\}$, $T=\{$tall people$\}$, $D=\{$dark people$\}$, $g=$George, $m=$Margaret, write sentences equivalent to these symbolic statements.

    a $g \in T \cap D$ **c** $D' \not\subset T'$ **e** $g \in T' \cup D'$

    b $T \subset D'$ **d** $m \in T' \cap D$ **f** $m \in T \cup D'$

4   If $\mathscr{E}=\{$musical instruments$\}$, $W=\{$woodwind instruments$\}$, $B=\{$brass wind instruments$\}$, $C=\{$clarinets$\}$, $T=\{$tubas$\}$, $S=\{$instruments in the Semibreve School Orchestra$\}$, write in symbolic form:

    a Clarinets are woodwind instruments.

    b Tubas are not woodwind instruments.

    c There are no tubas in the S.S.O.

    d All the instruments in the S.S.O. are woodwind or brass wind.

    e Some of the instruments in the S.S.O. are brass wind.

5   Take $\mathscr{E}=\{$foods$\}$, $L=\{$foods I like$\}$, and make up and name any other sets you wish. Write 5 symbolic statements about these sets, using all the symbols $\subset$, $\not\subset$, $\neq$, $\cap$, ϕ (and any others you wish). Write sentences equivalent to your symbolic statements.

6   Take $F=\{$flowers$\}$, $R=\{$roses$\}$, $W=\{$white flowers$\}$, and make up and name any other sets you wish. Then continue as in Question 5, above.

7 $\mathscr{E}=\{$animals$\}$, $W=\{$white animals$\}$, $R=\{$rabbits$\}$, $P=\{$animals with pink ears$\}$.

    a Write the following statement, using some of the symbols P, R, $\subset$, $\cap$, ϕ, $\neq$. Some rabbits have pink ears.

    b Write the statement $R \cap W$ in non-mathematical English.
Copy the Venn diagram (Figure 9.1) and label the sets so as to satisfy **a** and **b**. Shade the region representing white animals with pink ear.s

                                                                      (SMP)

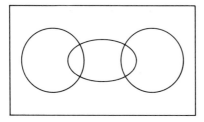

Figure 9.1

8   If $\mathscr{E}=$ {pigs}, $G=$ {greedy pigs}, $H=$ {healthy pigs}, $F=$ {fat pigs}, write the following statements in symbolic form.

   a   All healthy pigs are greedy.
   b   Some healthy pigs are not fat.
   c   All healthy pigs are greed and fat.
   d   All fat pigs are either greedy or healthy, or both.   (*LC*)

9   In this question $\mathscr{E}=$ {quadrilaterals}, $A=$ {quadrilaterals with all four sides equal}, $B=$ {quadrilaterals with at least three sides equal}, $C=$ {quadrilaterals with no axes of symmetry}. Marking any equal sides and showing any axes of symmetry, sketch a member of each of the following sets.

   (i) $A\cap C'$ (ii) $B\cap A'\cap C$ (iii) $B\cap A'\cap C'$ (iv) $C'\cap B'$

Express in symbolic form the following statements:

   a   There are no quadrilaterals with all four sides equal but no axes of symmetry.
   b   There are some quadrilaterals with three sides equal and no axes of symmetry.

Draw a Venn diagram to illustrate the relation between $\mathscr{E}$, A, B and C.
     (*LC*)

10   If $\mathscr{E}=$ {living creatures}, $M=$ {mammals}, $C=$ {cats}, $W=$ {water-creatures}, write the following statements in symbolic form.

   a   Some mammals are water-creatures.
   b   No cats are water-creatures.
   c   All cats are mammals.

Draw a single Venn diagram to illustrate these three statements.   (*LC*)

11 $\mathscr{E}=$ {people in the United Kingdom}, $A=$ {people over 17 years of age}, $B=$ {people who have passed a driving test}, $C=$ {people allowed to drive a car}. Write the following statements in set notation.

   a   People in the United Kingdom who are allowed to drive a car are those who are over 17 and who have passed a driving test.

b People in the United Kingdom who are not over 17 or who have not passed a driving test are among those who are not allowed to drive a car.   (*CD*)

12   A survey was made of the houses in a certain town, and some of the results are represented in the Venn diagram (Figure 9.2), in which *H*={houses with two or more storeys}, *B*={houses *without* bathrooms}, *D*={detached houses}.

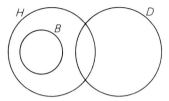

Figure 9.2

Copy the diagram and add a rectangle to represent a universal set. Write down a suitable title for this set.

The true statement $H \cap D \neq \phi$ is expressed by the sentence, 'Some of the detached houses had two or more storeys'. Make two other such true statements, one about the relation between *B* and *H* and one about that between *B* and *D*. Express each statement by a sentence. Given that
a some two-storey houses had garages,
b all non-detached houses were without garages,
c all single-storey houses with garages also had bathrooms,

represent clearly on your diagram the set *G*={houses with garages}. Write down a sentence, deduced from the above, about houses with garages and no bathrooms.   (*LC*)

13   In this question $\mathscr{E}$={pupils in a certain mixed school}, *B*={boys in the school}, *F*={pupils who play football}, *H*={pupils who play hockey}, *L*={pupils who play lacrosse}, *S*={pupils who swim}, *D*={pupils who dive}.

Express in symbols the sentences:

a All pupils play at least one of the games football, hockey and lacrosse.
b Only boys play football.
c No pupil dives who does not swim.

Write sentences to express the following symbolic statements.

d $L \cap S' = \phi$,
e $H \cap D = H$

If all the above five statements are true, name the activity in which all the girls take part, giving reasons for your answer.   (*LC*)

14   In the Venn diagram (Figure 9.3). *E*={imaginary animals}, *F*={fire-breathing animals}, *D*={dragons}, *J*={jabberwocks}. No region is

empty. Which of these statements
are consistent with the diagram
and which are inconsistent?

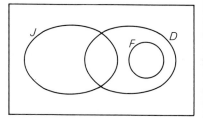
Figure 9.3

a $D \cup F = F$,
b $F \subset J'$,
c All dragons breathe fire.
d Some Jabberwocks are dragons.

(*SMP*)

Implication

Some more symbols used in mathematics are ⇒ meaning 'implies', ⇐
meaning 'is implied by' and ⇔ meaning 'implies and is implied by'.

These are conjunctions, as they join sentences. For example 'George is a
boy'⇒'George is a male human being' is correct, since {boys} ⊂ {male
human beings}, but we cannot replace ⇒ by ⇐ or ⇔ since the statement
'George is a boy' is **not** implied by 'George is a male human being': he
might be a grown-up man.

'ABCD is a square '⇔'ABCD has 4 equal sides and 4 equal angles' is
correct because {squares}={quadrilaterals with 4 equal sides and 4
equal angles}.

If $A \subset B$, then $x \in A \Rightarrow x \in B$, but **not** $x \in A \Leftarrow x \in B$.

Exercise 9.2

In all questions, state which, if any, of the symbols ⇒, ⇐ and ⇔ may
correctly be written between the two statements; if none of them may
correctly be written, write 'none'.

1 **a** Fido is a normal dog.   Fido has four legs.
    b Today is Monday.   Yesterday was Sunday.
    c Lucerne is in Switzerland.   Lucerne is in Europe.
    d Rectangle **p** has a longer perimeter than rectangle **q**.   Rectangle
    p has a larger area than rectangle **q**.
    e George is older than Margaret.   George is older than Herbert,
    who is older than Margaret.

2 x is a number (positive or negative).

a $x > 2$	$x > 3$	**e** $x^2 > 9$	$x > 3$
b $x > 2$	$-x > -2$	**f** $x^2 < 9$	$x < 3$
c $x + 3 = 8$	$x - 1 = 4$	**g** $x^2 = 3x$	$x = 3$
d $x^2 = 9$	$x = 3$	**h** $x = 0$	$x^2 \leqslant 0$

3 n is a positive integer

    a n is a multiple of 3 n is a multiple of 6
    b n is a multiple of 6 n is a multiple of 4
    c n is a prime number n is an odd number
    d $n > 5$ $n^2 > 30$
    e n is even $3n + 7$ is odd
    f $2n + 3 < 9$ $5 - n > 1$

4 ABC is a triangle

    a $AB = AC$ $\angle B = \angle C$
    b $AB = 3$ cm, $BC = 4$ cm, $AC = 5$ cm $\angle B = 90°$
    c $AB^2 + BC^2 = AC^2$ $\angle B = 90°$
    d $\angle A = 60°$ and $AB = AC$ ABC is equilateral
    e $\angle B = \angle C = 40°$ $\angle A = 100°$
    f $AB + BC > 10$ cm $AC = 5$ cm
    g $AB + BC > 5$ cm $AC = 5$ cm

5 A and B are sets

    a $x \in A$ $x \in B$ **d** $x \notin A$ $x \notin B$
    b $x \in A$ $x \in A \cap B$ **e** $x \notin A$ $x \notin A \cap B$
    c $x \in A$ $x \in A \cup B$ **f** $x \notin A$ $x \notin A \cup B$

6 PQRS is a quadrilateral

    a PQ is parallel to RS.   PQRS is a parallelogram.
    b PQ is parallel and equal to RS.   PQRS is a parallelogram.
    c $PQ = QR = RS = SP$.   PQRS is a square.
    d $PQ = QR = RS = SP$.   PQRS is a rhombus.
    e $PR = QS$.   PQRS is a rectangle.

Numbers in sets

Another piece of notation: $n(A)$ means the number of members of set A. Thus if $A = \{$Shem, Ham, Japhet$\}$, then $n(A) = 3$.

Again, if $P = \{1, 2, 3\}$ and $Q = \{2, 3, 4, 5\}$, then $n(P) = 3$, $n(Q) = 4$, $n(P \cap Q) = 2$, $n(P \cup Q) = 5$.

From a knowledge of the numbers of members of one or more sets, it is sometimes possible to calculate the numbers of members of other sets.

It is often useful to draw a Venn diagram and to write in each region the number of members of the set represented by that region.

Example 3   If $n(A) = 6$, $n(B) = 10$, find the largest and smallest possible numbers of members of $A \cap B$ and of $A \cup B$; find also $n(A \cup B)$ if $n(A \cap B) = 4$.

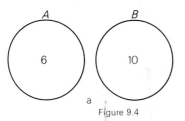
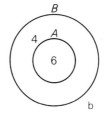
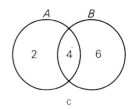

a

Figure 9.4

b

c

Answer

If $A \cap B = \emptyset$, $n(A \cap B) = 0$, and this is its smallest possible value (see Figure 9.4**a**). In this case $n(A \cup B) = 16$, and this is its largest possible value.

If $A \subset B$, then $A \cap B = A$, so $n(A \cap B) = 6$, and this is its largest possible value (see Figure 9.4**b**). In this case $n(A \cup B) = 10$, and this is its smallest possible value.

If $n(A \cap B) = 4$, then $n(A \cap B') = 2$ and $n(A' \cap B) = 6$ (see Figure 9.4**c**). In this case $n(A \cup B) = 4 + 2 + 6 = 12$.

Example 4   Of 55 pupils, 10 learn Latin and of these 3 also learn physics. 24 learn physics and of these 13 also learn geography. 33 learn geography and of these 5 also learn Latin. 2 learn all three of these subjects; how many learn none of them?

Answer

Let $L = \{$learners of Latin$\}$,
$P = \{$learners of physics$\}$,
$G = \{$learners of geography$\}$. We letter the regions of the diagram, and use each letter to denote the number of members of the set represented by that region.

g is the number of those learning all three subjects, so $g = 2$.

$f + g$ is the number of those learning Latin and physics, so $f + g = 3$ so $f = 1$.

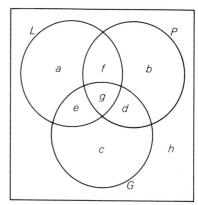

Figure 9.5

Similarly $d + g = 13$, so $d = 11$.

Similarly again, $e + g = 5$, so $e = 3$.

Now $n(L) = 10$ so $a + e + f + g = 10$, giving $a = 4$.

In the same way, $b = 10$ and $c = 17$.

$a + b + c + d + e + f + g = 48$; this is the total of all who learn any of the three subjects, so the number of those who learn none is $55 - 48 = 7$.

Exercise 9.3

1 Find the values of $n(A)$, $n(B)$, $n(A \cap B)$ and $n(A \cup B)$ in each of the following cases.

    a $A = \{L, M, N\}$, $B = \{N, O, P, Q, R\}$

    b $A = \{$prime numbers between 10 and 20$\}$
      $B = \{$odd numbers between 10 and 20$\}$

    c $A = \{$months of the year with 31 days$\}$
      $B = \{$months of the year whose names begin with J$\}$

    d $A = \{$letters of ROBIN$\}$, $B = \{$letters of WREN$\}$

    e $A = \{$letters of LION$\}$, $B = \{$letters of BEAR$\}$

    f $A = \{$letters of SCOTLAND$\}$, $B = \{$letters of COST$\}$

2 Find the values of $n(A)$, $n(B)$, $n(A')$, $n(B')$, $n(A \cap B')$ and $n(A \cap B)'$ in each of the following cases.

    a $\mathscr{E} = \{$positive integers between 20 and 40 inclusive$\}$, $A = \{$multiples of 3$\}$, $B = \{$multiples of 4$\}$

    b $\mathscr{E} = \{$letters of STARLING$\}$, $A = \{$letters of SING$\}$, $B = \{$letters of TAIL$\}$

3   **a** If $n(A) = 11$, $n(B) = 7$, $n(A \cap B) = 4$, find $n(A \cup B)$.
    b If $n(A) = 10$, $n(B) = 5$, $n(A \cup B) = 13$, find $n(A \cap B)$.
    c If $n(A) = 8$, $n(A \cap B) = 5$, $n(A \cup B) = 12$, find $n(B)$.
    d If $n(A) = a$, $n(B) = b$, $n(A \cap B) = c$, $n(A \cup B) = u$, find a formula for u in terms of a, b and c.

4 Out of a group of 35 children, 30 like sausages and 26 like fish-fingers.
    a Give the largest and smallest possible numbers of those who like both.
    b Give the largest and smallest possible numbers of those who like neither.
    c If 2 like neither, how many like both?

5 It is found that of a group of 50 people there are 14 who cannot speak English, but 27 who can speak French.
    a If 16 can speak both languages, how many can speak neither?
    b If 11 can speak neither language, how many can speak both?

6 A survey showed that, of the people questioned, 70% had watched BBC television on a certain evening and 65% had watched ITV.

    a What was the smallest percentage who could have watched both?
    b What was the largest percentage who could have watched neither?
    c If 45% watched both, what percentage watched neither?

7 100 members of a certain club play golf, and 74 do not. 29 of the golfers play cricket also, and 59 of them play tennis as well as golf. There are 68

cricketers and 106 tennis players, including 40 who play both of these games. 18 play all three games; how many play none?

8 In a certain examination there are four papers, named p, q, r and s. Every candidate must take two papers, which must be p and q, or p and r, or q and s: no other combination is allowed. If $\mathscr{E}=\{$candidates$\}$, $P=\{$candidates taking paper $p\}$, $Q=\{$candidates taking paper $q\}$, $R=\{$candidates taking paper $r\}$, $S=\{$candidates taking paper $s\}$, explain why

a $P'=S$ **b** $R\subset P$ **c** $P\cap S=\phi$

and write down three similar relations, concerning Q, R and S or their complements.

In a year when 500 candidates took paper p, 400 took paper q and 120 took paper r, find the total number taking the examination and the number taking paper s.   (*LC*)

9 Each day 45 trains leave a certain terminus. The next three stations are Aton, Beton and Ceton. Taking $\mathscr{E}=\{$all trains from the terminus$\}$, $A=\{$trains stopping at Aton$\}$, $B=\{$trains stopping at Beton$\}$, $C=\{$trains stopping at Ceton$\}$, write normal English sentences (not using technical words like 'set') to express the following symbolic statements.

a $n(A)=24$ **b** $C\subset B$

Write symbolic statements to express the following sentences.

c Some trains stop at all three stations   **d** 30 trains stop at Beton.

Use statements **b** and **c** to draw a Venn diagram to illustrate the relations between $\mathscr{E}$, A, B and C.

Given that 5 trains stop at none of the three stations, find the number which stop at both Aton and Beton.

Given also that 13 trains stop at Ceton, and 18 at Aton but not at Ceton, find the number that stop at Beton only.   (*LC*)

10 Each of the boys and girls leaving a certain school applied for admission to at least one of the Universities of Oxford, Cambridge and London. Taking
$\mathscr{E}=\{$all applicants$\}$,
$O=\{$Oxford applicants$\}$,
$C=\{$Cambridge applicants$\}$,
$L=\{$London applicants$\}$,
express the following statements of fact in set language.
a All applicants applied to at least one of the three universities named.

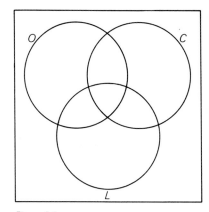

Figure 9.6

b All those who applied to both Oxford and Cambridge applied to London as well.

c In no case was Oxford the only one of the three to which application was made.

Copy the above Venn diagram (Figure 9.6), and indicate on it, by writing the symbol ϕ in the appropriate regions, the three of the eight subsets of $\mathscr{E}$ which are empty. Find a single set equivalent to $O \cap L$.

If $n(\mathscr{E}) = 40$, $n(C) = 26$, $n(L) = 38$, find $n(C \cap L)$.

If, also, 20 applicants applied to all three, and 10 to London only, find (i) the total number who applied to Oxford, (ii) the average number of applications per person.

(LC)

11   It is reported that of the children who take dinners at a certain school, 80% like fish, 85% like cheese dishes, and 75% like curry.

a It is known that the number who like cheese dishes is in fact 100. (i) Show that the given percentages cannot be exact. (ii) Assuming that each percentage figure is correct to the nearest whole number, find a possible value for the total number of children, and find the number who like fish.

b Find the largest and the smallest possible percentage who like all three of these foods. Find also the largest and smallest possible percentage who like none of them.

(LC)

12   In a survey of householders it was found that 42% took a newspaper, 42% took a comic and 42% took a magazine; 13% took a newspaper and a comic, 12% a comic and a magazine, and 5% a newspaper and a magazine. If x% took all three, draw a Venn diagram of this information, showing the percentage in each region.

If the remaining percentage who took none of the three was also x%, write down an equation and solve it to find x.

Hence find the percentage who took just one of the three.

(SB)

13   The readers of a comic were asked if they were satisfied or not with the cartoons section, the jokes section and the stories section. Of those interviewed, 52% liked the jokes, 46% liked the stories, 39% liked the cartoons, 19% liked the jokes and the stories, 15% liked the cartoons and the stories, and 13% liked the cartoons and the jokes. The percentage (x) who liked all three sections was equal to the percentage who disliked all three sections.

a Draw a Venn diagram, writing in the percentages, in terms of x, in all regions of the diagram.

b Write down an equation to find x.

c Solve the equation to find x.

d If 1400 people were interviewed, how many were satisfied with at least two of the three sections?

(*SB*)

14 In a certain school there are 87 boys of a particular year. Of these, 43 play hockey, 42 play football and 47 play tennis; 15 play tennis and hockey, 17 tennis and football, and 21 hockey and football. Each boy plays at least one of the three games and x boys play all three. Express these facts in a *large* Venn diagram, showing clearly the number in each region in terms either of x alone or, if you prefer, of x and other unknowns. Write down the equation(s) satisfied by the unknown(s) and hence find the value of x.

(*SMP*)

Chapter 10

Matrices and transformations

The picture may remind you of three kinds of transformations encountered in Book 1, namely reflection, rotation and enlargement (though the gnome affected by enlargement seems to have been treated to an enlargement with scale factor *less* than 1, since he has become *smaller*). In this chapter we shall see how transformations are connected with matrices – one of the main uses of matrices, at least so far as this course is concerned, is in connection with transformation geometry.

Position vectors

If we are to use matrices to work with geometrical elements, such as points, we must find some way of representing these elements by matrices.

The point P in Figure 10.1 can be represented by its coordinates (3, 1), but when we are using matrices we represent it by its *position vector*, the vector **OP**.

$$\mathbf{OP} = \begin{pmatrix} 3 \\ 1 \end{pmatrix}$$ which is a column vector and is also a column matrix. In the same way we can represent the points Q and R by the column vectors (column matrices)

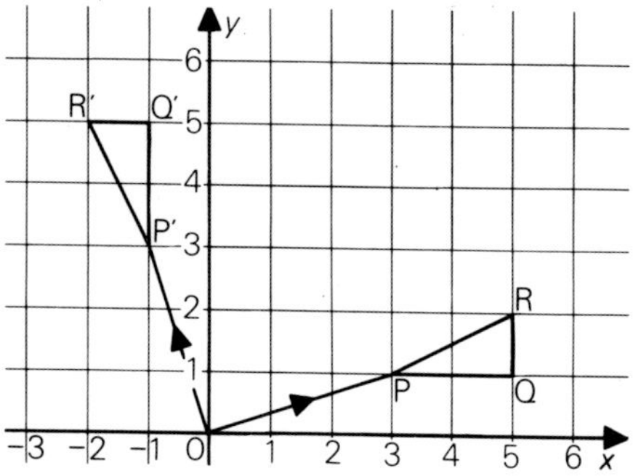

Figure 10.1

$$\begin{pmatrix} 5 \\ 1 \end{pmatrix} \text{ and } \begin{pmatrix} 5 \\ 2 \end{pmatrix}.$$

If we form these three column matrices into a single 2×3 matrix, $\begin{pmatrix} 3 & 5 & 5 \\ 1 & 1 & 2 \end{pmatrix}$, we have the *position vector matrix* of the triangle PQR.

Transformation matrices

Let us try the effect of pre-multiplying position vectors and matrices by a simple 2×2 matrix, for example $\begin{pmatrix} 0 & -1 \\ 1 & 0 \end{pmatrix}$, which we will call **M** for convenience.

We have $\mathbf{M} \begin{pmatrix} 3 \\ 1 \end{pmatrix} = \begin{pmatrix} -1 \\ 3 \end{pmatrix}$. The point P', whose position vector is $\begin{pmatrix} -1 \\ 3 \end{pmatrix}$ and whose coordinates therefore are $(-1, 3)$, is shown in Figure 10.1. However, there are many transformations which would transform P into P'; the nature of the transformation will be made clear if we multiply the position vector matrix of triangle PQR by **M**. This gives

$$\mathbf{M} \begin{pmatrix} 3 & 5 & 5 \\ 1 & 1 & 2 \end{pmatrix} = \begin{pmatrix} -1 & -1 & -2 \\ 3 & 5 & 5 \end{pmatrix}$$

The position vector matrix of the image triangle P'Q'R' is $\begin{pmatrix} -1 & -1 & -2 \\ 3 & 5 & 5 \end{pmatrix}$ and the coordinates of its vertices are $(-1, 3)$, $(-1, 5)$ and $(-2, 5)$. These points are plotted in Figure 10.1, and it can be seen that the transformation is a rotation of 90° about (0, 0).

M is the *transformation matrix* for this rotation.

Since matrix multiplication is non-commutative it is important to note the order of the matrices in the multiplication: the transformation matrix is written **before** the position vector matrix.

Exercise 10.1

In each of the examples 1 to 8:

1 Plot the given points and join them to form a figure.

2 Write down the position vector matrix of this figure.

3 Pre-multiply this position vector matrix by the given transformation matrix.

4 Plot the points whose position vectors are the columns of the position vector matrix found in 3, and join them to form the image figure.

5 Describe the transformation.

1 Points (1, 0), (3, 0), (3, 1), matrix $\begin{pmatrix} 0 & -1 \\ -1 & 0 \end{pmatrix}$

2 Points as in Question 1, matrix $\begin{pmatrix} 0 & 1 \\ 1 & 0 \end{pmatrix}$

3 Points (2, 1), (2, −1), (−1, 0), matrix $\begin{pmatrix} -1 & 0 \\ 0 & -1 \end{pmatrix}$

4 Points as in Question 3, matrix $\begin{pmatrix} 2 & 0 \\ 0 & 2 \end{pmatrix}$

5 Points (2, 1), (2, 2), (−1, 1), matrix $\begin{pmatrix} 1 & 0 \\ 0 & -1 \end{pmatrix}$

6 Points as in Question 5, matrix $\begin{pmatrix} -1 & 0 \\ 0 & 1 \end{pmatrix}$

7 Points (6, 0), (0, 6), (−6, 0), (0, −6), matrix $\begin{pmatrix} \frac{1}{2} & 0 \\ 0 & \frac{1}{2} \end{pmatrix}$

8 Points as in Question 7, matrix $\begin{pmatrix} -\frac{1}{3} & 0 \\ 0 & -\frac{1}{3} \end{pmatrix}$

9 The quadrilateral Q has vertices (2, 1), (4, 1), (5, 3) and (2, 3); the quadrilateral R has vertices (−2, 4), (−2, 8), (−6, 10) and (−6, 4). Show that the image of Q under the transformation whose matrix is $\begin{pmatrix} 0 & -1 \\ 1 & 0 \end{pmatrix}$ is the same as the image of R under that whose matrix is $\begin{pmatrix} \frac{1}{2} & 0 \\ 0 & \frac{1}{2} \end{pmatrix}$

10   Plot the points (2, 2), (2, −2), (−2, −2), and (−2, 2) and join them to form a square. Find the images of this square under each of the three transformations whose matrices are

a $\begin{pmatrix} 3 & 0 \\ 0 & 1 \end{pmatrix}$ b $\begin{pmatrix} 1 & 0 \\ 0 & 3 \end{pmatrix}$ c $\begin{pmatrix} 1 & 1 \\ 0 & 1 \end{pmatrix}$

These transformations are different from those you have encountered so far: describe each in words as well as you can.

11   Plot the points (0, 0), (10, 0), (10, 5) and (0, 5) and join them to form a rectangle. Write down the position vector matrix, and find the image of this rectangle under the rotation whose matrix is $\begin{pmatrix} 0.8 & -0.6 \\ 0.6 & 0.8 \end{pmatrix}$. Find the angle of this rotation, by drawing and measurement or by calculation.

12   Find the images of (3, 1), (6, 2) and (9, 3) under the transformation whose matrix is $\begin{pmatrix} 0.8 & 0.6 \\ 0.6 & -0.8 \end{pmatrix}$. Why do your results suggest that the transformation may be a reflection?

Draw the quadrilateral whose vertices are (0, 0), (5, 0), (3, −2) and (0, −2) and find its image under the transformation. If it is a reflection, draw the mirror-line and find its equation.

13   Repeat the second part of Question 12 but with the transformation matrix $\begin{pmatrix} -0.6 & 0.8 \\ 0.8 & 0.6 \end{pmatrix}$.

14   Repeat Question 12 but with the transformation matrix $\begin{pmatrix} \frac{5}{13} & \frac{12}{13} \\ \frac{12}{13} & \frac{-5}{13} \end{pmatrix}$, and beginning with the points (3, 2), (6, 4) and (9, 6).

15   Plot the points (0, 0), (2, 0), (2, 2) and (0, 2), and join them to form a square. On the same diagram, draw the images of this square under the transformations whose matrices are $\begin{pmatrix} 3 & 3 \\ 1 & -1 \end{pmatrix}$, $\begin{pmatrix} -3 & -3 \\ 1 & -1 \end{pmatrix}$, $\begin{pmatrix} 1 & -1 \\ 3 & 3 \end{pmatrix}$ and $\begin{pmatrix} 1 & -1 \\ -3 & -3 \end{pmatrix}$. Describe the symmetry of the pattern formed by the four images.

16   Plot the points (0, 0), (4, 0), (4, 2) and (0, 2), and join them to form a rectangle. Draw the image of this rectangle under the transformation whose matrix is $\begin{pmatrix} 1 & -1 \\ 1 & 1 \end{pmatrix}$.

This transformation consists of a rotation together with an enlargement. Find the angle of the rotation and the scale factor of the enlargement.

17 Plot the points (0, 0), (4, 0), (2, 2) and (0, 2), and join them to form a trapezium. Draw the image of this trapezium under the transformation whose matrix is $\begin{pmatrix} 3 & 4 \\ 4 & -3 \end{pmatrix}$. This transformation consists of a reflection together with an enlargement. Find the scale factor of the enlargement and draw the mirror line of the reflection. (This can be done by bisecting the angle between any line and its image.) Find the equation of the mirror line.

18 Plot the points (1, 1), (1, 3), (3, 3) and (3, 1), and join them to form a square. Draw the image of this square under the transformation whose matrix is $\begin{pmatrix} 1 & 2 \\ 2 & 4 \end{pmatrix}$. What is unusual about the result? Draw images of other figures of your own choosing under the same transformation.

$\begin{pmatrix} 1 & 2 \\ 2 & 4 \end{pmatrix}$ is an example of what is called a ***singular*** matrix. Can you see what is the special feature of the numbers forming the elements of the matrix, that makes it singular?

Try to compile another singular matrix, and transform the same figures with it.

Base vectors

In the previous section we saw how, in some cases, we could find the transformation associated with a given matrix. In this section we will look at the converse problem – that of how to find what matrix is associated with a given transformation. For this purpose it is convenient to use what are called the ***base vectors***, the vectors $\begin{pmatrix} 1 \\ 0 \end{pmatrix}$ and $\begin{pmatrix} 0 \\ 1 \end{pmatrix}$ (See Figure 10.2.)

The position vector matrix for the two base vectors is

$$\begin{pmatrix} 1 & 0 \\ 0 & 1 \end{pmatrix},$$

which is the 2 × 2 identity matrix. This means that when we

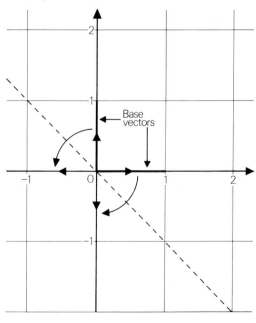

Figure 10.2

multiply this position vector matrix by any transformation matrix, the two columns of the product matrix (giving the images of the two base vectors) are the same as the two columns of the transformation matrix itself. If, therefore, we know the images of the two base vectors, we can write down the transformation matrix at onece.

Example 1   Find the matrix corresponding to a reflection in the line $x+y=0$.

Answer

If $\begin{pmatrix} 1 \\ 0 \end{pmatrix}$ is reflected in this line, its image is $\begin{pmatrix} 0 \\ -1 \end{pmatrix}$ (see Figure 10.2).

The first column of the transformation matrix is therefore $\begin{pmatrix} 0 \\ -1 \end{pmatrix}$. If $\begin{pmatrix} 0 \\ 1 \end{pmatrix}$

is reflected in the same line, its image is $\begin{pmatrix} -1 \\ 0 \end{pmatrix}$ · the second column of

the transformation matrix is therefore $\begin{pmatrix} -1 \\ 0 \end{pmatrix}$. The transformation matrix

is thus $\begin{pmatrix} 0 & -1 \\ -1 & 0 \end{pmatrix}$.

Example 2   Find the matrix of the transformation that transforms the rectangle whose vertices are (0, 0), (4, 0), (4, 2) and (0, 2) into the rhombus whose vertices (in the same order) are (0, 0), (4, −2), (8, 0) and (4, 2).

Answer

As the image of (4, 0) is (4, −2), the image of (1, 0) is $(1, -\tfrac{1}{2})$, and the

first column of the transformation matrix is $\begin{pmatrix} 1 \\ -\tfrac{1}{2} \end{pmatrix}$. As the image of

(0, 2) is (4, 2), the image of (0, 1) is (2, 1), and the second column of

the transformation matrix is $\begin{pmatrix} 2 \\ 1 \end{pmatrix}$. The transformation matrix is

$\begin{pmatrix} 1 & 2 \\ -\tfrac{1}{2} & 1 \end{pmatrix}$.

Unit square

The square of which two sides are formed by the base vectors is called the *unit square*.

Exercise 10.2

Find the matrices of the transformations which transform the unit square into each of the figures shown (Figure 10.3).

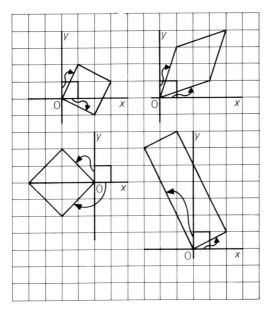

Figure 10.3

2 Find the images of the base vectors and hence find the matrices corresponding to each of the following transformations.

    a rotation of $-90°$
    b rotation of $180°$
    c reflection in the x-axis
    d reflection in the y-axis
    e reflection in the line $x=y$
    f enlargement with centre $(0, 0)$ and scale factor 4
    g enlargement with centre $(0, 0)$ and scale factor $-\frac{1}{2}$

3 Find the matrix of the transformation that transforms the rectangle whose vertices are $(0, 0)$, $(3, 0)$, $(3, 4)$, and $(0, 4)$ into the parallelogram whose vertices are $(0, 0)$, $(3, 6)$, $(5, 8)$ and $(2, 2)$ (in the same order).

4 Find the matrix of a transformation that transforms the unit square into a square of area 8 units lying on the positive side of the y-axis and with the x-axis as a diagonal. (There are two possible answers.)

5 Find the matrix of a transformation that transforms the rectangle whose vertices are $(0, 0)$, $(3, 0)$, $(3, 4)$ and $(0, 4)$ into a parallelogram whose vertices are $(0, 0)$, $(6, 3)$, $(10, 11)$ and $(4, 8)$. (There are two possible answers.)

6 Show that under a rotation of $20°$ about $(0, 0)$, the image of the first base vector is about $\begin{pmatrix} 0.94 \\ 0.34 \end{pmatrix}$. (Use trigonometry or measurement in a large scale diagram.) Find the image of the second base vector under this rotation. Write down the matrix of this transformation. Write down also the matrix corresponding to a rotation of $-20°$ about $(0, 0)$.

Combination of transformations

In Book 1 it was shown that two transformations carried out in succession may have the same effect as a single transformation. We will now consider the connection between the matrices of the separate transformations and the matrix of the combined transformation. If a figure whose position vector matrix is **P** is subjected to a transformation whose matrix is **M**, the position vector matrix of the image figure is **MP**. If this image figure is now subjected to a further transformation, with image **N**, the position vector matrix of the second image is **NMP**. Now **NMP** is the image of **P** under a transformation whose matrix is **NM**, so that *the matrix of the combined transformation is the product of the matrices of the separate transformations*. It is important to note that, in forming the product, the matrix of the transformation carried out second must be written first, and vice versa.

(The above work assumes that matrix multiplication is associative, a point mentioned in Chapter 3.)

Example 3   Show that the effect of a reflection in the x-axis followed by a reflection in the line $x=y$ is a rotation of 90°. What is the effect of reversing the order of the reflections?

Answer

The matrix corresponding to a reflection in the x-axis is $\begin{pmatrix} 1 & 0 \\ 0 & -1 \end{pmatrix}$: that corresponding to a reflection in $x=y$ is $\begin{pmatrix} 0 & 1 \\ 1 & 0 \end{pmatrix}$.

The product $\begin{pmatrix} 0 & 1 \\ 1 & 0 \end{pmatrix} \begin{pmatrix} 1 & 0 \\ 0 & -1 \end{pmatrix} = \begin{pmatrix} 0 & -1 \\ 1 & 0 \end{pmatrix}$, and this product matrix represents a rotation of 90°.

Reversing the order, the product $\begin{pmatrix} 1 & 0 \\ 0 & -1 \end{pmatrix} \begin{pmatrix} 0 & 1 \\ 1 & 0 \end{pmatrix}$ is $\begin{pmatrix} 0 & 1 \\ -1 & 0 \end{pmatrix}$, and this corresponds to a rotation of $-90°$.

Example 4   Find the matrix corresponding to a rotation of 90° combined with an enlargement with scale factor 3, the centres of both being $(0, 0)$. Is the result affected by the order in which the transformations are carried out?

Answer

The matrix for a rotation of 90° is $\begin{pmatrix} 0 & -1 \\ 1 & 0 \end{pmatrix}$ and that for the enlargement specified is $\begin{pmatrix} 3 & 0 \\ 0 & 3 \end{pmatrix}$. The products $\begin{pmatrix} 0 & -1 \\ 1 & 0 \end{pmatrix} \begin{pmatrix} 3 & 0 \\ 0 & 3 \end{pmatrix}$ and

$\begin{pmatrix} 3 & 0 \\ 0 & 3 \end{pmatrix} \begin{pmatrix} 0 & -1 \\ 1 & 0 \end{pmatrix}$ are both equal to $\begin{pmatrix} 0 & -3 \\ 3 & 0 \end{pmatrix}$: this is therefore the matrix of the combined transformation, and in this case the result is not affected by the order in which the transformations are carried out.

Exercise 10.3

1   For each of the following pairs of transformations, write down the two matrices and multiply them together, and so find the matrix of the combined transformations. Describe this combined transformation in each case. (The transformations are carried out in the order named.)

a   Rotation of 90°; rotation of 180° (both about (0, 0)).
b   Rotation of $-90°$ about (0, 0); reflection in the y-axis.
c   Reflection in $x + y = 0$; reflection in the x-axis.
d   Enlargement with scale factor 2; enlargement with scale factor -3, (both with centre (0, 0)).
e   Enlargement with scale factor -3; enlargement with scale factor $-\frac{1}{3}$, (both with centre (0, 0)).

2   For each transformation, write down the corresponding matrix and square it, and so find the matrix of the transformation carried out twice. Describe this double transformation in each case.

a   Rotation of 90° about (0, 0)
b   Reflection in the line $x = y$
c   Enlargement with scale factor -2, and centre (0, 0)

3   Each of the following matrices corresponds to an enlargement with centre (0, 0), combined with another transformation. In each case, find the scale factor of the enlargement, and find and describe the other transformation, taking the scale factor as positive.

a $\begin{pmatrix} 5 & 0 \\ 0 & -5 \end{pmatrix}$ **b** $\begin{pmatrix} 0 & -\frac{1}{2} \\ \frac{1}{2} & 0 \end{pmatrix}$ **c** $\begin{pmatrix} 0 & -3 \\ -3 & 0 \end{pmatrix}$

4   Repeat Question 3, but this time take the scale factor of each enlargement as *negative*.

5   **M** is the matrix $\begin{pmatrix} 1 & -1 \\ 1 & 1 \end{pmatrix}$.

Find **M**^{2} and describe it as a combination of two simple transformations. Hence find the transformations corresponding to

a M   **b M**^{3} **c M**^{4}

6   Repeat Question 5, but taking $\mathbf{M} = \begin{pmatrix} 1 & 1 \\ -1 & 1 \end{pmatrix}$.

7 $\mathbf{N}$ is the matrix $\begin{pmatrix} 3 & 4 \\ 4 & -3 \end{pmatrix}$. Find $\mathbf{N}^2$; what transformation does it represent? $\mathbf{N}$ represents an enlargement together with another transformation; what is the scale factor of the enlargement and what kind of transformation could the other be?

8   If you did Question 6 in Exercise 10.2, multiply together the two matrices you obtained, and explain your result. Also, multiply the matrix you obtained for a rotation of 20° by the matrix

$$\mathbf{P} = \begin{pmatrix} 0.34 & -0.94 \\ 0.94 & 0.34 \end{pmatrix}$$

and comment on this result. What transformation corresponds to $\mathbf{P}$?

Added vectors

Under any transformation which can be represented by a 2×2 matrix, the image of (0, 0) is always (0, 0), for if $\begin{pmatrix} a & b \\ c & d \end{pmatrix}$ is the matrix of the transformation, then $\begin{pmatrix} a & b \\ c & d \end{pmatrix}\begin{pmatrix} 0 \\ 0 \end{pmatrix} = \begin{pmatrix} 0 \\ 0 \end{pmatrix}$. (0, 0) is said to be an *invariant point* for such a transformation.

Clearly, this limits the range of transformations that can be dealt with by the use of 2×2 matrices; it excludes all translations, all rotations and enlargements for which the centre is not (0, 0) and all reflections whose mirror lines do not pass through (0, 0), as well as many other transformations. The most effective ways of dealing with this difficulty are outside the scope of this course, but one method is the use of an *added vector*. Consider for example the transformation

$$\begin{pmatrix} x \\ y \end{pmatrix} \rightarrow \begin{pmatrix} 0 & -1 \\ 1 & 0 \end{pmatrix}\begin{pmatrix} x \\ y \end{pmatrix} + \begin{pmatrix} 2 \\ 1 \end{pmatrix}$$

Under this transformation (0, 0)→(2, 1) and so (0, 0) is not invariant. The images of other points can easily be found: for example (1, 2)→(0, 2) and (3, 4)→(−2, 4).

In general $(x, y) \rightarrow (-y+2, x+1)$.

It can be seen that the transformation consists of a rotation of 90° about (0, 0) together with a translation of $\begin{pmatrix} 2 \\ 1 \end{pmatrix}$, and these will combine to give a rotation of 90° about another centre. To find the centre of this rotation, use the fact that it is invariant, so that its coordinates will map onto themselves. This gives $x = -y+2$ and $y = x+1$; solving these equations gives $x=\frac{1}{2}$ and $y=1\frac{1}{2}$, so the transformation is a rotation of $90°$ about the point $(\frac{1}{2}, 1\frac{1}{2})$.

Exercise 10.4

1 Find the images of (0, 0), (1, 3) and (3, 4) under the transformation

$$\begin{pmatrix} x \\ y \end{pmatrix} \rightarrow \begin{pmatrix} 0 & 1 \\ -1 & 0 \end{pmatrix} \begin{pmatrix} x \\ y \end{pmatrix} + \begin{pmatrix} -1 \\ 3 \end{pmatrix}$$

Find an expression for the image of (x, y). Find the invariant point, and describe the transformation.

2 Find the images of (0, 0), (−1, −3) and (4, 1) under the transformation

$$\begin{pmatrix} x \\ y \end{pmatrix} \rightarrow \begin{pmatrix} 3 & 0 \\ 0 & 3 \end{pmatrix} \begin{pmatrix} x \\ y \end{pmatrix} + \begin{pmatrix} 4 \\ -2 \end{pmatrix}$$

Find an expression for the image of (x, y). Find the invariant point, and describe the transformation.

3 Find the images of (0, 0), (−1, 5) and (3, −2) under the transformation

$$\begin{pmatrix} x \\ y \end{pmatrix} \rightarrow \begin{pmatrix} -1 & 0 \\ 0 & 1 \end{pmatrix} \begin{pmatrix} x \\ y \end{pmatrix} + \begin{pmatrix} 2 \\ 0 \end{pmatrix}$$

Find an expression for the image of (x, y). Show that any point on the line $x=1$ is mapped onto itself by this transformation ($x=1$ is called an *invariant line* of the transformation). Describe the transformation.

4 Find the images of (0, 0), (3, 4) and (−2, 5) under the transformation

$$\begin{pmatrix} x \\ y \end{pmatrix} \rightarrow \begin{pmatrix} 0 & 1 \\ 1 & 0 \end{pmatrix} \begin{pmatrix} x \\ y \end{pmatrix} + \begin{pmatrix} 2 \\ -2 \end{pmatrix}$$

Find an expression for the image of (x, y). Find the equation of the invariant line of this transformation, and describe the transformation.

Exercise 10.5 contains questions on all the topics of this chapter, taken from O-level papers of various boards.

Exercise 10.5

1 A transformation is represented by the matrix

$$\mathbf{M} = \begin{pmatrix} 2 & -1 \\ -1 & 2 \end{pmatrix}$$

a (i) On squared paper, using a scale of 1 cm to 1 unit for both x and y, and taking values on both axes from -8 to $+10$, draw the square S with vertices O(0, 0), A(2, 0), B(2, 2) and C(0, 2).

(ii) Work out the coordinates of the vertices of S_1, the image of S under the transformation, and draw S_1 on your diagram.

b Calculate $\mathbf{M}^2$, and draw S_2, the image of S under the transformation represented by $\mathbf{M}^2$.

c Find the image of (a, a) under the transformation represented by **M**. What does this tell you about the line $y=x$ under the transformation?

(*SMP*)

2   **a**   Describe the transformations whose matrices are

$$\mathbf{R} = \begin{pmatrix} -1 & 0 \\ 0 & 1 \end{pmatrix} \text{ and } \mathbf{S} = \begin{pmatrix} 0 & -1 \\ 1 & 0 \end{pmatrix}$$

Copy Figure 10.4 on squared paper and on it draw L and M, where $L = \mathbf{R}(K)$ and $M = \mathbf{S}(K)$. N is another image of K such that the figure formed by K, L, M and N has just one line of symmetry. Draw and label N on your diagram.

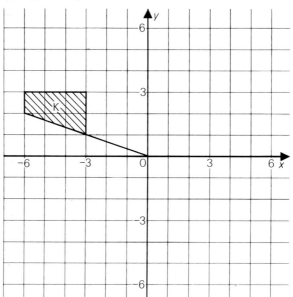

Figure 10.4

c   Describe the transformation that maps K onto N. If **T** is the matrix of this transformation, express **T** in terms of **R** and **S**, and compute **T**.

(*SMP*)

3   The vertices of an isosceles triangle E have coordinates A(0, 5), B(−1, 8), C(4, 8).

a   Using a scale of 1 cm to 1 unit, draw x- and y-axes, taking values of x from −2 to 14 and values of y from 0 to 16. Draw and label the isosceles triangle E.

b Transformation S is defined as

$$S: \begin{pmatrix} x \\ y \end{pmatrix} \rightarrow \begin{pmatrix} 2 & 0 \\ 0 & 2 \end{pmatrix} \begin{pmatrix} x \\ y \end{pmatrix}$$

(i) Draw and label the isosceles triangle $S(E)$ and the point $S(A)$.
(ii) Describe fully the single transformation S.
c Transformation U is defined as

$$U: \begin{pmatrix} x \\ y \end{pmatrix} \rightarrow \begin{pmatrix} -1.2 & 1.6 \\ 1.6 & 1.2 \end{pmatrix} \begin{pmatrix} x \\ y \end{pmatrix}$$

Draw and label the isosceles triangle $U(E)$ and the point $U(A)$.
d Describe fully in geometrical terms a single transformation that maps the triangle $U(E)$ onto the triangle $S(E)$ so that $U(A)$ maps onto $S(A)$.

(*SMP*)

4   Given that **M** is the matrix $\begin{pmatrix} 0 & 1 \\ 1 & 0 \end{pmatrix}$ calculate the matrix product

$$\mathbf{M} \begin{pmatrix} 3 & 5 & 5 \\ 2 & 2 & 6 \end{pmatrix}$$

and hence write down the coordinates of the points A′, B′, C′ which are respectively the images of points A(3, 2), B(5, 2), C(5, 6) under the transformation whose matrix is **M**.

On graph paper with a scale of 1 cm to 1 unit on each axis, draw the triangle T whose vertices are A, B, C and the triangle T′ whose vertices are A′, B′, C′. Describe fully the transformation whose matrix is **M**.

The triangle T′ is now reflected in the y-axis to give T″, whose vertices are A″, B″, C″. Draw the triangle T″, and write down the matrix **N** that represents this transformation.

Describe the transformation which maps T onto T″ and find the matrix to represent this transformation.

Given that $(\mathbf{NM})^p = \mathbf{I}$, where **I** is the identity matrix $\begin{pmatrix} 1 & 0 \\ 0 & 1 \end{pmatrix}$, find the smallest possible positive value of p.

(*LC*)

5   On graph paper or squared paper, with axes and scale (the same scale on both axes) so chosen that x and y can each range from -2 to 10, draw the square S whose vertices are (0, 0), (2, 0), (2, 2) and (0, 2).

Draw the image **T** of **S** under the transformation whose matrix is

$$\mathbf{M} = \begin{pmatrix} 2 & -1 \\ 1 & 2 \end{pmatrix}$$

and the image **U** of **S** under the transformation whose matrix is

$$\mathbf{N} = \begin{pmatrix} 2 & 1 \\ -1 & 2 \end{pmatrix}$$

Lable each image clearly with the appropriate letter.

Describe fully two different single transformations, either of which would map **T** onto **U**.

Form the product **MN**, and draw the image V of S under the transformation whose matrix is **MN**. Describe the single transformation that maps **S** onto V. (*LC*)

6 On graph paper, with a scale (the same on both axes) so chosen that x can range from 0 to 4, and y from -1 to 2, plot the points $(0, 0)$, $(1, 0)$, $(2, 1)$ and $(0, 1)$ and join them to form the quadrilateral Q.

Given that **M** is the matrix $\begin{pmatrix} 1 & 1 \\ 1 & -1 \end{pmatrix}$, form the product $\mathbf{M} \begin{pmatrix} 0 & 1 & 2 & 0 \\ 0 & 0 & 1 & 1 \end{pmatrix}$, and hence find and draw the image of Q under the transformation whose matrix is **M**. Calculate $\mathbf{M}^2$, and draw the image of Q under the transformation whose matrix is $\mathbf{M}^2$.

Describe the transformation whose matrix is $\mathbf{M}^2$.

The transformation whose matrix is **M** may be regarded as an enlargement with centre $(0, 0)$, followed by a reflection. Write down the scale factor of the enlargement, and by considering the angle between any side of Q and the image of that side (or otherwise), draw the invariant (mirror) line of the reflection, and write down its equation as accurately as you can. (*LC*)

7 On graph paper, with the scale of x ranging at least from 0 to 15 and the scale of y ranging at least from -4 to 5, draw the quadrilateral whose vertices are $O(0, 0)$, $A(1, 0)$, $B(3, 1)$ and $C(0, 1)$.

Find and draw the image $A'B'C'O$ of ABCO under the transformation whose matrix is $\mathbf{M} = \begin{pmatrix} 4 & 3 \\ 3 & -4 \end{pmatrix}$. Explain why OBB' is a straight line.

Find the value of n so that the transformation whose matrix is $\begin{pmatrix} n & 0 \\ 0 & n \end{pmatrix}$ transforms $A'B'C'O$ into a reflection of ABCO. Draw this reflection and find the equation of its mirror line. Hence describe briefly the transformation corresponding to **M**. (*LC*)

8 Find the image P' of the point $P(t, kt)$ under the transformation whose matrix is $\mathbf{M} = \begin{pmatrix} -1 & 1 \\ 4 & -1 \end{pmatrix}$.

Find the value of k if P' is the same point as P. Using this value of k, write down the equation of the invariant line of the transformation whose matrix is **M**.

Show that if $k = -2$ and O is the point $(0, 0)$, then POP' is a straight line, and find the ratio in which O divides PP'.

Form the matrix $\mathbf{M}^2$, and *verify* by matrix multiplication that the transformation whose matrix is $\mathbf{M}^2$ has the same invariant line as the transformation whose matrix is **M**.   (*LC*)

9   On graph paper draw the rectangle whose vertices are $(2, 0)$, $(2, 2)$, $(-2, 2)$ and $(-2, 0)$. Choose your scale and axes so that x can range from -4 to 6 and y from -2 to 2.

Draw the image of this rectangle under the transformation whose matrix is $\mathbf{M} = \begin{pmatrix} 2 & 1 \\ -1 & 0 \end{pmatrix}$.

By considering the equation $\mathbf{M} \begin{pmatrix} x \\ y \end{pmatrix} = \begin{pmatrix} x \\ y \end{pmatrix}$, or otherwise, show that the transformation whose matrix is **M** has an invariant line such that every point on it is transformed into itself. Give the equation of this invariant line, and show it on your diagram.

By considering the product $\mathbf{M} \begin{pmatrix} p \\ p \end{pmatrix}$, or otherwise, show that if P is any point on the line $x = y$, and P' is the image of P under the transformation whose matrix is **M**, then $PP' = 2PO$, where O is the origin.   (*LC*)

10   **a** Given that the transformation V maps triangle ABC onto triangle KLM, describe completely the transformation V, and find the 2×2 matrix which represents V.
b Given that the transformation W maps triangle KLM onto triangle PQR, describe completely the transformation W, and find the 2×2 matrix which represents W.
c Given that the transformation Z maps triangle ABC onto triangle PQR, describe completely the transformation Z.

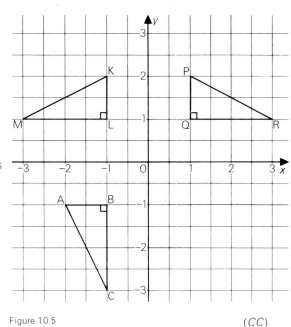
Figure 10.5

(*CC*)

11 Under a certain transformation, the image (x', y') of a point (x, y) is given by

$$\begin{pmatrix} x' \\ y' \end{pmatrix} = \begin{pmatrix} 2 & 1 \\ -1 & 1 \end{pmatrix} \begin{pmatrix} x \\ y \end{pmatrix} + \begin{pmatrix} 3 \\ 9 \end{pmatrix}$$

a Find the coordinates of A, the image of $(0, 0)$,
b Find the coordinates of B, the image of $(4, 3)$,
c Given that the image of the point (g, h) is $(0, 0)$, write down two equations each involving g and h. Hence or otherwise find the values of g and h. *(CD)*

12 Draw axes on graph paper showing values of x and y from 0 to $+10$, using a scale of 2 cm for 2 units on each axis. Mark triangle OAB on your diagram, where O is the origin, A is the point $(10, 0)$ and B is $(10, 5)$.

M is the matrix $\begin{pmatrix} 0.6 & 0.8 \\ 0.8 & -0.6 \end{pmatrix}$. Express **OA** and **OB** as column vectors, and multiply them by **M** to find the image points A' and B' under the transformation represented by **M**. Mark triangle OA'B' on your diagram also.

The geometrical transformation carried out is a reflection. Write down the equation of the axis of reflection (i.e. the mirror line).

Name the type of single geometrical reflection resulting from the following transformations applied one after the other: first triangle OAB is reflected in the x-axis, then the image is reflected in the line joining O to the original position of B. By multiplying the two appropriate matrices together in the correct order, or by some other method, find the single matrix representing this combined transformation. *(O52)*

13 The four points A$(1, 1)$, B$(-1, 1)$, C$(-1, -1)$ and D$(1, -1)$ form a square. The position vectors of A, B, C, D are transformed by premultiplying by the matrix $\mathbf{N} = \begin{pmatrix} 1 & -1 \\ 1 & 1 \end{pmatrix}$ in the usual way.

a Draw a diagram on graph paper showing the square ABCD and its image A'B'C'D' under the transformation carried out by the matrix **N**.
b Calculate the matrix $\mathbf{N}^2$ and show on your diagram the image A"B"C"D" of ABCD under the transformation carried out by $\mathbf{N}^2$.
c Given that the transformation carried out by $\mathbf{N}^2$ consists of an enlargement of factor k, followed by another transformation not involving an enlargement, find k.
d Describe as fully as you can the type of transformation **N** represents.
e Write down the images of $(1, 1)$ under the transformations represented by $\mathbf{N}^4$ and by $\mathbf{N}^8$. *(O52)*

Chapter 11

More equations

The farmer is in trouble because he did not realise that not all quadratic equations have solutions. However, we shall not encounter this point until later in the chapter.

In Chapter 13 of Book 1 it was shown how some quadratic equations can be solved by factorising, thus:

$$2x^2 + 7x - 15 = 0,$$

$$\Rightarrow (2x - 3)(x + 5) = 0,$$

$$\Rightarrow 2x - 3 = 0 \text{ or } x + 5 = 0,$$

$$\text{so } x = 1\tfrac{1}{2} \text{ or } x = -5$$

or we may write that the solution set of the equation is $\{1\tfrac{1}{2}, -5\}$.

As with most quadratic equations for which a solution can be found, the solution set has 2 members.

Many quadratic equations cannot be solved in this way; these equations have irrational roots, and other methods have to be found to solve them. A very simple example is

$$x^2 - 3 = 0$$

This can be written

$$x^2 = 3,$$

and clearly one root is

$$x = \sqrt{3} = 1.732$$

The other root is

$$x = -\sqrt{3} = -1.732$$

Another example is

$$(x - 4)^2 = 2$$

whence

$$x - 4 = \pm\sqrt{2} = \pm 1.414$$

(The sign $\pm$ is used to denote that the sign may be $+$ or $-$.)

$$\text{so } x = 4 + 1.414 = 5.414$$

$$\text{or } x = 4 - 1.414 = 2.586$$

(both answers correct to 4 sig. fig.)

Exercise 11.1

Give the solution sets of the following equations.

1 (By factors)

a $x^2 + 3x - 10 = 0$ c $x^2 - 7x + 10 = 0$ e $3x^2 - 14x - 5 = 0$

b $x^2 + 4x - 21$ d $2x^2 - 7x + 3 = 0$

2 a $x^2 - 7 = 0$ c $2x^2 - 5 = 0$ e $x^2 - \frac{1}{2} = 0$

b $x^2 - 10 = 0$ d $3x^2 - 1 = 0$ f $x^2 - \frac{3}{4} = 0$

3 (Give answers correct to 2 decimal places)

a $(x - 2)^2 = 3$ c $(x - 5)^2 = 30$ e $(x - 1\frac{1}{2})^2 = 3\frac{1}{4}$

b $(x + 1)^2 = 5$ d $(x + \frac{1}{2})^2 = 7$ f $(x + 2\frac{1}{2})^2 = 1\frac{3}{4}$

Completing the square

Clearly, most quadratic equations are not given in the form of those in

Question 3, above, which are quite easy to solve. The equation in **3a** is equivalent to

$$x^2 - 4x + 4 = 3$$

i.e. to

$$x^2 - 4x + 1 = 0$$

and is much more likely to be given in this form. The problem is to reverse the above process, and to get a given equation into the form $(x+a)^2 = b$, where a and b are some numbers. The following examples show how this is done.

Example 1   Solve the equation $x^2 - 6x + 3 = 0$.

Answer
The solution will involve the identity

$$x^2 - 6x + 9 = (x - 3)^2$$

(The -3 in the bracket is half the coefficient of x in the equation.)

To make the left hand side of the given equation a perfect square we must add 6 to it, and we must also do the same to the right hand side, giving

$$x^2 - 6x + 9 = 6$$

i.e.

$$(x - 3)^2 = 6$$

The equation is now in the required form and can be solved, giving

$$x - 3 = \pm\sqrt{6} = \pm 2.45$$

so

$$x = 3 \pm 2.45 = 5.45 \text{ or } 0.55$$

Example 2   Solve the equation $x^2 + 5x - 2 = 0$.

Answer
Here the coefficient of x is **odd** and we must use $x^2 + 5x + 6\frac{1}{4} = (x + 2\frac{1}{2})^2$.

(Again half the coefficient of x in the equation is put in the bracket.)

To complete the square, $8\frac{1}{4}$ must be added to each side of the equation, giving

$$x^2 + 5x + 6\frac{1}{4} = 8\frac{1}{4}$$

i.e. $(x + 2\frac{1}{2})^2 = 8\frac{1}{4} = \frac{33}{4}$

so $x + 2\frac{1}{2} = \dfrac{\sqrt{3}}{\pm 2} = \pm\dfrac{5.74}{2}$

and $x = \dfrac{-5 \pm 5.74}{2} = -5.37 \text{ or } 0.37$

Example 3   Solve the equation $2x^2 - 3x - 7 = 0$.

Answer
Here the coefficient of x^2 is not 1 but 2. We must first divide the equation through by 2, giving

$$x^2 - 1\tfrac{1}{2}x - 3\tfrac{1}{2} = 0$$

We must use

$$x^2 - 1\tfrac{1}{2}x + \tfrac{9}{16} = (x - \tfrac{3}{4})^2$$

The quantity to be added to both sides is $3\tfrac{1}{2} + \tfrac{9}{16} = \tfrac{65}{16}$ this gives

$$x^2 - 1\tfrac{1}{2}x + \tfrac{9}{16} = \tfrac{65}{16}$$

i.e.

$$(x - \tfrac{3}{4})^2 = \tfrac{65}{16}$$

Proceeding as before, we arrive at the solution set $\{2.77, -1.27\}$.

Exercise 11.2

Give all answers correct to 2 decimal places. Solve the equations.

1	$x^2 - 6x + 1 = 0$		**11**	$x^2 + 5x - 7 = 0$
2	$x^2 + 10x - 7 = 0$		**12**	$x^2 - 9x + 3 = 0$
3	$x^2 + 4x + 2 = 0$		**13**	$x^2 - 3x + 1 = 0$
4	$x^2 - 12x + 10 = 0$		**14**	$x^2 + 3x - 8 = 0$
5	$x^2 - 2x - 5 = 0$		**15**	$x^2 + x - 3 = 0$
6	$x^2 + 6x - 3 = 0$		**16**	$x^2 - 13x + 7 = 0$
7	$x^2 + 8x + 4 = 0$		**17**	$x^2 - 7x - 2 = 0$
8	$x^2 - 20x + 17 = 0$		**18**	$x^2 - x - 9 = 0$
9	$x^2 - 16x - 10 = 0$		**19**	$x^2 - 5x + 2 = 0$
10	$x^2 + 14x - 6 = 0$		**20**	$x^2 + 11x - 6 = 0$

Rewrite the following equations in the form $x^2 + bx + c = 0$ and then solve them, giving the answers correct to 2 decimal places.

21	$x^2 - 3x = 5$		**26**	$(x - 1)(x + 4) = 15$
22	$x^2 - 7 = 2x$		**27**	$(x + 5)(x - 1) = 2x$
23	$4x - x^2 = 1$		**28**	$x(5 - x) = 2$
24	$x(x + 1) = 9$		**29**	$(x - 4)(x - 5) = x + 7$
25	$x(8 - x) = 5$		**30**	$x(2x + 1) = (x + 1)(x - 8)$

The formula

It is possible to obtain a general formula for the solution to a quadratic equation. The equation

$$ax^2 + bx + c = 0$$

can be made to represent *any* quadratic equation, by giving suitable values to a, b and c.

Dividing through by a, we have

$$x^2 + \frac{b}{a}x + \frac{c}{a} = 0$$

Now $\qquad x^2 + \frac{b}{a}x + \frac{b^2}{4a^2} = \left(x + \frac{b}{2a}\right)^2$

so to both sides of the original equation add

$$\frac{b^2}{4a^2} - \frac{c}{a}$$

This gives

$$x^2 + \frac{b}{a}x + \frac{b^2}{4a^2} = \frac{b^2}{4a^2} - \frac{c}{a}$$

i.e. $\qquad \left(x + \frac{b}{2a}\right)^2 = \frac{b^2}{4a^2} - \frac{c}{a} = \frac{b^2 - 4ac}{4a^2}$

so $\qquad x + \frac{b}{2a} = \frac{\pm\sqrt{b^2 - 4ac}}{2a}$

and $\qquad x = \frac{-b\sqrt{b^2 - 4ac}}{2a}$

This formula can be used to solve any quadratic equation, as shown in Example 4.

Example 4 Solve the equation $2x^2 - 3x - 7 = 0$.

Answer
Here $a = 2$, $b = -3$, $c = -7$. So

$$x = \frac{3 \pm \sqrt{(-3)^2 - (4 \times 2 \times -7)}}{2 \times 2}$$

$$= \frac{3 \pm \sqrt{9 + 56}}{4}$$

$$= \frac{3 \pm \sqrt{65}}{4}$$

$$= \frac{3 \pm 8.06}{4}$$

$$= \frac{11.06}{4} \text{ or } \frac{-5.06}{4}$$

$$= 2.77 \text{ or } -1.27$$

Exercise 11.3

Give all answers correct to 2 decimal places. Solve the following equations, using the methods of Example 3 or Example 4.

1 $2x^2 + 3x - 4 = 0$ **9** $2x^2 - 13x + 5 = 0$
2 $2x^2 - 5x + 1 = 0$ **10** $7x^2 + 9x - 11 = 0$
3 $2x^2 + 7x + 2 = 0$ **11** $6x^2 + 2x - 1 = 0$
4 $3x^2 - 2x - 6 = 0$ **12** $3x^2 - 20x + 7 = 0$
5 $3x^2 - x - 5 = 0$ **13** $10x^2 - 3x - 8 = 0$
6 $3x^2 + 4x - 8 = 0$ **14** $9x^2 + 17x + 4 = 0$
7 $5x^2 - 9x + 3 = 0$ **15** $4x^2 + 8x - 7 = 0$
8 $4x^2 + x - 7 = 0$

Rewrite the following equations in the form $ax^2 + bx + c = 0$, and solve them, giving the answers correct to 2 decimal places.

16 $3x^2 + 5x = 17$ **20** $(x+4)(3x-5) = 50$
17 $2x^2 - 3x = 10$ **21** $(x-1)(7-x) = x^2$
18 $x(2x-3) = 6$ **22** $2x(x-5) = 7(x-2)$
19 $(2x+1)(x-5) = 12$ **23** $(x-6)(5x+6) = 40$

Problems

In Chapter 13 of Book 1, problems were solved by the use of quadratic equations: all those equations could be factorised, but the equations arising from the problems in the following exercise cannot be solved in this way. Completing the square, or the formula, will have to be used.

Example 5   A rectangular enclosure of area 250 m² is to be made using an existing wall for one side and flexible fencing, of which 50 m are available, for the other three. What should be its dimensions?

Answer

Let the lengths of the sides be x m, $(50-2x)$ m and x m, as shown in Figure 11.1. The area is then $x(50-2x)$ m², so

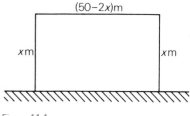

Figure 11.1

$$x(50-2x)=250$$

This gives

$$50x-2x^1=250$$

or, rearranging and dividing through by 2,

$$x^2-25x+125=0$$

Solving gives

$$x=\frac{25}{2}\pm\frac{\sqrt{125}}{2}$$

$= 18.1$ or 6.9 correct to 1 decimal place.

So the possible dimensions are 18.1 m × 13.8 m, or 6.9 m × 36.2 m.

Example 6   The coordinates of A and B are respectively (0, 1) and (8, 4), and P is a point on the x-axis such that PB = 2PA. Find the coordinates of the two possible positions of P.

Answer
Let P be $(x, 0)$: then by Pythagoras' Theorem

$$PA^2=x^2+1 \text{ and } PB^2=(8-x)^2+16.$$

As PB = 2PA, $PB^2=4PA^2$, and we have

$$(8-x)^2+16=4(x^2+1)$$

$$\Rightarrow 64-16x+x^2+16=4x^2+4$$

$$\Rightarrow -3x^2-16x+76=0$$

or $3x^2+16x-76=0$

Solving this gives $x=3.0$ or -8.4. The coordinates are (3.0, 0) and (−8.4, 0).

Exercise 11.4

1   If a projectile is thrown up with a velocity of 20 m/s, its height h m at time t seconds later is given by $h=20t-5t^2$. Find to the nearest tenth of a second the times

a for which $h=10$ **b** for which $h=18$

2   The arch of a bridge is an arc of a circle: if the width is w m, the greatest height is h m and the radius of the circle is r m, then $4h(2r-h)=w^2$. Find h (to 2 sig. fig.)

a if $w=14$, $r=10$ **b** if $w=r=15$

3 Find to the nearest millimetre the dimensions of a rectangle whose area is 20 cm² and whose perimeter is 20 cm.

4 X is a point on the line AB such that AB:AX=AX:XB. Find AX to the nearest mm if AB=10 cm. (X is said to divide AB in *golden section*.)

5 The height of a triangle is 2 cm more than the length of its base, and its area is 16 cm². Find the length of its base, to the nearest mm.

6 ABC is a right-angled triangle. AB is 3 cm longer than AC, which is 2 cm longer than BC. Find, to the nearest mm, the lengths of all the sides.

7 The lengths of the sides of a triangle are (in centimetres) 2, 4 and $x+1$. Those of the corresponding sides of a similar triangle are y, $8x$ and 7. Find x and y to 2 sig. fig.

8 A is (2, 0), B is (2, 8) and Q is a point on the y-axis such that BQ=3AQ. Find to 3 sig. fig. the coordinates of the two possible positions of Q.

9 The diagonals of the kite ABCD cross at right angles at O, and each diagonal is 2 cm long. Given that AB=2BC, find the length of AO to 3 sig. fig. (O is the mid-point of BD.)

10 Figure 11.2 shows a rectangle 10 cm long, with two semicircles, the diameter of each of which is equal to the width of the rectangle. Find the width of the rectangle to the nearest millimetre if the area of the whole figure is 100 cm².

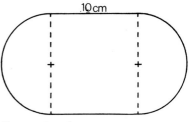

Figure 11.2

Roots and no roots

Returning to Example 5, suppose that the area to be enclosed is 350 cm² instead of 250 m². The equation will now be

$$x(50-2x) = 350$$

giving

$$50x - 2x = 350$$

or, rearranging and dividing through by 2,

$$x^2 - 25x + 175 = 0$$

Completing the square, we use

$$x^2 - 25x + 156\tfrac{1}{4} = (x - 12\tfrac{1}{2})^2$$

giving

$$(x - 12\tfrac{1}{2})^2 = -18.75$$

or if we use the formula,

$$x = \frac{25 \pm \sqrt{25^2 - (4 \times 175)}}{2}$$

$$= \frac{25 \pm \sqrt{-75}}{2}$$

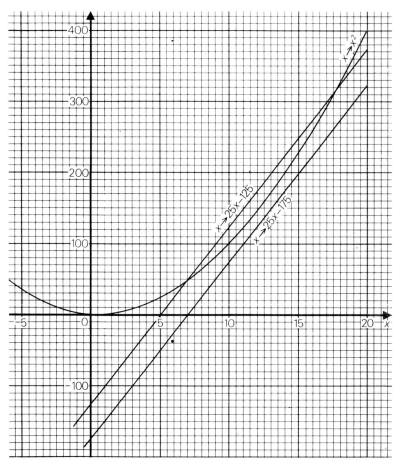

Figure 11.3

Either way, we are faced with the square root of a negative number; as a negative number has no square root, this means that the equation has no solution, and it is impossible to enclose 350 m² of ground with 50 m of fencing in the manner described. (This is the situation depicted at the head of this chapter.)

As we see, a quadratic equation may have no roots; strictly, we should say that it has no **real** roots, or that its solution set is ϕ when $\mathscr{E}=\{$real numbers$\}$. 'Real numbers' means all numbers used in this course (or any other main-school course) – integral and fractional, positive and negative, rational and irrational. The student of this book is unlikely to be concerned with non-real numbers until a much later stage, and so it will usually be assumed that $\mathscr{E}=\{$real numbers$\}$, and we shall often say that an equation has 'no roots' rather than 'no real roots'.

The equation arising out of Example 5 could be solved approximately by graphical methods, possibly by using the intersections of the graph of $x\rightarrow x^2$ with that of $x\rightarrow 25x-125$ (see Figure 11.3).

If we try to use the graph to solve the equation $x^2-25x+175=0$, we have to draw the graph of $x\rightarrow 25x-175$, and, as can be seen, this does not cut the graph of $x\rightarrow x^2$ at all, showing again that the equation has no solution.

Sets of numbers

The solution of an equation is sometimes required as a subset of some universal set other than the whole set of real numbers.

Example 7   Give the solution set of $(x+1)(2x-3)(x^2-3)=0$

a if $\mathscr{E}=\{$real numbers$\}$ c if $\mathscr{E}=\{$positive numbers$\}$
b if $\mathscr{E}=\{$rational numbers$\}$ d if $\mathscr{E}=\{$positive integers$\}$

Answer
a By the same argument as that used in solving quadratic equations by factors, either

$x+1=0$, giving $x=-1$, or

$2x-3=0$, giving $x=1\frac{1}{2}$, or

$x^2-3=0$, giving $x\pm\sqrt{3}$.

The solution set is therefore $\{-1, 1\frac{1}{2}, \sqrt{3}, -\sqrt{3}\}$.
b In rational numbers the solution set is $\{-1, 1\frac{1}{2}\}$.
c In positive numbers it is $\{1\frac{1}{2}, \sqrt{3}\}$.
d In positive integers it is ϕ, since none of the solutions is a positive integer.

Exercise 11.5

1 Find which of the following equations have no roots.

a $x^2 - 6x + 2 = 0$,   **c** $x^2 - 6x + 9 = 0$,   **e** $x^2 - 6x + 16 = 0$
b $x^2 - 6x + 10 = 0$,   **d** $x^2 - 6x = 0$,

2 Show that if $k > 25$, the equation $x^2 + 10x + k = 0$ has no roots. What happens when $k = 25$?

3 Find the range of values of p for which the equations $x^2 + 8x + p = 0$ has no roots.

4 Using the formula given in Question 1 of Exercise 11.4 (page 00), try to find the time at which the projectile is at a height of 22 m. What conclusion do you draw?

5 Try to find the dimensions of a rectangle whose perimeter is 20 cm and whose area is 30 cm². What conclusion do you draw?

In Questions 6, 7, 8 and 9 give the solution set of each equation

a if $\mathscr{E} = \{$real numbers$\}$ **c** if $\mathscr{E} = \{$positive numbers$\}$
b if $\mathscr{E} = \{$rational numbers$\}$ **d** if $\mathscr{E} = \{$integers$\}$

6 $(x - 6)(x + 3)(x^2 - 2) = 0$

7 $(2x + 1)(2x + 5)(x^2 - 5) = 0$

8 $(x^2 - 9)(x^2 - 3) = 0$

9 $(x^2 - 4x + 3)(x^2 - 4x + 2) = 0$

Equations of higher degree

The last four equations in the above exercise are of the fourth degree, that is, if each equation were multiplied out, it would contain a term in x^4.

This presents no difficulty here, since the equations are all given in a ready factorised form. Equations of degree higher than the second cannot be solved by elementary methods unless they can be factorised.

We will write $f(x) = 0$ for an equation of this kind, where $f(x)$ is a polynomial in x (that is, an expression consisting of a sum of multiplies of positive integral powers of x, together with possibly a constant; e.g. $3x^3 - 4x^2 + 5x - 6$).

If we can find, by trial and error or otherwise, a number a such that $f(a)=0$, then a is a root of the equation and $x-a$ is a factor of $f(x)$. (This result is sometimes called the **factor theorem**.)

For example, suppose we have to solve the equation

$$f(x)=x^3-7x^2+13x-6=0$$

and suspect that one root is an integer. Call this root a; then $x^3-7x^2+13x-6=(x-a)(x^2+bx+c)$, where b and c are some other numbers, still unknown. If we were to multiply out the right hand side, the constant term would be $-ac$, so $-ac=-6$. The possible values of a are the factors of 6, i.e. ±1, ±2, ±3 and ±6. Trying these in turn:

$f(1)=1\neq0$, so 1 is not a root,

$f(-1)=-27\neq0$, so -1 is not a root,

$f(2)=0$, so 2 *is* a root, and $(x-2)$ is a factor.

So

$$x^3-7x^2+13x-6=(x-2)(x^2+bx+c)$$

Now

$$-6=-2c, \text{ so } c=3.$$

If we were to multiply out the right hand side, the terms in x^2 would be bx^2-2x^2 and these must combine to make $-7x^2$, so $b=-5$.

The equation can now be written

$$(x-2)(x^2-5x+3)=0$$

So either

$$x-2=0 \text{ or } x^2-5x+3=0$$

The equation

$$x^2-5x+3=0$$

can be solved as described earlier in the chapter, giving $x=4.30$ or 0.70 (to two decimal places), so the solution set is $\{2, 4.30, 0.70\}$.

Exercise 11.6

Solve the following equations, given that each has at least one root which is an integer. Give any irrational roots correct to 2 decimal places.

1 $x^3-3x^2-3x+1=0$ **3** $x^3+2x^2-13x-6=0$

2 $x^3-39x+70=0$ **4** $x^3+3x^2-10x-24=0$

5 $x^3 + 5x^2 - 13x + 7 = 0$

6 $2x^3 + 3x^2 - 14x - 15 = 0$

7 $x^3 - 10x^2 + 26x - 5 = 0$

8 $x^4 - 5x^2 + 4 = 0$ (all the roots are integers)

9 $x^4 + 2x^3 - 13x^2 - 14x + 24 = 0$ (all the roots are integers)

10 $x^4 - 6x^3 + 9x^2 - 4 = 0$ (two of the roots are integers)

Chapter 12

Loci

The man in the boat is trying to fix his position by taking the bearing of the landmark. The bearing is 260: if we look at the map (Figure 12.1), we can see that if he has no further information about his position, he may be at R, or at Q, or anywhere along the line ORQ.

This line forms the set of his possible positions, and is called the *locus* of these positions.

A locus is a set of points satisfying some given condition. Being a set, it may be named with a letter of the alphabet and described in set notation. The above locus could be named and described as $S = \{P: \text{bearing of L from P is 260}\}$.

If the boatman wishes to locate his exact position, he can find it by measuring the bearing of some other point, say M (see map). The bearing of M is 200, so the boat lies on the locus (shown dotted on the map) $T = \{P: \text{bearing of M from P is 200}\}$.

The position of the boat is at $S \cap T$, i.e. at the point marked Q.

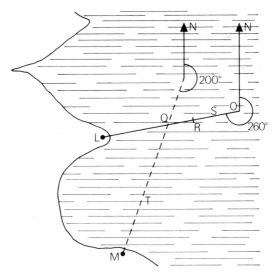

Figure 12.1

Example 1   A point X is 5 cm from a line l. Draw the loci $L = \{P:PX = 3\ cm\}$ and
$M = \{P:P$ is 3 cm from $l\}$, and hence find the points which are 3 cm from
X and 3 cm from l.

Answer
The locus L consists of all points which are 3 cm from X, and these
points lie on a circle with centre X and radius 3 cm (see Figure 12.2).

L is therefore this
circle.

The locus M consists of
all points which are 3
cm from l, and these
points lie on two lines,
each parallel to l, and
3 cm from it on either
side: M is therefore
these two lines.

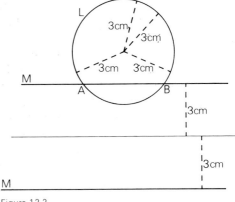

Figure 12.2

The set $L \cap M$ consists
of the two points
marked A and B, and
these are the points
which are 3 cm from
X and 3 cm from l.

Basic loci

Example 1 illustrates the use of two important loci which may be regarded as basic.

1 If X is a fixed point, then {P:PX=r} is a circle with centre X and radius r.

2 If ℓ is a fixed line, then {P:P is d cm from ℓ} is two lines, each parallel to ℓ and d cm from it on either side.

Two other basic loci are now described.

3 Given two fixed points, A and B, find the locus N={P:PA=PB}.

Figure 12.3 shows three possible positions of P.

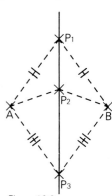

These can easily be located, using intersecting arcs (as indicated in the figure), and the locus is seen to be the perpendicular bisector of AB. The perpendicular bisector is an axis of symmetry for the figure, B being the image of A under reflection in it.

Figure 12.3

4 Given two fixed line-segments, OA and OB, find the locus X={P:distance of P from OA=distance of P from OB}.

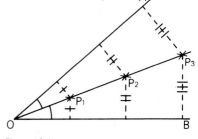

Again three positions of P are shown, and it is clear that the locus is the bisector of the angle AOB, which forms an axis of symmetry of the whole figure. Note that if, instead of line segments, we have two lines **crossing** at O, the locus consists of **two** lines – the bisectors of both the acute and the obtuse angle formed at O.

Figure 12.4

Exercise 12.1

1 Mark two points A and B, 10 cm apart. Draw the loci L={P:PA=8 cm}, and M={P:PB=6 cm}. Mark the two members of $L \cap M$, and measure the distance between them.

2   Mark two points X and Y, 12 cm apart on a horizontal line, with Y to the right of X. These represent, on a scale of 10 000:1, two points on a coastline, Y being due east of X. Draw the loci

    a {points from which the bearing of X is 330}
    b {points from which the bearing of Y is 040}

Mark the point of intersection of these two loci. This point represents the position of a boat: find its distances from X and Y.

3   Draw a triangle ABC with AB=8 cm, BC=10 cm, CA=12 cm. Draw the loci

    a $R = \{P:PB = PC\}$
    b $S = \{P:$perpendicular distance of P from AB=perpendicular distance of P from AC$\}$

$R \cap S$ comprises just one point: measure its distances from A, B and C.

4   Draw an acute-angled triangle XYZ. Draw the loci $U = \{P:PX = PY\}$ and $V = \{P:PY = PZ\}$. Why must the point $U \cap V$ lie on the locus $W = \{P:PZ = PX\}$? Draw the locus W and verify that it does so. What special circle can be drawn with its centre at the point $U \cap V \cap W$?

(This example gives a method for drawing a circle through three given points.)

5   Draw a triangle LMN. Draw the locus of points equidistant from LM and MN, and the locus of points equidistant from LM and LN. Why must the point of intersection of these two loci lie on the locus of points equidistant from MN and LN? What special circle can be drawn with its centre at this point?

6   Draw a line-segment AB, 6 cm long. Draw the loci

    a $\{P: \angle PAB = 30°\}$
    b $\{P:$area of triangle PAB$= 18 \text{ cm}^2\}$

Hence draw a triangle ABC such that $\angle CAB = 30°$ and the area of the triangle is 18 cm², and measure its other sides and angles.

7   Draw a line-segment QR, 5 cm long. Draw the locus {P:triangle PQR is isosceles} (this locus consists of three parts).

8   Aylesbury is 50 km due west of Hertford, and Banbury is 44 km from Aylesbury, on bearing 309. On a suitable scale, draw a map showing these three towns. Use intersecting loci to find a point equidistant from all three. Measure the distance of this point from each of the towns.

9   A and B are fixed points. Describe the locus of a variable point P

a if A can be mapped onto B by a rotation about P

b if A can be mapped onto B by an enlargement with centre P.

10 ∕ is a fixed line, and P′ is the image of P under reflection in ∕. Describe the locus of P if PP′ = 8 cm.

11 A pole 5 m high stands on level ground. Describe the following loci.

a {points on the ground from which the bearing of the pole is 045}

b {points on the ground from which the angle of elevation of the top of the pole is 45°}.

12 ∕ and m are two fixed lines. A circle touches both of them. Describe the locus of the centre of this circle

a if ∕ and *m* are parallel

b if ∕ and *m* are not parallel.

13 ABC is a fixed isosceles triangle, with AB = AC. Describe the locus {P:PBAC is a kite}.

14 ABCD is a variable rectangle. Describe the loci

a of C and D, if A and B are fixed.

b of B and D, if A and C are fixed.

15 Mark two points X and Y, 6 cm apart. Find and mark the points A and P′ such that PX = P′X = 6 cm, PY = P′Y = 3 cm; also the points Q and Q′ such that QX = Q′X = 8 cm, QY = Q′Y = 4 cm, and several other points belonging to the locus {P:PX = 2PY}. Sketch this locus freehand. Given that the locus is a circle, try to locate its centre and to draw it with a compass. Measure its radius, and the distance of its centre from Y.

Region loci

The conditions satisfied by the points of a locus may involve one of the signs <, ≤, > or ≥ instead of the equals sign. In this case the locus will be a region and not a line or a curve. For example, if O is a fixed point the locus P:OP < 5 cm is the region inside a circle with centre O and radius 5 cm. Since the sign < is used, the locus does not include the circumference of the circle, but if the sign ≤ were to be used, the circumference would be included. The locus P:OP > 5 cm is the region *outside* the circle.

A region locus is usually indicated by shading in a diagram the region concerned. It is necessary to begin by drawing the line or curve forming the **boundary** of the region, and then to decide which side of the boundary to shade.

Example 2

Given that $\mathscr{E}=\{$points inside the triangle ABC$\}$, shade the loci $\{P:\angle PBC<\angle PCB\}$ and $\{P:$ area of $\Delta PAB<\frac{1}{2}$ area of $\Delta ABC\}$.

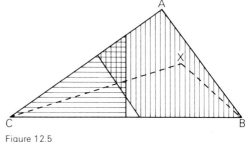

Figure 12.5

Answer

If $\angle PBC=\angle PCB$, then $PB=PC$, so the boundary of the locus is the perpeniduclar bisector of BC. Choose at random any point inside the triangle (e.g. X in the figure). Since $\angle XBC>\angle XCB$, X does not belong to the locus, which is therefore on the other side of the boundary. The locus is shaded horizontally. If area of $\Delta PAB=\frac{1}{2}$ area of ΔABC, the height of ΔPAB is half the height of ΔABC (since they have the same base) and P lies on the line parallel to AB and half as far from AB as C is. This line is the boundary of the locus, which is the region between it and AB. This locus is shaded vertically.

The constant angle locus

Draw a line-segment AB, about 8 cm long, and with AB as base construct a number of triangles ABP with $\angle P=90°$. (What can be said about the sizes of the angles you will have to make at A and B, in order that $\angle P$ may be 90°?)

What sort of locus is $P:\angle APB=90°$?

(You can also obtain this locus by laying your paper on a board, sticking in two drawings pins – not right up to their heads – about 8 cm apart, inserting your set-square between them and moving it round: the right-angle corner of the set-square will trace out the locus. (See Figure 12.6).

Now repeat the above, but make angle APB 60° instead of 90°. (If you use the set-square method, use the 60° corner of the set-square; you may have to put the drawing-pins closer together.)

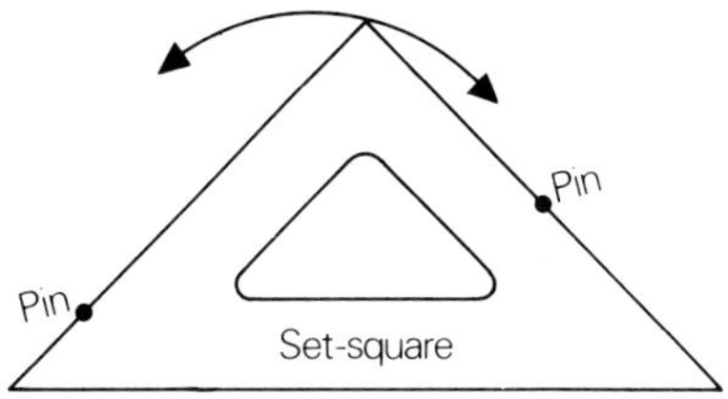

Figure 12.6

You should reach this conclusion:

If A and B are fixed points, then $\{P\angle PAB=\text{constant}\}$ is two arcs of equal

circles, one on each
side of AB. If ∠APB is
a right-angle, the two
arcs are semi-circles
and form a complete
circle, but otherwise
they do not. (See
Figure 12.7.)

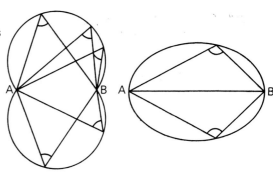

Figure 12.7

Exercise 12.2

1 Draw a square ABCD. With $\mathscr{E}=\{$points inside the square$\}$, shade in
different ways the loci

  a $\{P:PA>PB\}$ **b** $\{P:PA>AB\}$.

2 Draw a triangle XYZ. Shade the locus of points inside the triangle which
are nearer to XY than to either of the other two sides of the triangle.

3 Draw a rectangle LMNO with LM = 8 cm, MN = 6 cm. With $\mathscr{E}=\{$points
inside the rectangle$\}$ shade the loci $X=\{P:PL<PN\}$ and $Y=\{P:P$ is more
than 5 cm from LO$\}$. Find the area of the region $X\cap Y$.

4 In Figure 12.8, describe each of
the shaed regions as an
intersection of two basic loci,
taking $\mathscr{E}=\{$points inside the
rectangle$\}$.

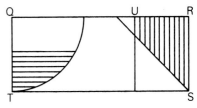

Figure 12.8

5 Draw a rhombus ABCD with each side 5 cm long and the diagonal AC
also 5 cm long. Shade the locus of points inside the rhombus which are
nearer to A than to any of the other three vertices of ABCD.

6 Draw a circle and mark a diameter AB. Describe as loci involving the
angle APB

  a the set of points P on the circumference of the circle,
  b the set of points P inside the circle,
  c the set of points P outside the circle.

7 Draw a square ABCD, and draw two circles, one with centre B and the
other with centre D, both passing through A and C. Mark some points
P_1, P_2, P_3 etc. on the circumference of either circle but outside the

square. Measure the angles AP_1C, AP_2C, AP_3C etc. Describe as loci involving the angle APC

a the set of points P on the circumference of either circle but outside the square,

b the set of points P inside either circle (or inside both),

c the set of points P outside both circles.

8 With the same figures as in Question 7, mark points Q_1, Q_2, Q_3 etc. on the circumference of either circle but *inside* the square. Describe as loci involving the angle AQC

a the set of points Q on the circumference of either circle and *inside* the square,

b the set of points Q inside both circles,

c the set of points Q which are not inside both circles.

9 Draw an isosceles triangle XYZ with XY=XZ and $LX=50°$. Draw a circle with centre X, passing through Y and Z. Part of this circle is part of the locus $\{P:LYPZ=x°\}$, where x is a certain number. What is the value of x

a when P is on the larger arc of the circle,

b when P is on the smaller arc of the circle?

10 Repeat Question 9 with another value for angle X. Try to find the connection between LX and the two values of x.

11 Draw a line AB, 8 cm long. Construct the loci

a $\{P:LAPB=90°\}$ **b** $\{P:\text{area of } LAPB=8 \text{ cm}^2\}$.

Hence draw a triangle ABC, right-angled at C and with area 8 cm². How many such triangles could be drawn?

12 A tall box which cannot be tilted has a square base 1.2 m × 1.2 m. Someone is trying to get it through a doorway 1 m wide. Find the area of that part of the floor, on the far side of the doorway, which it is possible for any part of the box to reach.

13 Copy Figure 12.9 accurately. X and Y represent landmarks on a coastline, and the shaded region represents a region of the sea which it is dangerous for boats to enter. Navigators are to be instructed not to allow the angle XBY (where B is the position of the boat) to rise above a certain value. Suggest what this value should be (allow a certain margin

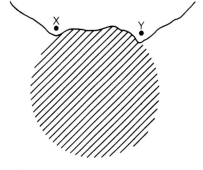

Figure 12.9

of safety). If this value is chosen, draw the boundary of the region which boats will not enter, if the instruction is obeyed.

Locus as the path of a 'moving point'

It is sometimes convenient to regard a locus as the path of a moving point, rather than as a set of fixed points.

Example 3

The square ABEF is to be rotated into the position of the square BCDE. Trace the path of the vertex A if the centre of rotation is **a** B, **b** X, the mid-point of BE, **c** E.

Answer

The three paths are shown by the broken-lined arcs marked **a**, **b** and **c**.

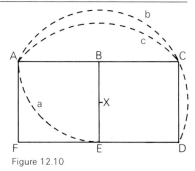

Figure 12.10

Example 4

A bead is attached to one end of a thread 8 cm long: the other end of the thread is attached to the corner A of a square reel ABCD, each side of which is 2 cm. To start with, the thread is wound round the reel so that the bead is at A and the point of the thread 3 cm from A is at B. The thread is then unwound, always remaining taut and horizontal. Trace the path of the bead, and find the total distance it travels, as far as the point where the bead is in line with BA.

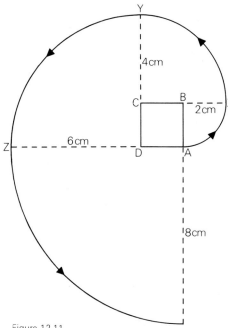

Figure 12.11

Answer

At first the bead leaves A and moves in a quarter-circle with centre B and radius 2 cm, until it reaches the point marked X in Figure 12.11. The length of thread between B and C now leaves the reel, and the bead moves in a quarter-circle with centre C and radius 4 cm, until it reaches

Y. The bead then moves in two more quarter-circles with centres D and A and radii 6 cm and 8 cm until it reaches Z.

The length of the path is

$$\tfrac{1}{4} \times 2\pi(2+4+6+8) \text{ cm} = 10_\pi \text{ cm} = \text{about } 31.4 \text{ cm.}$$

Exercise 12.3

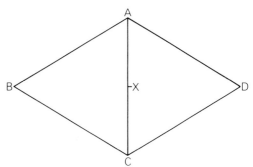

Figure 12.12

1 In Figure 12.12, the triangle ABC is to be rotated into the position of triangle ACD. Copy the figure, and trace the path of the vertex B if the centre of rotation is
   a A,
   b X, the mid-point of AC,
   c C.

2 A dog is tethered by a chain 4 m long to one corner of a square shed, measuring 2 m × 2 m. Draw a plan, and shade the entire region over which the dog can go. Find the area of this region.

3 A man walks all round a rectangular building which is 12 m long and 10 m wide. He always keeps 2 m from the nearest point of the building. On a plan, draw the route travelled by this man, and find its length.

4 Draw each of the following figures. For each figure, draw the path of a point which moves, if possible, so as to be always 2 cm from the nearest point of the figure (i) outside and (ii) inside the figure.

   a A square of side 6 cm,
   b An equilateral triangle of side 6 cm,
   c A circle of diameter 6 cm.

5 ABCD is a rectangular field with AB = 30 m, BC = 40 m. Someone walks from A to B in such a way as to be always equidistant from the two nearest edges of the field. Describe the route taken by this person, and find its length. Another person walks from A to B in such a way that ∠APB is always 90°, where P is the person's position. Describe this second route, and find its length. How many points have the two routes in common?

Three-dimensional loci

Loci may consist of points in three dimensions (i.e. in all space) in
stead of only in two (i.e. in a plane such as the surface of this page).
The locus $\{P:PX=5 \text{ cm}\}$, where X is a fixed point, consists of a circle if
P is restricted to lie in the plane of the paper, but if P is allowed to rise
above the plane or to sink below it, the locus is the surface of a sphere
of radius 5 cm. Similarly, the locus $\{P:PX<5\}$ cm is the interior of the
sphere.

Exercise 12.4

1   O is a fixed point on a fixed line ℓ. X is the locus of points in space 6 cm
from ℓ; Y is the locus of points in space 10 cm from O.

Describe the loci

a X,   **b** $X \cap Y$.

2   Describe the loci of points in a room which are

    a 1 m above the floor,
    b equidistant from the floor and the ceiling,
    c 1 m from the front wall,
    d equidistant from the floor and the front wall,
    e equidistant from the floor, the ceiling and the front wall.

3   A model aeroplane is attached to a wire 10 m long, the other end of
which is attached to a point on the ground (supposed horizontal).
Describe the locus of possible positions of the aeroplane

    a when the wire is taut,
    b when the wire is not taut,
    c when the aeroplane is 6 m above the ground, and the wire is taut.

4   A and B are two fixed points. Describe the following loci in three
dimensions.

    a $\{P:PA=PB\}$ **c** $\{P:\angle PAB=60°\}$
    b $\{P:\angle PAB=90°\}$ **d** $\{P:\angle APB=90°\}$

5   One end of a string 30 cm long is attached to a bead, the other end to a
ring which can slide along a straight wire 50 cm long. Describe the
region in space that forms the locus of all possible positions of the bead.

6   T is the top of a vertical mast TB, which is 10 m high. From a point P
the angle of elevation of T is $e°$ and the angle of depression of B is $d°$.
Describe the following loci in three dimensions.

a $\{P:e=45\}$ **b** $\{P:d=45\}$ **c** $\{P:d=e\}$ **d** $\{P:d+e=90\}$

Other curves

All the two-dimensional loci encountered so far have been straight lines or circles (or parts of circles), or made up of straight lines and parts of circles. Many loci are curves other than circles, and a very few of these will be met with in the following examples.

Example 5   O is a fixed point 2 cm from a fixed line l. Draw the locus $\{P:OP=$perpendicular distance of P from $l\}$.

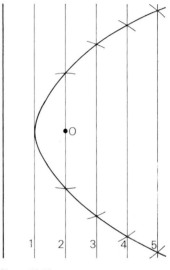

Figure 12.13

Answer
Draw a series of lines parallel to l and at distances 1, 2, 3. . . . cm from l. Number these lines 1, 2, 3. . .

With centre O and radius 1 cm draw an arc to touch line 1, and mark the point of contact.

With centre O and radius 2 cm draw arcs to cut line 2, and mark the points of intersection.

With centre O and radius 3 cm draw arcs to cut line 3, and mark the points of intersection.

Continue in this way for as long as possible. All the points you have marked lie on the required locus.

Draw a smooth curve through the points. This curve is a *parabola*: you will often have drawn parabolas before, for example in drawing the graph of $x\rightarrow x^2$.

Exercise 12.5

1   Draw a circle and a diameter AB. Draw a number of chords QXQ', perpendicular to AB, with X on AB. For each chord mark P and P', the mid-points of QX and XQ' respectively. Trace the locus of P and P': this curve is an *ellipse*.

Different ellipses can be drawn by taking, for example, $XP=\frac{1}{3}XQ$ and $XP'=\frac{1}{3}XQ'$ instead of making P and P' the mid-points of QX and XQ'.

2   Begin as in Question 1, above, but this time extend the chord QXQ' to R and (in the other direction) to R', so that XR = 2XQ and XR' = 2QX'. Trace the locus of R and R'. What kind of curve is it?

3   Draw two lines OX and OY at right-angles (graph paper is suitable for this question).

Draw a rectangle AOBC with A on OX and B on OY, and with the lengths of OA and OB so chosen that the area of the rectangle is 12 cm². Repeat with other rectangles with the same area. Trace the locus of C. This is part of a **rectangular hyperbola**. Repeat with other areas for the rectangles, but keeping the area the same when drawing any one curve.

4   A ladder stands against a vertical wall, with its foot on a horizontal floor. The foot of the ladder is moved away from the wall, and the ladder slips down until it is lying on the floor. Draw a diagram showing various positions of the ladder as it slips. Draw the loci of some of the points of the ladder. These loci form parts of curves you have drawn while answering a previous question. What are they?

5   Draw a circle and a diameter AB. Mark a point Q on the circumference of the circle. Join AQ and extend it both ways, to P and to P' so that QP = QP' = AB. Repeat this for many positions of Q, and trace the locus of P and P'. This curve is a **cardioid**.

6   Repeat Question 5, above, but with the difference that the length of QP and QP', though still fixed, is not equal to that of AB. This will give a **limaçon**. The exact shape will of course vary according to the length you choose for QP and QP'.

7   Mark two points X and Y, 10 cm apart, and mark some points belonging to the locus {P:PX − PY = 2 cm}. Draw a smooth curve through them. This is part of a **hyperbola**: another part is formed by the locus {P:PY − PX = 2 cm}. Other hyperbolas can be drawn by using distances other than 2 cm.

8   Mark two points A and B, 8 cm apart. These are to represent two railway stations 16 km apart in open country. The members of a rambling club arrive at A: they decide they have time to walk 24 km before catching a train at B. Locate two points P such that AP = 7 cm, PB = 5 cm: these represent two of the points that the ramblers could just reach. Locate several other such points and draw the boundary of the region accessible to the ramblers. What sort of curve is formed by this boundary?

The chapter concludes with some examples from former O-level papers.

Exercise 12.6

1 The square ABCD is divided into four equal parts named p, q, r and s. A point X lies inside the square ABCD.

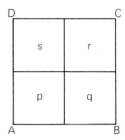

Figure 12.14

a If XA > XD, name the regions representing the possible positions of X.

b Write down two different inequalities, each involving XA, if the region representing the possible positions of X is square p.

(*CC*)

2 A circle PQRS of radius *r* is inscribed in a square ABCD.

Indicate clearly on the diagram below the region in which the point X must lie, within the square ABCD, if RX ⩽ PX, SX ⩽ QX and OX ⩾ *r*.

(*CD*)

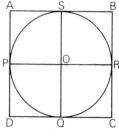

Figure 12.15

3 Two squares, ABEF and BEDC, are drawn side by side. $\mathscr{E}$ = {all points inside the rectangle ACDF}. Draw this figure, and

a shade M = {P:PA > PC},

b draw N = {Q:FD = 90°}, and label it,

c using just three of the symbols M, N, >, <, =, ∩, ∪, ⊂ describe the quarter circle between B and D with radius BE and centre E. (*SMP*)

4 A circle is inscribed inside a square ABCD. Any point of the circle is joined to any point Q of the square and PQ is produced to R, so that PR = 2PQ. Describe and illustrate

a the locus of R as Q moves round the square for any fixed point P not a point of contact,

b the locus of R as P moves round the circle for any fixed point Q not a point of contact. (*LC*)

5 The points X and Y are 1 metre apart on the horizontal floor of a room. Describe briefly each of the following loci in space.

a {P:PX = PY}

b {P:PX = PY and P is 80 cm above the floor}

c {P:PX has length 1 metre}

d {P:PX has length 1 metre and P is 80 cm above the floor} (*LC*)

6   The line ∕ is a tangent at T to the circle with centre O and radius 5 cm. A variable point P lies on the line ∕, and OP meets the circle at Q, where Q lies between O and P. The mid-point of the perpendicular from Q onto OT is M.

Draw the figure accurately.

Mark three possible positions of P and the corresponding positions of M. Sketch the locus of M.   (*LC*)

7   Figure 12.16 shows a side view of an 'up-and-over' garage door PQ, 210 cm high, in a partly open position. U is a fixed point on the edge of the door, 140 cm from P. U slides vertically along AB, an edge of the door-frame, while P slides horizontally to the right from its closed position A.

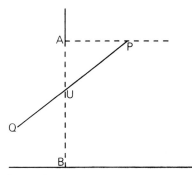

Figure 12.16

a Using a scale of 1:20, make an accurate drawing showing the door in five positions: fully open; with U at 40 cm; 80 cm; and 120 cm below A; fully closed.

b Sketch and label the locus of Q.

c Explain why, as the door is opened, the mid-point of PU moves on a circle with centre A.   (*SMP*)

8   Two landmarks, *A* and *B* stand on a coastline, *B* is 11 km from *A* on bearing 020. On graph paper, using a scale of 1 cm to 1 km, draw a map showing *A* and *B*, and indicating the north direction. (Have the line *AB* well to the right of your map.)

A small boat with a valuable cargo has sunk in the sea to the west of *AB*. Before it sank, the crew noted that the bearings of *A* and *B* were respectively 170 and 100. Supposing that these bearings are correct, locate and mark on your map the point where the boat sank, and find the distances of this point from *A* and *B*.

Divers fail to find the sunken boat at this point, and it is decided to search the whole region in which the boat could be, if the bearings given had been accurate only to the nearest 10°. Shade this region on your map, and make a rough estimate of its area, stating how your estimate was obtained.

The boat still cannot be found, and it is suggested that its compass may have suffered from a fault which would have meant that, although the difference between the bearings was in fact 70°, the bearings themselves were wrongly given. Draw on your map the locus of possible positions of the boat, if this supposition is correct.   (*LC*)

9 The diagram is a plan of a field
with a straight hedge *XY* and a
post *P*, 7 metres from the hedge. A
goat *G* is tethered to the post by a
rope of such a length that the goat
can reach points up to 14 metres
from *P*. The points *X* and *Y* are the
further points of the hedge that the
goat can reach. Taking $\pi = \dfrac{22}{7}$,
calculate

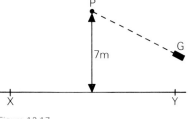

Figure 12.17

a the length *XY*,
b the area of the triangle *PXY*,
c the total area that the goat can graze if it encounters no obstacle
other than the hedge.

In order to stop the goat from damaging the hedge, the post is replaced
by a length of fencing *OPQ*, parallel to the hedge and 7 m from it, with
the same rope attached to the middle point of the side of the fencing
away from the hedge.

The second diagram
shows three possible
positions of the goat
when the rope is taut.
Calculate
d the shortest length
of fencing will keept
the goat from reaching
the hedge.

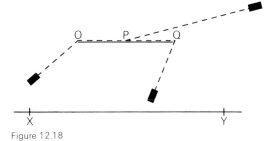

Figure 12.18

e the area that the goat can now graze, if this shortest length of fencing
is used.   (*LC*)

Chapter 13
More probability

In Chapter 14 of Book 1 the idea of probability was introduced and some simple problems were solved. Each of these problems involved only one 'trial'. A trial, it will be remembered, is an operation like tossing a coin or throwing a die, which can have more than one possible outcome.

Probability space. The set of possible outcomes is sometimes called the *probability space* or the *possibility space* or the *sample space*.

In this chapter we shall encounter some rather more elaborate problems, each involving more than one trial.

The multiplication rule

A coin is tossed and a die is thrown: what is the probability that the result will be a head and a six? We can summarise all the possible results in a table.

From die	1	2	3	4	5	6
From coin						
Heads	H1	H2	H3	H4	H5	H6
Tails	T1	T2	T3	T4	T5	T6

(H1 means 'heads on the coin and 1 on the die' and so on.) Since tossing the coin has two possible outcomes and throwing the die has six, the total number of possible outcomes is $2 \times 6 = 12$: of these only 1 gives the outcome 'a head and a six', so the probability of this outcome is $\frac{1}{12}$.

We see that $\frac{1}{12} = \frac{1}{2} \times \frac{1}{6}$, i.e. the probability of a head $\times$ the probability of a six.

Another example: a number is chosen at random from each of the sets A and B, where $A = \{1, 2, 3, 4, 5\}$ and $B = \{6, 7, 8, 9, 10\}$, and the two are multiplied together. What is the probability that the product is odd?

In order for the product to be odd, each separate number must be odd. There are 25 possible pairs of numbers, and of these the only ones which give odd products are those containing one of the 3 odd numbers in A and one of the 2 odd numbers in B. There are $3 \times 2 = 6$ of these, so the probability is $\frac{6}{25}$. This is $\frac{3}{15} \times \frac{2}{25}$ (probability of an odd number from A $\times$ probability of an odd number from B).

These examples illustrate the *multiplication rule* which may be stated as follows:

If the probability of a certain outcome of one trial is p, and the probability of another certain outcome of another trial is q, then the probability that *both* outcomes will occur is pq, the product of the separate probabilities.

The same rule holds when more than two trials are involved.

Complementary probability

If the probability of a certain event is p, then the probability that this event will *not* occur is $1 - p$, and the two probabilities are said to be *complementary*. Similarly, if two events cannot both occur and their separate probabilities are p and q, then the probability that neither will occur is $1 - p - q$.

For example, a sweet is chosen at random from a bag: it is known that the probability of its being red is $\frac{1}{3}$ and that the probability of its being green is $\frac{1}{4}$. Then the probability that it will be neither red nor green is $1-\frac{1}{3}-\frac{1}{4}=\frac{5}{12}$.

Example 1   Three dice are thrown. Find the probability

    a   that all will show 6,

    b   that none will show 6,

    c   that at least one will show 6.

Answer

a   The probability that the first will show 6 is $\frac{1}{6}$; the probability that the second will show a 6 is also $\frac{1}{6}$, and similarly for the third. The probability that all three will show 6 is therefore

$$\tfrac{1}{6}\times\tfrac{1}{6}\times\tfrac{1}{6}=\tfrac{1}{216}$$

or about 0.0046.

b   If none shows a 6, then each shows a 'non-6', and the probability of a 'non-6' is $\frac{5}{6}$. The probability of three 'non-6's' is

$$\tfrac{5}{6}\times\tfrac{5}{6}\times\tfrac{5}{6}=\tfrac{125}{216}\text{ or about 0.58.}$$

c   This is the complementary probability to that found in **b**, so the answer is

$$1-\tfrac{125}{216}=\tfrac{91}{216}\text{ or about 0.42.}$$

The outcome of the first trial may affect the probability of the second, as in the following example.

Example 2   A box contains 4 hard and 3 soft chocolates. Three of these are chosen at random: what is the probability that they will be

    a   all hard,   **c**   at least one hard and at least one soft?

    b   all soft,

Answer

a   The probability that the first is hard is $\frac{4}{7}$. If the first *is* hard, there are now 6 left of which 3 are hard, so the probability that the second will also be hard is $\frac{3}{6}=\frac{1}{2}$.

If both the first two are hard, there are now 5 left of which 2 are hard, so the probability that the third will be hard is $\frac{2}{5}$.

By the multiplication rule, the probability that all three will be hard is $\frac{4}{7}\times\frac{1}{2}\times\frac{2}{5}=\frac{4}{35}$.

b   In the same way, the probability that the first is soft is $\frac{3}{7}$; if the first is soft, the probability that the second is soft is $\frac{2}{6}=\frac{1}{3}$, and if the first two are soft the probability that the third is soft is $\frac{1}{5}$.

The probability that all three are soft is $\frac{3}{7} \times \frac{1}{3} \times \frac{1}{5} = \frac{1}{35}$.

c If the chocolates are not all hard, and not all soft, then there must be at least one of each kind. The answer here is therefore the complementary probability to the previous two, i.e.

$$1 - \tfrac{4}{35} - \tfrac{1}{35} = \tfrac{30}{35} = \tfrac{6}{7}$$

Exercise 13.1

1 A die is thrown and at the same time a card is drawn from a pack. Find the probability that the die shows a six and the card is an ace.

2 Two numbers are chosen, one from the set $P = \{1, 2, 3, 5\}$ and the other from $Q = \{4, 6, 7, 8\}$. Find the probability

    a that the product of the two numbers is odd
    b that the product is even
    c that the product is not a multiple of 3 (this will be the case if neither number is a multiple of 3)
    d that the product *is* a multiple of 3

3 A letter is chosen from {letters of CART}, and a letter is chosen from {letters of HORSE}. Find the probability

    a that the same letter is chosen each time
    b that both are vowels
    c that both are consonants
    d that one is a vowel and the other a consonant

4 Three coins are tossed. Find the probability

    a that all come down heads
    b that all come down tails
    c that there is at least one head and at least one tail

5 Two cards are drawn from different packs. Find the probability

    a that the first is a heart and the second an ace
    b that both are hearts
    c that both are aces
    d that neither is a heart
    e that neither is an ace

6 Three people are chosen at random. Find the probability that their birthdays

    a are all in June (assume that all months are equally probable)
    b are none of them in June

7 In planning their cricket festival, the Much Slogging club learn from the Meteorological Office that the probability that the first Saturday in June will be wet is $\frac{1}{6}$, and that the corresponding probabilities for the second, third and fourth Saturdays in June are $\frac{1}{5}$, $\frac{1}{4}$ and $\frac{1}{3}$. Find the probability

  a that all four Saturdays in June will be wet
  b that none of these Saturdays will be wet
  c that at least one, but not all, will be wet

8 A student of football results states that the probability of the home team winning a match is $\frac{1}{2}$, while the probability of the away team winning is $\frac{1}{3}$. Supposing that he is right, what is the probability of a draw? Still supposing this, find the probability that of three matches

  a all will be won by the home teams
  b all will be won by the away teams
  c all will be drawn
  d not all will have the same kind of result

9 Bag A contains 3 red, 2 white and 4 blue balls; bag B contains 2 red, 4 white and 3 blue ones. One ball is drawn at random from each bag; find the probability that

  a both will be red   **d** they will be of different colours
  b both will be white   **e** they will be of the same colour
  c both will be blue

10 Repeat Question 9, but this time **both** the balls are drawn from bag A and the first is not replaced before the second is drawn.

11 A hand of cards contains 4 spades, 2 hearts and 1 club. Two cards are drawn from it at random; find the probability that they are

  a both spades   **c** both clubs
  b both hearts   **d** of different suits

12 Six boys and four girls draw lots for the last two places on a school outing. Find the probability that those who go are

  a both boys   **b** both girls   **c** one boy and one girl

13 Two **different** numbers are chosen at random from the set {2, 3, 4, 5, 6, 7} and multiplied together. Find the probability that the product is

  a odd   **c** not a multiple of 3 (see Question 2)
  b even   **d** a multiple of 3

14 The probability that it will rain today is 0.2. If it rains today, the probability that it will rain tomorrow is 0.15. If it does not rain today, the probability that it will not rain tomorrow is 0.9.

a   List all the possible combinations of weather for the two days and calculate the associated probabilities.

b   What is the probability that at least one of the two days will be fine?

(*SMP*)

15   A bag contains 4 red balls and x blue balls. A ball is drawn at random; write down the probability that it is red.

This ball is not replaced, and a second ball is drawn. Show that the probability that both are red is $\dfrac{12}{(4+x)(3+x)}$.

Given that this probability is in fact $\frac{1}{11}$, find the value of x.

16   A bag contains 5 black balls and y white ones. Two balls are drawn at random (the first is not replaced before the second is drawn). The probability that both are white is $\frac{2}{9}$. Find the value of y.

17   Balls are drawn at random from a bag containing 6 red and 4 green balls. Find the probability that

a   the first ball drawn will be green,

b   the first two balls drawn will both be green. (The first ball is not replaced before the second is drawn.)

The balls are all replaced and then more green balls are added, and it is now found that the probability of drawing a green ball is $\frac{2}{3}$. Find how many more green balls have been added.

Another bag contains r red and g green balls. The probability of drawing a green ball at random is $\frac{3}{7}$. Find a relation between r and g. If, in addition, the probability that when two balls are drawn both are green is $\frac{6}{35}$, show that $5(g-1)=2(r+g-1)$. (Again, the first ball is not replaced before the second is drawn.) Hence find the values of r and g.

(*LC*)

The addition rule

In order to find other probabilities – for example, that of scoring a total of 17 with three dice – it is necessary to use the *addition rule*. In order to illustrate this rule, consider the following problem: a card is drawn from a pack; what is the probability that it is a spade, or a red ace, or the queen of hearts?

There are 13 spades, so the probability of a spade is $\frac{13}{52}=\frac{1}{4}$.

There are 2 red aces, so the probability of a red ace is $\frac{2}{52}=\frac{1}{26}$.

There is 1 queen of hearts, so the probability of drawing it is $\frac{1}{52}$.

The total number of outcomes which satisfy the conditions of the question is $13+2+1=16$, so the required probability is $\frac{16}{52}=\frac{4}{13}$. It can easily be seen why this is the sum of the separate probabilities, i.e. $\frac{1}{4}+\frac{1}{26}+\frac{1}{52}$.

It is very important to note that the probability that one or other of several events will occur is given by the sum of their separate probabilities *only if no two of the events can occur together*. The above result held because a card cannot be a spade and also a red ace, or a spade and also the queen of hearts, or a red ace and also the queen of hearts. If, instead of a red ace, the above problem had involved a *black* ace, the answer would have been different, since a card *can* be a spade and also a black ace (if it is the ace of spades).

A set of events of which no two can occur together are said to be *mutually incompatible* (or sometimes, for brevity, just 'incompatible').

The addition rule may be stated as follows:

If the probabilities of two outcomes of a trial are p and q, and the outcomes are mutually incompatible, then the probability that one or other outcome will occur is $p+q$, the sum of the separate probabilities.

The same rule holds when more than two outcomes are involved.

Example 3   Find the probability of scoring a total of 17 with three dice.

Answer
A score of 17 can be obtained in the following ways:

6 on the first die, 6 on the second, 5 on the third,

6 on the first die, 5 on the second, 6 on the third,

5 on the first die, 6 on the second, 6 on the third.

The probability of 6, 6 and 5 is $\frac{1}{6}\times\frac{1}{6}\times\frac{1}{6}=\frac{1}{216}$.

The probability of 6, 5 and 6 is clearly the same, as is that of 5, 6 and 6.

These three outcomes are mutually incompatible, and the probability that one or other will occur is

$$\frac{1}{216}+\frac{1}{216}+\frac{1}{216}=\frac{3}{216}=\frac{1}{72}$$

Exercise 13.2

1   Which of the following pairs of outcomes are mutually incompatible?

    a When two dice are thrown, a 6 on one die and a total of 7,
    b When two dice are thrown, a 6 on one die and a total of 6,
    c A card is drawn from a pack; it is a heart, it is a diamond,
    d A card is drawn from a pack; it is a heart, it is a queen,

e A number is chosen; it is prime, it is even

f A number more than one is chosen; it is prime, it is a perfect square

g A number more than 8 is chosen; it is prime, it is a multiple of 7

h A number more than 9 is chosen; it is a multiple of 7, it is a multiple of 8.

2 A card is drawn from a pack. Find the probability that it is a red king, or a club, or a heart which is not a 'picture card'.

3 A day in a (non-leap) year is chosen at random. Find the probability that it is

a in January   **c** either in January or a Sunday in February

b a Sunday in February

4 Ann and Bert throw dice. Find the probability that either Ann's die shows a 5, or the total is 5.

5 Three dice are thrown. Find the probability that the total is 4.

6 Three dice are thrown. Write down all the ways in which a total of 16 can be made up, and hence find the probability that the total is 16.

7 Two balls are drawn from a bag containing 2 red, 2 white and 2 blue balls; find the probability that they are the same colour.

8 Three coins are tossed; find the probability that they fall the same way up.

9 Each of two people chooses a number at random from the set {1, 2, 3, 4, 5}. Find the probability that they choose the same number.

10 Four coins are tossed; find the probability that they show three heads and a tail.

Probability trees

In solving problems involving more than one trial it is sometimes useful to draw a diagram of a kind known as a *probability tree*. For example: from a bag containing 4 red, 3 yellow and 2 green balls, a ball is drawn and then a second ball is drawn without the first one being replaced. Find the probability of each combination of colours.

We begin by drawing three 'branches' representing the first draw.

Each possible
outcome, with its
associated probability,
is written along one of
the lines, or 'branches'.

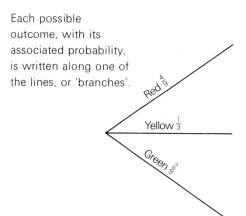

Figure 13.1

Now we consider the
second draw, if the
result of the first has
been 'red', and add
three more 'branches'.

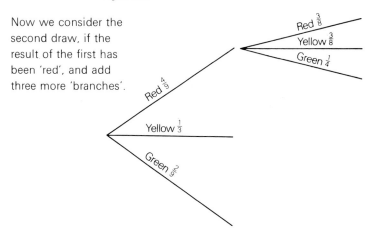

Figure 13.2

The tree is then
completed in the same
way.

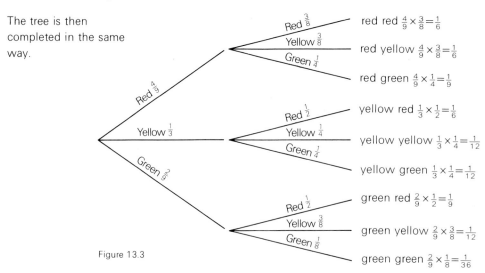

red red $\frac{4}{9} \times \frac{3}{8} = \frac{1}{6}$

red yellow $\frac{4}{9} \times \frac{3}{8} = \frac{1}{6}$

red green $\frac{4}{9} \times \frac{1}{4} = \frac{1}{9}$

yellow red $\frac{1}{3} \times \frac{1}{2} = \frac{1}{6}$

yellow yellow $\frac{1}{3} \times \frac{1}{4} = \frac{1}{12}$

yellow green $\frac{1}{3} \times \frac{1}{4} = \frac{1}{12}$

green red $\frac{2}{9} \times \frac{1}{2} = \frac{1}{9}$

green yellow $\frac{2}{9} \times \frac{3}{8} = \frac{1}{12}$

green green $\frac{2}{9} \times \frac{1}{8} = \frac{1}{36}$

Figure 13.3

The probability of two reds is found by 'running up the tree' from the start to the point marked, multiplying the probabilities found on the way, i.e. $\frac{4}{9}$ and $\frac{3}{8}$: this gives $\frac{1}{6}$ as the probability of two reds. In the same way the probabilities of all the other final outcomes are found.

If, as may well be the case, the order of drawing does not matter, so that 'red yellow' is the same as 'yellow red', the probability of 'red and yellow in either order' can be found by adding the probabilities of 'red yellow' and 'yellow red', (since these are mutually incompatible outcomes). This gives a probability $\frac{1}{3}$: similarly the probability of red and green is $\frac{2}{9}$ and that of yellow and green is $\frac{1}{6}$.

Example 4

(In this example, the outcome of the second trial is not affected by that of the first.)

I travel by bus to the station and there hope to catch a train. The probabilities that the bus will arrive at the station at 10.58, 11.00 and 11.02 are respectively $\frac{1}{2}$, $\frac{1}{3}$ and $\frac{1}{6}$. The probabilities that the train will leave at 10.59, 11.01 and 11.03 are respectively $\frac{2}{3}$, $\frac{1}{4}$ and $\frac{1}{12}$. Allowing 1 minute to get from the bus to the train, find the probability that I shall catch the train.

Answer
See Figure 13.4.

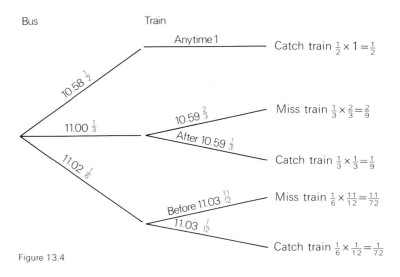

Figure 13.4

The probability of catching the train is $\frac{1}{2}+\frac{1}{9}+\frac{1}{72}=\frac{5}{8}$.

Exercise 13.3

1 A box contains 10 electric torches, 3 of which are faulty. Two are chosen from the box. Complete the tree in Figure 13.5 and find the probabilities

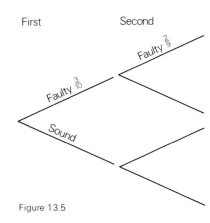

a that both are faulty
b that neither is faulty
c that just one is faulty

Figure 13.5

2 A nurseryman finds that when he sows seeds from a certain batch, the probability that any one will germinate is $\frac{3}{4}$. In each pot he sows 3 seeds: complete the tree (Figure 13.6) and find the probabilities

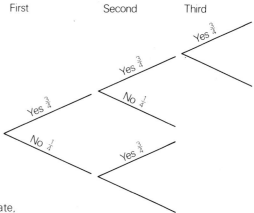

a that all will germinate,
b that 2 will germinate,
c that only 1 will germinate,
d that none will germinate.

Figure 13.6

3 Five equal discs, numbered 1, 2, 3, 4 and 5 respectively, are placed in a bag. A disc is drawn out of the bag and then a second disc is drawn out without replacing the first. Find the probability that

a the first disc is the 4,   **b** the first disc is not the 4,
c the first disc is the 4 and the second is the 5.   (CC)

4 A particle P is placed at (0, 0), and is then subjected to a series of translations. The probability that any translation will be $\begin{pmatrix} 0 \\ -1 \end{pmatrix}$ is $\frac{2}{3}$, and the probability that it will be $\begin{pmatrix} -2 \\ 0 \end{pmatrix}$ is $\frac{1}{3}$. Find

a the coordinates of the three possible positions of P after the second translation,
b for each position, the probability that P will be at that position.   (LC)

5   (In this question give all your answers as exact decimals.)

To reach school I travel first by train and then by bus. The train is punctual nineteen times out of twenty. On these occasions I arrive at the bus-stop at 8.29; otherwise at 8.31. The probability that the bus leaves at 8.28 is 0.1; that it leaves at 8.30 is 0.5; that it leaves at 8.32 is 0.4.

a For a school day chosen at random find the probabilities that
(i) at 8.29 the bus has not left the bus-stop;
(ii) I shall arrive at the bus-stop at 8.29;
(ii) I shall arrive at the bus-stop at 8.29 *and* catch the bus.

b Calculate
(i) the probability that, on a school day chosen at random, I shall catch the bus;
(ii) the number of days in a term of 64 school days on which I should expect to miss the bus.   (*SMP*)

6   (In this question all probabilities should be expressed as fractions.)

Each member of a class of 30 boys supports one and only one of three football teams; 13 boys support City, 10 support Rovers and 7 support United.

a If a boy is to be chosen at random, what is the probability that he will support City?
b If two boys are to be chosen at random, what is the probability that they will both support City?

Draw a tree diagram to show all the possible outcomes of choosing two boys at random, showing the probability of each outcome.

Hence find

c the probability that the two boys chosen will support the same team,
d the probability that the two boys chosen will support different teams.
                                                                       (*LB*)

7 Figure 13.7 shows a circular disc, of fixed centre O, with an arrow marked on its surface. A die is thrown. If the number 1 is thrown, the disc is rotated *clockwise* through 90°; otherwise it is not moved. Given that the arrow points initially to position A, write down, as a fraction, the probability that the arrow is pointing

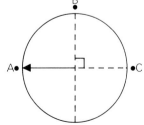

Figure 13.7

a to position A after 1 **throw,**
b to position C after 2 throws.
c to position B after 2 throws.
                        (*CC*)

8   In a school year, consisting of three terms, the pupils are to be given one extra day's holiday in each term. The day chosen, in each case, is equally likely to fall on any day of the week from Monday to Friday. Find the probability that

  a the first day chosen will be a Friday
  b the three holidays will all occur on Fridays
  c the three holidays will all occur on the same day of the week
  d at least one of the holidays will occur on a Friday   (*JMB*)

9   The diagram is a plan of a factory-building patrolled by a night-watchman. In order to make his movements unpredictable, the watchman is supplied with two coins and is given the following instructions:

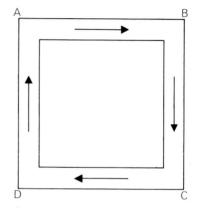

'Begin your patrol at A at 8 p.m.. At 8 p.m., and at 8.10, 8.20 and so on at 10-minute intervals, toss your two coins and proceed as follows:

Figure 13.8

'If both show heads, move on to the next corner in the direction of the arrows, reaching it in time for the next tossing. If both show tails, move to the next corner in the opposite direction to that of the arrows, reaching it in time for the next tossing. If one shows heads and the other tails, stay where you are until the next tossing.'

Write down the probabilities that at 8.10 p.m. the watchman is

  a at A   **b** at B   **c** at D

Calculate the probabilities that at 8.20 p.m. he is

  d still at A, not having moved from there   **g** at B
  e back at A after visiting B   **h** at C
  f at A, whether or not he has moved   **i** at D   (*LC*)

10 The probability that a seed from a certain packet will produce a pink flower is $\frac{1}{4}$ while the probability that it will produce a blue flower is $\frac{1}{5}$. Assuming that every seed produces a flower, find the probability that a particular seed will produce a flower which is either blue or pink.

Find the probability that a group of three seeds will produce

  a three pink flowers
  b two pink flowers and one blue flower   (*CC*)

11 A bag containing three red and three green sweets will be passed alternately to two children, Alice and Brenda. Alice has first choice, and will always choose at random, but Brenda will look into the bag and will take a red sweet if one is available, but will otherwise take a green sweet. By drawing a tree diagram, or otherwise, find the probability that

  a the first sweet taken will be red,
  b the first two sweets taken will be both red,
  c the first three sweets taken will be all red,
  d Alice's first sweet will be red, but Brenda will have the other two red ones,
  e Brenda will have all the red sweets,
  f Brenda will have only one red sweet. *(LC)*

12 When I drive from my home to the station I have the choice of using either the main road or a side road. If there are no delays, it takes 25 minutes by either road.

  a On the side road there are two possible delays (independent of each other). I may be held up by a tractor outside one farm F (probability $\frac{1}{6}$); or by animals outside another farm G (probability $\frac{2}{15}$). Draw a tree diagram to show the four possibilities – delay by animals and tractor; delay by animals only; delay by tractor only; no delays – and calculate the probability for each of these four.

  b Animals delay me by 6 minutes; a tractor by 2 minutes. If I allow 28 minutes by the side road, calculate the probability of reaching the station on time.

  c On the main road there is one possible delay – being held up by a lorry (probability $\frac{1}{9}$) – which lengthens the journey by 5 minutes. State, with reason, which road I should use if I leave home with 28 minutes in which to reach the station. *(SMP)*

13 In a certain game, a turn consists of a player spinning a top in the shape of a regular pentagon divided as shown. If the top rests on a red section, the player scores 0, but if it rests on a green section the player continues his turn by throwing a die and scoring the number shown. Find the probability of

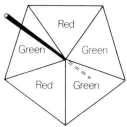

Figure 13.9

  a a score of 0 in one turn,
  b a score of 2 in one turn,
  c a score of 0 in the first turn and 2 in the second turn,
  d a score of 1 in each of two successive turns,
  e a total score of 2 in two turns.

Find the probability that a player will score more than 10 in two turns.

(LC)

14   A six-faced die is numbered from 1 to 6 in the usual way, but its faces have been weighted so that the probability of scoring the number n is proportional to n.

a Show that the probability of scoring the number 1 is $\frac{1}{21}$.
b What is the probability of scoring a number greater than 4?
c What is the probability of scoring an even number?
d If the die is rolled twice, what is the probability that the sum of the two numbers scored is at least 11?   (O52)

15   On his journey to school a teacher has to pass through two sets of traffic lights A and B. The probabilities that he will be stopped at these are $\frac{2}{7}$ and $\frac{1}{6}$ respectively, with corresponding delays of 1 minute and 3 minutes. Without these delays his journey takes 30 minutes.

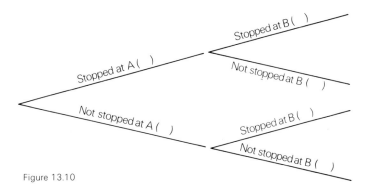

Figure 13.10

a Copy and complete the tree-diagram, entering the appropriate one-stage probabilities in the given brackets.
b Find the probabilities that
(i) the journey takes no more than 30 minutes;
(ii) the teacher encounters just one delay.
c On a particular morning the teacher has only 32 minutes to reach school on time. Find the probability that he will be late.   (SMP)

The electronic calculator and probability problems

There are many interesting problems whose solution would be tedious without the help of a calculating aid, but which can be solved in reasonable time with the use of a calculator.

Example 5   What is the probability that a die thrown 10 times will not give even one 6? How many times must the die be thrown before the probability that there will not be even one 6 falls below a millionth?

Answer

Probability of no 6 on first throw $= \frac{5}{6}$

Probability of no 6 on first 2 throws $= (\frac{5}{6})^2$,

Of no 6 on first 10 throws $= (\frac{5}{6})^{10} = 0.1615 \ldots (1)$

The probability of no 6 on first n throws is $(\frac{5}{6})^n$ so we must have $(\frac{5}{6})^n < 10^{-6}$.

One way of solving this inequality is by some form of trial and error, e.g. by repeated squaring of equation (1).

$(\frac{5}{6})^{20} = 2.608 \times 10^{-2}$; not nearly small enough.

$(\frac{5}{6})^{40} = 6.804 \times 10^{-4}$; still not small enough.

$(\frac{5}{6})^{80} = 4.629 \times 10^{-7}$; just too small.

Now 'come back' by *dividing* by $\frac{5}{6}$, i.e. multiplying by 1.2:

$(\frac{5}{6})^{79} = 5.555 \times 10^{-7}$; still too small.

$(\frac{5}{6})^{78} = 6.666 \times 10^{-7}$; still too small.

$(\frac{5}{6})^{77} = 7.999 \times 10^{-7}$; still too small.

$(\frac{5}{6})^{76} = 9.599 \times 10^{-7}$; just too small.

$(\frac{5}{6})^{75} = 1.151 \times 10^{-6}$; just over 10^{-6}.

The smallest value of n for which $(\frac{5}{6})^n < 10^{-6}$ is therefore 76.

Alternatively, logarithms can be used, considerably shortening the procedure. If this method is to be employed, it is convenient to 'turn the inequality upside down', giving

$$(\tfrac{6}{5})^n > 10^6$$

taking logarithms $n \log 1.2 > 6$,

i.e. $n \times 0.07918 > 6$,

so $n > \dfrac{6}{0.07918} = 75.76$;

since n is a whole number,

$n = 76$ as before.

Example 6   What is the probability that a hand at bridge (13 cards) will be

a all hearts   **b** all of the same suit?

Answer

a The probability that the first card is a heart is $\frac{13}{52}$; if it is, then the probability that the second card is a heart is $\frac{12}{51}$; if these are both hearts, then the probability that the third card is a heart is $\frac{11}{50}$ and so on.

The probability that all 13 cards are hearts is

$$\frac{13 \times 12 \times 11 \times 10 \times 9 \times 8 \times 7 \times 6 \times 5 \times 4 \times 3 \times 2 \times 1}{52 \times 51 \times 50 \times 49 \times 48 \times 47 \times 46 \times 45 \times 44 \times 43 \times 42 \times 41 \times 40}$$

This gives plenty of scope for cancelling, but with a calculator, cancelling may not be thought worthwhile. The answer is 1.57×10^{-12}.

b As the above result is the same for each suit, the probability that the hand will contain cards all of any one of the four suits is

$$4 \times 1.57 \times 10^{-12} = 6.30 \times 10^{-12}$$

Exercise 13.4

1 Four cards are drawn at random from a pack. Find the probability that they

a are all aces   **c** contain at least one ace.
b are none of them aces

2 A card is drawn from a pack and then replaced, and this process is repeated 12 times. Find the probability that no ace has been drawn. Find how many times the process must be repeated for the probability that no ace has been drawn to fall below a thousandth.

3 Eight boys and ten girls draw lots for the eight places on a school visit. Find the probability that those successful will be

a all boys   **b** all girls.

4 If two people are chosen at random, what is the probability that both their birthdays are in January? What is the probability that both their birthdays are in the same month? (Assume that all months are equally likely.) What is the probability that they are in **different** months? If 3 people are chosen at random, find the probability that their birthdays are in different months. What is the corresponding result for 12 people?

5 Find the probability that, if three people are chosen at random, their birthdays are on different **days** (ignoring leap years).

A number of people are in a room. It is more likely than not that there are at least two whose birthdays are on the same day. Find the smallest possible number of people in the room.

6 An examination paper consists of ten questions, in each of which the candidate has to choose the correct answer from five given possible answers. One candidate knows nothing about the subject and answers entirely at random. Find the probability that this candidate will

    a give all the correct answers   **c** give just one correct answer
    b give 9 of the correct answers   **d** give all the answers wrong

7 A nurseryman sows three seeds of a certain kind in each of 100 pots. He records the number of seeds in each pot that germinate, and tabulates the results as follows.

Number of seeds germinating	3	2	1	0
Number of pots	34	44	20	3

Find the total number of seeds that germinated, and hence calculate the experimental probability that a seed will germinate.

If 4 seeds are planted in each of 100 larger pots, calculate the expected numbers of pots in which

    a all the seeds will germinate
    b three of the seeds will germinate
    c none of the seeds will germinate
    d only one of the seeds will germinate
    e just two of the seeds will germinate

8 $G = \{$Greek capital letters$\}$, and $n(G) = 24$.
$C = \{$Greek capital letters which also appear in the Roman alphabet$\}$, and $n(C) = 14$.

    a State the relation between the sets C and G.
    b If a letter is chosen at random from G, state as a fraction the probability that it belongs to C.
    c If two letters (not necessarily different) are chosen at random from G, evaluate as a decimal the probability that they are both from C. (Keep all the figures in your answer at this stage.)
    d Number plates on Greek cars have two letters on them. A tourist visiting Greece notices that the letters on the first four cars he sees are all from C. Show that the probability that this would happen if the letters were chosen at random from G is less than 0.02.
    e The tourist forms the theory that the letters on Greek cars are always chosen from C, and this is apparently confirmed when he has seen a total of n cars. The probability that this would happen if the letters were chosen at random from G is less than 10^{-6}. Write down an inequality for n and solve it.   (*SMP* (slightly adapted))

Chapter 14

Number bases

The sums on the blackboard look wrong, but if you look at the creatures' 'hands' you will see why. Because *we* have *ten* fingers, and our remote ancestors used their fingers for counting, we use a system of numbers based on *ten*, and called the decimal system. When we write 11 the first 1 does not mean 'one' at all, but 'ten'; creatures with *eight* fingers would probably use a system based on *eight*, and called the *octal* system. When an octal creature writes 11, the first 1 means 'eight' not 'ten', so that 11 means, not ten plus one but eight plus one, i.e. nine, and so $3 \times 3 = 11$ is correct in octal. Is the other sum on the blackboard also correct?

In the octal system, 35 for example means 3 eights and 5, i.e. 29 in the decimal system. In a 3-digit number like 274, the first digit denotes not hundreds but sixty-fours (because sixty-four is the square of eight just as a hundred is the square of ten); similarly in a four digit number the first digit denotes multiples of five hundred and twelve (because that is

the cube of eight) and so on. A small suffix 8 can be used to show that a number is in the octal, and not the decimal, system, thus 274_8.

Example 1   Express the octal number 1265_8 as a decimal number.

Answer
The 5 denotes 5, as in any system;
The 6 denotes 6×8 $= 48$ in decimal;
The 2 denotes $2 \times 8 \times 8$ $= 128$ in decimal;
The 1 denotes $1 \times 8 \times 8 \times 8$ $= 512$ in decimal;
So $1265_8 = 5 + 48 + 128 + 512$ $= 693$ in decimal.

Example 2   Express the decimal number 375 as an octal number.

Answer
Method 1
As $375 < 512$, only 3 digits are needed.

$375 \div 64 = 5$, rem. 55, so the first digit is 5, with 55 still to be put into octal.

$55 \div 8 = 6$ rem. 7, so the second digit is 6 and the third 7, giving the answer 567.

Method 2
Divide 375 repeatedly by 8:

8)375   The answer is found by reading the remainders
————   upwards: thus 567.

8) 46 rem. 7

8)   5 rem. 6

     — rem. 5

Arithmetical processes in octal

Addition, subtraction, multiplication and division are carried out in octal exactly as in decimal, except that whenever any 'carrying' or 'borrowing' is done, the number 'carried' or 'borrowed' is always eight and never ten.

Example 3   Add: $355_8 + 476_8$.

Answer:
  355        $5 + 6 = $ eleven, which in octal is 13; write down the 3 and
  476   carry the 1, thus
 ————

355
476

$5+7+1$ (carried) = thirteen, which in octal is 15; write down the 5 and carry the 1.

3
1

355
476

Finally, $3+4+1$ (carried) = 8, which in octal is 10.

1053
11

The answer is 1053_8

Example 4   Subtract: $3052_8 - 475_8$.

Answer

Method 1

3052
475

5 from 2 requires borrowing; borrow 1 and the 2 becomes 12 which is octal for ten:

4
30$\cancel{5}$2
475

subtracting 5 leaves 5.

5

274
$\cancel{3}\cancel{0}\cancel{5}$2
475

Borrowing from the 5 makes it a 4; 7 from 4 again requires borrowing, but the next digit is 0; we must therefore change the 3 to a 2 and the 0 to a 7.

5

274
$\cancel{3}\cancel{0}\cancel{5}$2
475

The 4 becomes 14 which is octal for twelve: subtracting 7 leaves 5. The rest of the subtraction can be done without borrowing.

2355

The answer is 2355_8.

Method 2

3052
475

5 from 2 requires borrowing; borrow 1 and the 2 becomes 12 which is octal for ten;

3052
58
$\cancel{4}7$5

subtracting 5 leaves 5.

Adding 1 to the 7 gives 8; 8 from 5 again requires borrowing. The 5 becomes 15 which is octal for thirteen:

55

subtracting 8 leaves 5.

3052
158
$\cancel{4}7$5

Continuing to borrow, 5 from 10 (octal for eight) leaves 3, and 1 from 3 leaves 2.

2355

The answer is 2355_8.

Example 5   Divide 312_8 by 7.

Answer

7)312   7 will not go into 3, but 7 into 31_8 goes 3 with remainder 4.

7)31^42

   3   7 into 42_8 goes 4 with remainder 6.

7)31^42

   34 rem. 6 The answer is 34_8, remainder 6.

Exercise 14.1

(All numbers in this exercise are in octal, unless stated to be decimal.)

1   Write as octal numbers

   a the number of x's here: xxxxxxxxxxx
   b the number of x's here: xxxxxxxxxxxxxx
   c the total number of x's in both **a** and **b**, above
   d the number of months in a year
   e the number of days in January
   f the number of minutes in an hour
   g your age in years and months

2   Convert (mentally if possible) the following octal numbers to decimal numbers.

   a 14   **c** 31   **e** 63   **g** 100
   b 63   **d** 50   **f** 77   **h** 111

3   Convert the following octal numbers to decimal numbers.

   a 121   **c** 371   **e** 1234   **g** 2107
   b 206   **d** 1000   **f** 2053   **h** 2222

4   Convert (mentally if possible) the following *decimal* numbers to octal numbers.

   a 9   **c** 16   **e** 25   **g** 64
   b 14   **d** 20   **f** 32   **h** 100

5   Convert the following *decimal* numbers to octal numbers.

   a 105   **c** 200   **e** 287   **g** 511
   b 127   **d** 256   **f** 299   **h** 1000

6 Carry out (mentally if possible) the following calculations with octal numbers.

a $5+4$	**c** 3×4	**e** $12 \div 5$	**g** 3×13
b $10-1$	**d** 4×6	**f** 2×13	**h** $100-7$

7 Add the following pairs of octal numbers.

a $112+233$	**c** $564+337$	**e** $5632+7046$
b $345+226$	**d** $1056+767$	**f** $2647+5131$

8 Carry out the following subtractions of octal numbers.

a $765-345$	**c** $541-165$	**e** $725-136$
b $322-217$	**d** $1000-1$	**f** $1453-67$

9 Write out the 'three times table' in octal, as far as 3×12.

10 Write out the 'four times table' in octal, as far as 4×12. Which of the 'ordinary' multiplication tables does this resemble? Why?

11 Write out the 'seven times table' in octal, as far as 7×12. Which of the 'ordinary' multiplication tables does this resemble? Why?

12 Carry out the following multiplications of octal numbers.

a 213×2	**c** 372×4	**e** 624×6
b 436×3	**d** 507×5	**f** 777×7

13 Carry out the following divisions of octal numbers.

a $642 \div 2$	**c** $452 \div 4$	**e** $2056 \div 6$
b $317 \div 3$	**d** $1742 \div 5$	**f** $4315 \div 7$

The binary system

Obviously ten and eight are not the only possible bases for numbers: any positive integer more than 1 will serve as a base. Probably the most important system, next to the decimal, is the *binary* system, based on 2. In the binary system the only digits used are 0 and 1, and for this reason it is particularly suitable for use in computers. Anything which can be in one or other of two states – a conductor which can carry, or not carry, an electric current; an iron core which can be magnetised one way or the other; a section of paper tape which may or may not have a hole in it – can represent a binary digit. Such a device may be called a *bit* or a *flip-flop*.

The binary system has also the advantage that calculations are very simple since no numbers except 0's and 1's are involved, but it has the drawback that even quite small numbers need very many digits to express them: thus a hundred is 1 100 100 in the binary scale.

A suffix 2 may be used to show that a number is in the binary scale.

In binary work it is particularly important to ensure that the digits are kept in their correct vertical columns.

Example 6   Convert the binary number $1\,011\,011_2$ to decimal.

Answer
Reading from right to left the digits of a binary number denote 1, 2, 4, 8, 16, 32, 64. In this number the 1's represent 1, 2, 8, 16 and 64, totalling 91.

Example 7   Convert the decimal number 237 to binary.

Answer
Method 1
The highest power of 2 we need is 128: denote this by 1, leaving $237 - 128 = 109$ to be converted.

We also need 64: denote this by 1, leaving 45. Denote 32 by 1, leaving 13.

We do *not* need 16, so write 0, but we *do* need 8, so write 1 next, leaving 5.

5 in binary is 101, so the complete answer is 11 101 101.

Method 2
Divide repeatedly by 2

2) 237
2) 118 rem 1   Reading the remainders upwards, the answer is
2) 59 rem 0   11 101 101.
2) 29 rem 1
2) 14 rem 1
2)   7 rem 0
2)   3 rem 1
2)   1 rem 1
     0 rem 1

Example 8   Subtract $11\,011_2$ from $100\,010_2$.

Answer

Method **1**

```
        2
100 0/0
 11 011
_____
      1
```

1 from 0 requires borrowing: borrow the 1 which becomes 2 in the right hand column, and $2-1=1$.

In the next column, 1 from 0 again requires borrowing, but the only 1 available is that at the beginning (far left) of the number: change that for 1's in the next three columns, but a 2 in the 5th.

```
  11 12
1̸00 0̸/0
 11 011
_____
000 111
```

The subtraction can now be completed without further borrowing, giving 000 111.

Method **2**

```
100 010
122 12
1̸1̸ 0̸1̸1̸
_____
000 111
```

In this method, borrowing is done as in method 1, but after each borrowing, 1 is 'repaid' by being *added* to the *lower* digit in the next column to the left.

Example 9   Multiply 10 101 by 1101.

Answer

This is done by 'long multiplication'.

```
        10 101
         1 101
       _____
        10 101
      1 0101
     10 101
    _____
    100 010 001
    11 111
```

Example 10   Divide 111 011 by 101.

Answer

This is done by 'long division'.

```
          1 011
     _____
101 )111 011
     101
     _____
      1001
      1 01
      _____
      1 001
        101
        _____
        100
```

The answer is 1011, remainder 100.

Conversion between octal and binary scales

Numbers can easily be converted from octal to binary or vice versa (this is sometimes useful, as binary numbers are used in computers whereas octal numbers are less cumbrous).

For example, suppose 237_8 is to be converted to binary.

The 7 in binary is 111. 3 in binary is 011, but as this 3 means 3×8, this in binary is 011 000.

Similarly, the 2 means $2 \times 8 \times 8$, and this in binary is 10 000 000. So $237_8 = 10 011 111_2$.

This simply means that each digit of the octal number in turn is converted to binary and gives three digits of the binary equivalent. For another example,

$$5416_8 = 101\ 100\ 001\ 110_2$$

Conversely, to change $111\ 010\ 011\ 100_2$ into octal, each group of three digits is changed into the equivalent single octal digit, giving 7234.

Exercise 14.2

(All numbers in this exercise are in binary, unless stated to be decimal or octal.)

1 Write as binary numbers all the numbers in Question 1 of Exercise 14.1 (page 215)

2 Convert (mentally if possible) the following binary numbers to decimal numbers.

a 11	**c** 101	**e** 1000	**g** 1011
b 100	**d** 111	**f** 1001	**h** 1111

3 Convert the following binary numbers to decimal numbers.

a 10 101	**c** 10 001	**e** 111 111
b 11 100	**d** 110 011	**f** 1 010 101

4 Convert (mentally if possible) the following *decimal* numbers to binary numbers.

a 2	**c** 10	**e** 13	**g** 16
b 6	**d** 12	**f** 14	**h** 17

5 Convert the following *decimal* numbers to binary numbers.

a 23	**c** 75	**e** 99	**g** 121
b 31	**d** 83	**f** 100	**h** 345

6   Add the following pairs of binary numbers.

a 111 + 101   **c** 1101 + 1011   **e** 111 111 + 11 010
b 1010 + 1100   **d** 10 101 + 11 001   **f** 110 011 + 101 011

7   Carry out the following subtractions of binary numbers.

a 111 − 101   **c** 1000 − 11   **e** 10 001 − 1101
b 1010 − 1001   **d** 11 011 − 1110   **f** 10 000 000 − 1

8   Carry out the following multiplications of binary numbers.

a 111 × 101   **c** 1101 × 110   **e** 11 011 × 1101
b 101 × 11   **d** 1001 × 111   **f** 1 010 101 × 1011

9   Carry out the following divisions of binary numbers.

a 1001 ÷ 11   **c** 110 011 ÷ 111
b 1110 ÷ 101   **d** 1 010 101 ÷ 1001

10   Convert the following *octal* numbers directly into binary numbers.

a 73   **c** 142   **e** 311   **g** 634
b 55   **d** 260   **f** 452   **h** 777

11   Convert the following binary numbers directly into octal numbers.

a 110   **c** 101 100   **e** 1 101 110
b 11 101   **d** 111 011   **f** 111 101 001

A simple binary abacus

The device described here can be made very simply out of cardboard, and can be used to display binary numbers and also to carry out addition and subtraction in the binary scale.

Take a rectangular-piece of cardboard, about 20 cm long and about 13 cm wide. Draw two lines along its whole length, parallel to the long sides and about 3 cm from them. Lightly score these lines, so that the cardboard can be folded along them. Draw a series of parallel lines, equally spaced (2 cm apart is suitable), parallel to the short sides of the cardboard and running between the long edges and the lines first drawn (see Figure 15.1). Cut along each of these lines, forming a series of flaps, each about 3 cm × 2 cm, and each of which can be folded onto the body of the card, or opened out flat.

Write two rows of 0's along the central part of the card, in such a way that each 0 is concealed by one flap, when it is folded in. On the back of each flap write a 1, in such a way that when the flap is folded in, the 1's form a row with the 0's. By folding the flaps in or out, two rows of binary numbers can be formed: in the figure the numbers formed are 1 100 011 010 and 0 111 001 011. The decimal equivalents of the numbers may be written between the rows.

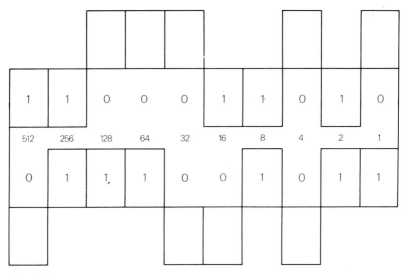

1	1	0	0	0	1	1	0	1	0
512	256	128	64	32	16	8	4	2	1
0	1	1	1	0	0	1	0	1	1

Figure 14.1

To add two numbers, proceed as follows.

1 Set the two numbers on the two rows of the abacus.

2 Working from right to left with the lower number, whenever you come to a flap turned in and reading 1, turn it out and at the same time change the corresponding flap on the upper row. (To 'change' a flap means to turn it in if it is out, and vice versa). At the same time, follow instruction 3.

3 Whenever you turn a flap *out* in the upper row, so changing a 1 to a 0, change the flap next on the left; if this change is a turning out, also change the *next* flap to the left, and so on.

4 Continue until all the flaps on the lower row have been turned out, showing 0's. The upper row now gives the sum of the two numbers.

To subtract one number from another, set the larger number on the upper row and the smaller number on the lower. Then proceed as for addition, *except* that instruction **3** now reads:

Whenever you turn a flap in the upper row *in*, so changing a 0 to a 1, change the flap next on the left; if this change is a turning in, also change the next flap on the left, and so on. At the end, the upper row gives the **difference** of the two numbers.

Some other bases

As stated before, any positive integer larger than 1 can be used as a base: this section contains examples on the use of various numbers as bases. Sometimes it is required to find out the base in which a given calculation has been performed.

Example 11   Find the base of the following addition sum and complete it.

$$234+$$
$$145$$
$$\overline{2}$$

Answer
Since $3+5=8$ and 2 is written down, it follows that 6 must have been carried. 6 could be carried if the base were 2, 3 or 6, but since the digits 3, 4 and 5 appear in the sum, the base cannot be 2 or 3, so it must be 6. The sum can now be completed.

$$243+$$
$$415$$
$$\overline{1102}$$
$$11$$

Point fractions

In the decimal system, numbers such as 3.25 are called 'decimal fractions'. We can have corresponding fractions in other bases. They could be called 'octal fractions' and so on, but we shall use the general name 'point fractions'.

In octal, 0.1 means 'one-eighth',

0.13 means 'one-eighth and 3 sixty-fourths'
or (in octal) $\frac{13}{100}$, or (in decimal) $\frac{11}{64}$.

In binary 0.1 means 'half', 0.101 means 'half plus one-eighth' or 'five-eighths', and so on.

Exercise 14.3

1   Write the following numbers in decimal.

    a 14_6 **c** 22_5 **e** 61_7 **g** 50_6
    b 32_9 **d** 33_4 **f** 21_3 **h** 121_4

2   Write each of the decimal numbers: 9, 27, 50,

    a in base 6   **b** in base 4   **c** in base 9   **d** in base 3

3   Convert the following numbers to decimal.

    a 2332_5 **c** 1221_3 **e** 2332_4

    b 4145_6 **d** 2085_9 **f** 4532_7

4   Convert the decimal number 1000,

    a to base 6   **b** to base 5   **c** to base 9   **d** to base 4

5   Give the bases of the following calculations.

    a $4+4=12$ **c** $2 \times 2 \times 2 = 22$ **e** $6 \times 16 = 124$ **g** $3 \times 33 = 231$

    b $5 \times 4 = 22$ **d** $100 - 1 = 66$ **f** $31 \div 4 = 4$ **h** $\sqrt{321} = 15$

6   In base six calculate

    a $453 + 525$ **b** $1321 - 504$ **c** 23×32 **d** $3422 \div 5$

7   In base five calculate

    a $234 + 432$ **b** $2033 - 441$ **c** 104×24 **d** $1044 \div 4$

8   In base three calculate

    a $2121 + 2002$ **b** $2012 - 1122$ **c** 102×201 **d** $1111 \div 21$

9   In base nine calculate

    a $874 + 655$ **b** $1670 - 872$ **c** 227×8 **d** $2056 \div 7$

10   In base four calculate

    a $1332 + 3103$ **b** $1013 - 223$ **c** 103×301 **d** $3221 \div 13$

11   Find the base of each of the following calculations, and complete the calculations.

    a $\begin{array}{r} 234+ \\ 145 \\ \hline 1 \end{array}$ **c** $\begin{array}{r} 234 \times 13 \\ 13 \\ \hline 3 \end{array}$ **e** $\begin{array}{r} 112+ \\ 212 \\ 122 \\ 222 \\ 132 \\ \hline 1 \end{array}$

    b $\begin{array}{r} 301- \\ 124 \\ \hline 2 \end{array}$ **d** $4)\overline{31\,221} \\ 45$ **f** $\frac{1}{2} + \frac{1}{10} = 12$

12   Express the following as vulgar fractions (i.e. non-point fractions such as $\frac{1}{2}$ or $\frac{2}{3}$) in base ten.

    a 0.11_2 **c** 0.011_2 **e** 1.11_3 **g** 2.3_6 **i** 4.6_8

    b 0.101_2 **d** 0.1_3 **f** 0.101_3 **h** 3.4_6

13   Express as point fractions in the binary scale.

    a $\frac{1}{4}$ **c** $\frac{7}{8}$ **e** $\frac{5}{16}$ **g** $\frac{1}{32}$

    b $\frac{3}{8}$ **d** $\frac{3}{16}$ **f** $\frac{11}{16}$ **h** $\frac{17}{32}$

14   Express as point fractions in bases.

    a $\frac{2}{3}$ **b** $\frac{5}{9}$ **c** $\frac{8}{9}$ **d** $\frac{11}{27}$

15   Express one-half as a point fraction in each of the following bases (correct to 3 places where necessary).

    a 4   **b** 8   **c** 3   **d** 5

Bases larger than ten

The student will have noticed that whereas the decimal system uses ten digits (including 0), the octal system uses eight, the binary only two, and so on. If a base larger than ten is to be used, more than ten digits will be needed. We shall have to use a symbol for ten, a symbol for eleven and a symbol for each other number below the base. Any symbols can be used, but the most common practice is to use *a* for ten, *b* for eleven and so on. We shall refer to only two bases of this kind, namely twelve and sixteen.

The *duodecimal system* is based on twelve, and requires the letters *a* and *b* as well as the ten decimal digits.

In many ways, twelve is a more convenient base than ten, as is shown by our habit of counting in dozens, and by many relations between units only recently superseded by the metric system, (and for many other groups, from the members of a jury to the days of Christmas, we often seem to think in terms of twelve rather than in terms of ten).

The *hexadecimal system* is based on sixteen and so uses the letters *a*, *b*, *c*, *d*, *e* and *f* as well as the decimal digits. Its great advantage is that numbers in it, like those in the octal system, are very easily converted into binary numbers and vice versa. This corresponds to the advantage of the old imperial measure of sixteen ounces to the pound; the pound could be repeatedly halved, always giving a whole number of ounces down to one ounce.

Example 12   Add the numbers 1*a*3*f* and *cd*4*e* in the hexadecimal system, and convert the answer to binary.

Answer

1*a*3*f*   *f* + *e* means fifteen plus fourteen, i.e. twenty-nine, which
*cd*4*e*   in hexadecimal is 1*d*. Write down *d* and carry 1.
‾‾‾‾
*e*78*d*
1 1

$3+4+1=8$.

a + *d* means ten plus thirteen, i.e. twenty-three, which in hexadecimal is 17. Write down 7 and carry 1.

$1+c+1=e$ (thirteen), so completing the addition.

In binary

	e (thirteen) = 1101
7	= 0111
8	= 1000
d (twelve)	= 1100

So the answer in binary is 1 101 011 110 001 100.

Exercise 14.4

1 Convert to decimal the following duodecimal numbers

    a 11   **b** 1*a*   **c** *a*2   **d** 2*b*   **e** *ab*   **f** *ba*

2 Convert to duodecimal the following decimal numbers.

    a 14   **b** 23   **c** 120   **d** 132   **e** 144   **f** 154

3 Convert to decimal the following duodecimal numbers.

    a 1*a*1   **b** 2*b*3   **c** 3*ab*   **d** *aaa*   **e** *a*3*b*   **f** *b*01

4 Convert to duodecimal the following decimal numbers.

    a 79   **b** 121   **c** 295   **d** 266   **e** 1451   **f** 1727

5 In duodecimal calculate

    a $2a7+39b$ **c** $1035-a8b$ **e** $459 \times b$
    b $796+895$ **d** $1735-746$ **f** $36bb \div a$

6 Convert to decimal the following hexadecimal numbers.

    a 12   **b** 1*e*   **c** 2*f*   **d** *a*0   **e** 3*b*   **f** 33

7 Convert to hexadecimal the following decimal numbers.

   a 13   **b** 17   **c** 27   **d** 161   **e** 256   **f** 268

8 Convert to decimal the following hexadecimal numbers.

   a 34   **b** *ab*   **c** *ed*   **d** 144   **e** *2fc*   **f** *abc*

9 Convert to hexadecimal the following decimal numbers.

   a 79   **b** 121   **c** 176   **d** 225   **e** 525   **f** 1000

10 In hexadecimal calculate

   a $3be + a1f$ **c** $1027 - edc$ **e** $3a7 \times d$
   b $987 + a7c$ **d** $3220 - 1897$ **f** $24b3 \div b$

11 Convert to binary the following hexadecimal numbers.

   a 23   **b** 143   **c** *2af*   **d** *ed0c*

12 Convert to hexadecimal the following binary numbers.

   a 10110111   **c** 1010101011011
   b 11110000101011   **d** 10000111000011

13 Express as vulgar fractions in decimal the following point fractions in duodecimal.

   a 0.3   **b** 0.4   **c** 0.6   **d** 0.*a*   **e** 0.69

14 Express as vulgar fractions in decimal the following point fractions in hexadecimal.

   a 0.2   **b** 0.8   **c** 0.*c*   **d** 0.08   **e** 0.88

Miscellaneous problems

Example 13   Find in what base the number 121 denotes the decimal number 49. Show also that 121 is a perfect square in any base.

Answer

Let the base be n: then the first 1 of 121 denotes n^2, the 2 denotes $2n$, and the last 1 simply means 1; thus

$$121_n = n^2 + 2n + 1.$$

We therefore have $n^2 + 2n + 1 = 49$,

$$\Rightarrow n^2 + 2n - 48 = 0,$$
$$\Rightarrow (n + 8)(n - 6) = 0,$$
$$\Rightarrow n = -8 \text{ or } n = 6$$

Since a base cannot be negative, $n=6$; the base is 6.

Also, $n^2+2n+1=(n+1)^2$ for all values of n. This means that $121=11^2$, i.e. 121_n is a perfect square for any value of n, and its square root is one more than the base number n.

Exercise 14.5

1   Find in what base 32 is equal to each of the following decimal numbers.

    a 14   **b** 23   **c** 29   **d** 38   **e** 50

2   Find in what base the number 144 denotes the decimal number 100. Also, show that 144 is a perfect square in any base which uses its digits (i.e. any base larger than 4). Find some other 3-digit numbers which are perfect squares in any bases that use their digits.

3   Find in what base the number 143 denotes the decimal number 120. Also, show that 143 cannot be a prime number, whatever the base. Find some other 3-digit numbers for which this is true.

4   Find the decimal number equal to 1331 if the base is

    a 4   **b** 5   **c** 6   **d** 9

    What do these answers have in common?

5   In which number bases is the following statement true:

    last digit of a number is even $\Rightarrow$ the number is even?

    In which, if any, of these bases can the sign $\Rightarrow$ be replaced by the sign $\Leftrightarrow$?

    Are there any number-bases in which the following statement is true:

    last digit of a number is even $\Rightarrow$ the number is odd?

    If so, which bases are they?

6   In decimal numbers it is found that, if the sum of the digits of a number is divisible by 9, then so is the number, and the same applies to divisibility by 3. Find the corresponding rules for numbers

    a in base 6   **b** in base 9   **c** in base sixteen

    Make up a general rule which applies to all bases, (except 2).

7 In decimal numbers it is found that, if the sum of the alternate digits of a number is equal to the sum of the remaining digits, then the number is divisible by 11, (e.g. 2475 is divisible by 11, for $2+7=4+5$). Find the corresponding rule for numbers

a in base 8   **b** in base 6   **c** in base 2

8 In decimal numbers it is found that a perfect square must always have last digit 0, 1, 4, 5, 6 or 9; the last digit can never be 2, 3, 7 or 8. Find the corresponding rule for perfect squares.

a in base 6   **b** in base 8   **c** in base twelve

9 An old-fashioned sweet-shop proprietor has a set of weights of 1, 2, 4 and 8 ounces. Make a table showing how he can weight out any exact number of ounces up to 15. What connection has this with the binary scale? Supposing that weights of 16 and 32 ounces are also available, show how the following total weights can be made up.

a 30 ounces   **b** 57 ounces   **c** 63 ounces

10 A still more old-fashioned shopkeeper has a weight of 1 ounce, a weight of 3 ounces, and one other weight: with these he can weigh out an amount of any whole number of ounces up to 13, by putting weights in **both pans** of his scales when necessary. What is the third weight? Make a table showing how each amount up to 13 ounces is weighed out. What should be the size of the next larger weight, in order to extend the range?

11 The *complement* of a binary number is the number obtained by replacing all its 0's by 1's and all its 1's by 0's: thus, the complement of 1 100 101 011 is 0 011 010 100.

One way (in fact the way used in a computer) of subtracting one binary number (say x) from another (say y) is to **add** the complement of x to y and then to carry out two alterations. These alterations are the same in every case: by carrying out the process and checking against normal subtraction, and repeating this several times with different numbers, find out what the alterations are.

12 If the number of entrants in a knock-out tournament is not an exact power of 2, some of them have to take part in a preliminary round: only the winners of this round go on to the first round proper, and in this they are joined by the other entrants, who are said to have 'byes' into the first round.

Continue the following table, at least as far as 12 entrants.

Number of entrants		Number of rounds	Number of games in preliminary round	Number of entrants with 'byes'
Decimal	Binary			
3	11	2	1	1
5	101	3	1	3
6	110	3	2	2
7	111	3	3	1

Verify that each number in the last column is (in decimal) the complement of the corresponding number in the second column, with 1 added.

Find how the numbers in the third and fourth columns may be derived from those in the second columns.

13   Find the product of 102 and 12, giving the number bases for which your result is not true.

If $102_n \times 12_n = 2001_n$ find the number base n.   (LC)

14   Given that

$B_p = \{$binary numbers with p digits, whose first digit is 1$\}$,
$Z_p = \{$binary numbers containing p zero digits$\}$

write down all the members of $B_4 \cap Z_1$, and calculate their sum.

Find $n(B_2)$, $n(B_3 \cap Z_2)$, $n(B_5 \cap Z_1)$ and $n(B_4 \cap Z_4)$.

Write down $n(B_p \cap Z_{p-1})$ and find an expression in terms of p for the number of members of $B_p \cap Z_1$.

Show that all members of the set Z_0 are, when expressed in a non-binary scale, of the form $2^k - 1$, where k is a positive integer.   (LC)

15   Express the number 9

a in base 2,   **b** in base 3.

On parallel scales, with domain set $\{2, 3, 4, 5, 6\}$, draw arrows to represent the mapping

$x \rightarrow$ (last digit of the number 9 expressed in base x). Name four digits which will never appear in the range of this mapping, however far the domain is extended.   (LC)

16   **a** Calculate 3^1, 3^2, 3^3, 3^4, 3^5, giving your answers in base six.
   b What do you think are the last two figures of 3^{30} and those of 3^{31}, when written in base six?

                                                                          (SMP)

Revision Exercises

On the work of Chapters 11–15, Book 1

Exercise IS (Short questions)

1 Find two possible values for x if $x^2 - 3x = 0$.

2 The sides of a triangle are 3 cm, 4 cm and 5 cm. Find the tangents of the two acute angles of the triangle.

3 Give the median of the set {1.3, 5.7, 3.6, 2.4, 0.9}.

4 If $P = \{$letters of PIG$\}$ and $G = \{$letters of GOAT$\}$, give the members of $P \cap G'$.

5 A letter is chosen at random $P \cup G$ (see Question 4). What is the probability that it is a member of P?

6 From a point 10 m (measured horizontally) from a tower, the angle of ·elevation of the top is 45° and the angle of depression of the foot is 11°. Given that tan 11° = 0.2, find the height of the tower.

7 If $A \subset B$, which, if any, of the following sets must be empty: $A \cap B$, $A \cap B'$, $A' \cap B$, $A' \cap B'$, $A' \cup B$, $A \cup B'$?

8 6 people each contributed £4, and 4 people each contributed £6. What was the mean contribution?

9 Give the three factors of $k^3 - 9k$.

10 A card is drawn at random from a pack. What is the probability that it is a heart, or a diamond, or a black ace?

11 Dunstable is 40 km east of Bicester, and Bedford is 28 km north of Dunstable. Given that tan 35° = 0.7, find the bearing of Bedford from Bicester.

12 If $\mathscr{E} = \{$even numbers$\}$, $P = \{$multiples of 4$\}$ and $Q = \{$multiples of 6$\}$ give the three smallest members of $P' \cap Q'$.

13 Find three different positive integers whose mean is 4 and whose median is 5.

14 Some of the spades, but no other cards, are missing from a pack, and now the probability that a card drawn from the pack will be a spade is three-sixteenths. How many spades are missing?

15 State what must be written in the squares to make the following correct.

$$(x-a)(x+ \square)=x^2 - \square + 2bx - \square$$

16 Name the set
represented by the
shaded region.

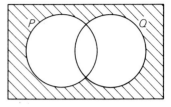

Figure R1

17 The mean of five numbers is 17 and the mean of the same five numbers
together with a sixth number is 18. What is the sixth number?

18 Two coins are tossed. What is the probability that at least one of them
will fall 'heads'?

19 The window of a house is 8 m above ground level. Opposite the
window, and 24 m away horizontally, is a wall 16 m high. Find the
tangent of the angle of elevation of the top of the wall from the window.

20 Solve the equation $(x-2)(x+3) = (x-2)(5-x)$.

Exercise IA (Medium length questions)

1A — 1 BT is the perpendicular from the vertex B to the side AC of the triangle
ABC. Given that BT$=8$ cm, $\angle A=58°$, TC$=12$ cm, calculate

  a the length of AT, to 3 sig. fig.
  b the size of $\angle C$, to the nearest degree
  c the area of the triangle, to 3 sig. fig.

2 $\mathscr{E}=\{1, 2, 3, 4, 5, 6\}$. The sets P, Q and R each contain two elements and
$P\cap Q\cap R=\phi$. Given that $(Q\cup R)'=\{1, 2\}$ write down

  a the set P **b** a possible set Q and the corresponding set R **(CC)**

3 The universal set is the set of
positive integers less than 14.
Subsets are defined as follows.
$T=\{$Multiples of 3$\}$
$F=\{$Multiples of 4$\}$
$P=\{$Prime numbers$\}$
Note: 1 is not a prime number.

  a Using at least half a page, copy
and complete the given Venn
diagram, writing the numerals 1 to
13 in the appropriate regions.

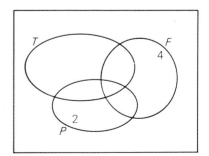

Figure R2

b If a number is chosen at random from the integers 1 to 13 (inclusive), write down the probability that the number is (i) a multiple both of 3 and of 4; (ii) a multiple of 3, or of 4, or of both.   (*SMP*)

4 **a** Factorise $x^2 + 3x - 10$
  b Factorise $p^2 + pq - 2q - 2p$
  c Solve the equation $x^2 - x - 20 = 0$
  d Simplify $(2x + 3)(3x - 2) - (2x - 3)(3x + 2)$

5 The mean of the numbers 1, 1, 1, 2, 2, 3, x is 1 more than the median: find x. (Assume $x > 3$). Give also the mode of these numbers.

6 From a position on level ground 15 m away from the foot of a tree, a boy observes the angle of elevation of the top of the tree to be 38°. Calculate the height of the tree.

To check his result, he walks 5 m further away from the tree. What should the angle of elevation be now if his first observation was correct?

7 The set $A = \{1, 2, 4, 8\}$. Write down the four subsets of A, each of which contains three elements. If one of these subsets is chosen at random, find the probability

  a that the mean of the elements of the subset is more than 3,
  b that the median element of the subset is more than 3.   (*LC*)

8 The mappings f and g are defined as follows:

$$f: x \to x^2, \qquad g: x \to 2x + 3.$$

Find the members of each of the following sets (each set has two members).

  a $\{x : fg(x) = 9\}$ **b** $\{x : gf(x) = 35\}$ **c** $\{x : f(x) = g(x)\}$

1A — 2

1 On a certain island the average rainfall per month for the first 9 months of the year was 0.62 cm. In the 10th and 11th months the rainfall was 4.72 cm and 4.88 cm respectively. What was the rainfall for the 12th month if the average for the whole year was 1.49 cm?   (051)

2 The dots on the figure below are such that each shows one of the 36 possible results when a red cubical die and a black cubical die are thrown together once only. The scores are then added together. Thus the dot marked as ⊙ shows that the black die is a 6 and the red die is a 2, giving a total of 8. (This score of 8 could have been obtained in other ways.)

By using the figure, or otherwise,
calculate the probability (as a
fraction) of scoring in one throw
of the two dice

a   a total of 2
b   a total of 8
c   a double, i.e. *both* dice showing
the same score
d   a double *or* a total of 8
e   a double *and* a total of 8

(16+)

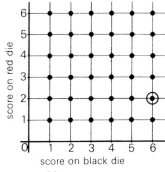

Figure R3

3   In a triangle PQR, PQ = PR = 13 cm, and QR = 10 cm. Calculate

a   the length of the perpendicular from P to QR
b   the size of each angle of the triangle
c   the size of the triangle
d   the perpendicular distance from Q to PR

4 N is the set of natural numbers. $N = \{1, 2, 3\ldots\}$ When r is a positive
integer, the set rN is defined by $rN = \{rn:\ n \in N\}$.

a   Write down three members of $5N$
b   Write down the smallest member of the set $5N \cap 3N$
c   Give examples of positive integers s and t such that $sN \cap tN \neq (st)N$

(052)

5   Find the factors of

a $2n^2 + 9n + 9$ **b** $100n^2 - 9$

Use your results to find a pair of factors for each of these numbers: 299,
20 909, 9991, 999 991.

6   A tin contains 500 wrapped sweets, some of which are toffees and the
others chocolates. Of the first 20 sweets taken out, 12 are toffees and 8
chocolates. Write down the experimental probability of taking each kind
of sweet, when drawing at random, and make an estimate of the total
number of each kind in the tin.
Supposing that your estimate is correct, find the probability of taking
each kind of sweet if the contents of the tin are mixed with those of a
tin containing 200 toffees only, and a sweet drawn at random.

7   250 pupils from a certain school entered for an examination. The
following table shows how many entered for each number of subjects
(for example, 12 entered for only 1 subject).

Number of subjects	1	2	3	4	5	6	7	8
Number of pupils	12	15	27	35	50	56	30	25

Find the mode, the median and the mean of this distribution.

8 A rectangular plot of land was originally twice as long as it was broad. Later its length was increased by 9 m and its breadth by 3 m, and this had the effect of doubling its area. Find its original dimensions.

Exercise 1B (Longer questions)
1B — 1

1 In the diagram,
$PQ = (3y-5)$ cm,
$QR = (y+20)$ cm,
$RS = (2x-2)$ cm,
$SP = (x-6)$ cm,
$PR = (x+12)$ cm
and $\angle PSR = 90°$.

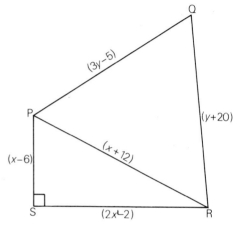

a Write down and simplify an expression for the perimeter of the quadrilateral PQRS in terms of x and y

b Given that $PQ = QR$, calculate the value of y.

Figure R4

c Using the right-angled triangle PSR write down an equation for x and show it reduces to $x^2 - 11x - 26 = 0$. Solve this equation for x.

Use your results to calculate the numerical value of the perimeter of the quadrilateral PQRS.   (CB)

2 The number x is chosen at random from the set {16, 17, 18, 19, 20}, and the number y is chosen at random from the set {1, 2, 3, 4, 5}. Show graphically the points {x, y} of the sample space* of possible outcomes.

Find the probability of each of the following events:

a x is a prime number
b xy is a square number
c $xy > 40$
d x is exactly divisible by y (NC)

3 In this question $\mathscr{E} = ${positive integers less than 100}, $M_1 = ${multiples of 2 less than 100}, $M_3 = ${multiples of 3 less than 100}, and M_4, M_5 etc. have similar meanings.

---

* For the meaning of 'sample space', see page 194.

    a Name all the members of $M_5 \cap M_6$

    b Name all the members of $M_9 \cap M'_{18}$

    c State which of the M sets is the same as (i) $M_2 \cap M_3$, (ii) $M_2 \cap M_4$ (iii) $M_4 \cap M_6$

    d Give the smallest value of n for which $M_9 \cap M_n = \phi$

    e Draw a Venn diagram showing the relationship between $\mathscr{E}$, M_6, M_9 and M_{12}

4 A vertical mast stands on a horizontal plane. From X in the plane, 80 m south of the foot of the mast, the angle of elevation of the top of the mast is 13.9°. Y is a point in the plane 150 m east of X. Calculate

    a the height of the mast

    b the distance of Y from the foot of the mast

    c the angle of elevation of the top of the mast from Y

    d the bearing of the mast from Y   (051)

5 The functions f and g map x onto $3x - 2$ and $2x^2 + 1$ respectively. Show that fg maps x onto $6x^2 + 1$, and find the mapping of the function gf.

A third function, h, maps x onto $ax + b$, where a and b are positive constants, and is such that fgh maps x onto $6x^2 + 12x + 7$.

Find the values of a and b and also that of fgh (-2).

Find the two values of x for which $fgh(x) = 25$.   (*LC*)

6 On a Monday, 88 letters were posted to an address in Cornwall. 40 of these arrived on the following day, Tuesday. 28 took two days and arrived on Wednesday; 9 arrived on Thursday, 6 on Friday, and the rest on Saturday.

    a Draw a bar chart to illustrate this information

    b Give the modal number of days taken for the letters to arrive

    c Give the median number of days taken for the letters to arrive

    d What percentage of the letters took more than two days to arrive?   (*SMP*)

1B — 2

1 The digits 1, 2, 3 are arranged in random order to form a 3-digit number. Write down all the 3-digit numbers that could be so formed. Find the probability that the number is

    a odd   **c** more than 220   **e** a multiple of 5

    b even   **d** a multiple of 3

2   A tourist wishes to estimate the height, *h* metres, of a tower and the width, *w* metres, of a moat that surrounds it. Taking the shortest route, he walks from C to a point A on the bank of the moat. At B he estimates the angle of elevation of the top T of the tower to be 45°. At A he estimates it to be 60°. He measures the distance AB as 16 metres to the nearest metre.

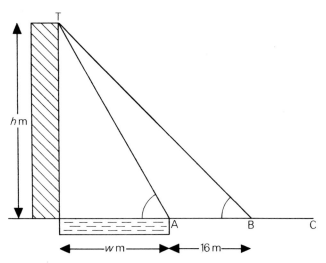

Figure R5

a   Write down two expressions for *h* in terms of *w*.
b   Hence calculate the values he obtains for *w* and *h*.

On enquiry at an information office, the tourist is told that the height of the tower is 40 m and the width of the moat 25 m.

c   Calculate the correct angle of elevation at A.
d   Find the percentage error in the estimation of the height, giving your answer correct to 1 significant figure.   (*SMP*)

3   The members of the set *A* are the integers {3, 4, 7, 9, 12, 21, 24, 38, 45}.

Those members of *A* which are factors of some *other* member of the set form a subset *F*, and those members of *A* which are multiples of some *other* member of the set form a subset *M*.

List the members of

     a *F*   **b** *M*   **c** *F*∪*M*   **d** *F*∩*M*   **e** *F'*∩*M'*   **f** (*F*∩*M*)'

                                                         (051)

4   A local authority has 200 houses of a certain type (Type A). The following table gives an analysis of the numbers of houses in which 1, 2, 3, 4, 5 or 6 people live. (This type of house will not hold more than six people.)

Number of people	1	2	3	4	5	6
Number of houses	5	25	40	75	33	22

Calculate the mean number of people per house.

Calculate what percentage of this population is living fewer than four to a house.

The authority also has 100 houses of another type (Type B); the mean number of people living in each of these is $2 \cdot 12$. Find the mean number of people per house in all 300 houses.

It is suggested that all those who live fewer than four in a Type A house should be moved to other houses, and their houses filled by larger families. Find the largest possible increase in the number of people living in Type A houses, if this were done.   *(LC)*

5 The faces of two dice, instead of carrying numbers, carry letters; on the faces of one are inscribed the letters of METHOD, and on those of the other, the letters of MUDDLE. The two dice are thrown in the usual way; find the probability that

   a both dice show M
   b one die shows M and the other E
   c one die shows M and the other O
   d one die shows M and the other D
   e both dice show O
   f both dice show the same letter
   g both dice show consonants

6 Find the factors of $x^2 - 2xy - 3x + 6y$. Hence show that if $x^2 - 2xy - 3x + 6y = 0$, then either $x = ay$ or $x = b$; where a and b are numbers to be found. Hence find the four pairs of values of x and y which satisfy both the equations

$$x^2 - 2xy - 3x + 6y = 0$$

$$x^2 + 3xy + y^2 = 19$$

On the Work of Chapters 1–5, Book 2

Exercise 2S (Short questions)

1 Give the value of $16^{-\frac{3}{4}}$.

2 Find f^{-1} if f: $x \rightarrow 4x + 7$.

3 Find the gradient of the line joining $(1, 5)$ and $(7, -1)$.

4   Calculate **AB** if $\mathbf{A} = (2 \;\; -1)$ and $\mathbf{B} = \begin{pmatrix} -3 \\ -5 \end{pmatrix}$.

5   Transform the formula $V = \frac{1}{3}\pi r^2 h$ to make r the subject.

6

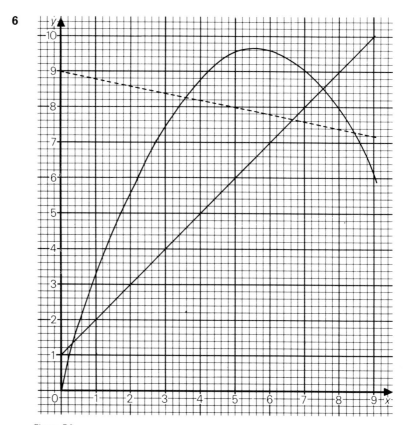

Figure R6

From the graph (i.e. the curve) estimate the value of y when $x = 3$.

7   From the same curve, estimate the two values of x for which $y = 7$.

8   Given that $\log_{10} 6 = 0.78$ and $\log_{10} 5 = 0.70$, find $\log_{10}\sqrt{1.2}$.

9   Find the gradient of the line $3x + 4y = 24$.

10 Given that g: $x \to 3 - x$ and h: $x \to 3 + x$, find the mapping hg. Of the mappings g, h and hg, which are self-inverse?

11 **A** and **B** have the same meanings as in Question 4, and $\mathbf{C} = \begin{pmatrix} 4 & -1 \\ 0 & 3 \end{pmatrix}$.
Of the products **BA**, **AC**, **CA**, **BC** and **CB**, which can be formed?

12 A particle moves in a straight line in such a way that, t seconds after it starts, its distance s metres from a fixed point O is given by $s = 35 - 7t$. With what speed is the body moving? For how long does it move towards O?

13   If y is a linear function of x, which of the following pairs of values is wrong?

x	2	3	4	5	6	7	8
y	8.4	7.1	5.8	4.5	3.4	1.9	0.6

14   Given that $ab^x = 3$ and $ab^{x+2} = \frac{1}{3}$, find the value of ab^{x-4}.

15   The price of a commodity has been increasing throughout the last five years, but is now increasing more slowly than at any time during this period. Which of these graphs illustrates the above statement?

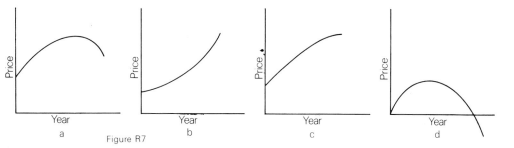

a   Figure R7   b   c   d

16   Find x and y if $\begin{pmatrix} 3 & 0 \\ 1 & 1 \end{pmatrix} \begin{pmatrix} x \\ y \end{pmatrix} = \begin{pmatrix} 9 \\ 2 \end{pmatrix}$.

17   For a domain set of men and a range set of cats, the relation 'is the brother of the mother of the owner of' is defined. Give the inverse of this relation, and give also the associated mapping.

18   Find the equation of the line that passes through the point $(1, -2)$ and has gradient 2.

19   A, B and C are points on a logarithmic scale, and $AB = BC$. A represents 4 and C represents 9: what number does B represent?

20   Calculate the matrix product $\begin{pmatrix} 6 & 2 \\ 3 & 1 \end{pmatrix} \begin{pmatrix} 1 & -2 \\ -3 & 6 \end{pmatrix}$.

Exercise 2A (Medium length questions)
2A — 1

1   It is given that $\mathbf{A} = \begin{pmatrix} 2 & 0 \\ 3 & 1 \end{pmatrix}$ and $\mathbf{B} = \begin{pmatrix} 1 & x \\ y & -1 \end{pmatrix}$.

a Find the matrix product **AB**,

b Given that $\mathbf{B} + p\mathbf{A} = \begin{pmatrix} 7 & 5 \\ 13 & z \end{pmatrix}$, find the values of x, y, z and p.   (*CC*)

2 Figure R6 shows the graph of $y = 3.4x - 0.3x^2$.

a Find the equation of the (continuous) straight line graph.
b Find, and give in its simplest form without fractions of decimals, the quadratic equation in x whose roots are given by the intersection of the curve with the straight line graph mentioned in **a**.
c Use the graph to give the roots of this equation correct to 1 place of decimals.

3 The cooking time (t minutes) for a joint of meat is given by

$$t = \frac{2000(4W + 3)}{H}$$

where W kg is the weight of meat and $H°C$ is the cooking temperature.

a Calculate the cooking time for a joint weighing 2 kg at a temperature of 160°C.
b Rearrange the formula to give H in terms of W and t.
c Rearrange it to give W in terms of H and t.   (*SMP*)

4 Find the value of $x^{p/q}$,

a when $x = 2$, $p = -2$, $q = 1$ d when $x = 1$, $p = 7$, $q = 5$
b when $x = 7$, $p = 0$, $q = 5$ e when $x = 9$, $p = -3$, $q = 2$
c when $x = 8$, $p = 2$, $q = 3$

5 $\mathbf{X} = \begin{pmatrix} 3 & -1 \\ 0 & 2 \end{pmatrix}$, $\mathbf{Y} = \begin{pmatrix} 1 & 0 & 3 & -1 \\ 0 & 2 & 1 & 0 \end{pmatrix}$.

a Calculate whichever can be calculated of **XY** and **YX**.
b Write down **X′** and **Y′**, the tranposes of **X** and **Y**.
c Calculate whichever can be calculated of **X′Y′** and **Y′X′**.
d Describe the connection between the matrices you obtained in answer to **a** and **c**.

6 a P and Q are the points whose coordinates are (8, 2) and (−4, 7) respectively. Calculate the length of PQ and the gradient of PQ.
b The point whose coordinates are (3, 7) lies on the line $y = 5x + c$. Calculate the value of c.   (*OC*)

7 f: $x \to \frac{1}{4}x$, and g: $x \to \frac{4}{x}$.

Give the values of f(6), g(6), fg(6), $f^{-1}(6)$, $g^{-1}(6)$ and $g^{-1}f^{-1}(6)$.

Express as single mappings fg, gf, $f^{-1}g$ and gf^{-1}. Which of these are self-inverse? Express $x \to \frac{64}{x}$ in terms of f or f^{-1} and g.

8 The quantities x and y are connected by the equation $y=pq^x$, where p and q are certain numbers. When $x=1$, $y=0.5$, and when $x=3$, $y=312.5$.

    a Find p and q.
    b Find the values of y corresponding to the following values of x: 2, 0, $\frac{1}{2}$, -1.
    c Find the smallest integral value of x for which $y>1\,000\,000$.

2A-2

1 Repeat Question 2 of Exercise 2A-1 (page 240), but this time with reference to the **broken** straight line graph.

2 A molecule of water consists of two atoms of hydrogen and one of oxygen; a molecule of carbon dioxide, of one atom of carbon and two of oxygen; and a molecule of glucose, of six atoms of carbon, twelve of hydrogen, and six of oxygen. Complete the matrix **M** which summarises this information.

$$
\begin{array}{c}
\\
\text{Water} \\
\text{Carbon dioxide} \\
\text{Glucose}
\end{array}
\begin{array}{ccc}
\text{H} & \text{O} & \text{C} \\
\left(\begin{array}{ccc}
2 & 1 & 0 \\
\\
\\
\end{array}\right)
\end{array}
$$

Form a 3×1 matrix **N** which gives the information that the masses of an atom of hydrogen, an atom of oxygen and an atom of carbon are respectively 1, 16 and 12 of a certain unit.

Form the product **MN** and state what information it gives.

3 Solve the equations

    a $\dfrac{17}{1+x^2}=1.7$,   **b** $\sqrt{(10-4x^2)}=3$.

4 The equations of two straight lines are

$$y=x+4$$
$$y=6x-11$$

    a Calculate the coordinates of their point of intersection.
    b Find the distance between the points at which these lines cut the y-axis.   (*CC*)

5 Given that $\log_3 4=1.262$, find the logarithms to base 3 of the following numbers.

    a 16   **b** 12   **c** 2   **d** 8   **e** $\frac{1}{4}$

6   Given that $f:x \rightarrow 3x$ and $g:x \rightarrow x-4$, write down, in the form $x \rightarrow ...$, the inverse function f^{-1} and the composite function $f^{-1}g$.

Find a value of x for which $f^{-1}g(x)=f(x)$.   *(LB)*

7   On squared paper draw the lines whose equations are $x+y=6$, $y-x=1$ and $y=x+3$. Draw a fourth line such that the four lines enclose a square region, and write down the equation of this fourth line.

Write down the four inequalities which are satisfied by the coordinates of all points in the square region.

8   An Inspector of Weights and Measures checked an old kitchen scale (re-marked in metric units), using accurate masses of 1, 2 and 3 kg. His results are shown in the graph below.

a What were the readings on the scale for the accurate masses of 1, 2 and 3 kg?
b What is the true mass of an object when the reading on the scale is 2.7 kg?
c What is the increase in the reading on the scale when an accurate mass of 1 kg is added?
d Which reading on the scale is accurate?

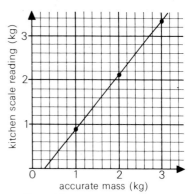

Figure R8

(SMP)

Exercise 2B (Longer questions)
2B-1

1   The volume V of a beaker is given by the formula $V=\frac{1}{3}\pi h(2R^2-r^2)$, where R is the radius of the top, r the radius of the bottom and h the vertical height of the beaker, all in centimetres.

a Taking π as 3.142, and showing the steps in your calculations, find the volume when $h=11$, $R=4$ and $r=2$.
b Make R the subject of the formula.
c Given that the volume V can also be expressed by the formula $V=\frac{7}{3}\pi r^2 h$, express R in terms of r.   *(LD)*

2   Each of four football teams, A, B, C and D, plays each other team once. The matrix **M**, which forms a table showing how many games were played, won, drawn and lost by each team, is as partly shown below.

$$\mathbf{M} = \begin{matrix} A \\ B \\ C \\ D \end{matrix}$$

$$\begin{matrix} \text{Played} & \text{Won} & \text{Drawn} & \text{Lost} \\ \begin{pmatrix} 3 & 2 & 1 & 0 \\ 3 & 1 & 2 & 0 \\ 3 & 0 & 2 & 1 \end{pmatrix} \end{matrix}$$

Copy and complete the matrix **M**.

If $\mathbf{P} = \begin{pmatrix} 0 \\ 2 \\ 1 \\ 0 \end{pmatrix}$ and $\mathbf{Q} = \begin{pmatrix} 1 \\ -1 \\ -1 \\ -1 \end{pmatrix}$, evaluate **MP** and

give a possible meaning for it.

Without evaluating **MQ**, explain why it must be a zero matrix.

If $\mathbf{R} = (1 \quad 1 \quad 1 \quad 1)$, explain why the second and fourth elements of **RM** must be equal.   (*LC*)

3 **a** Given that $y = \dfrac{2}{x}$, copy and complete the following table.

x	-2	-1	-0.5	0.5	1	2	3	4	5
y	-1	-2		4			0.7	0.5	0.4

Using scales of 1 cm to represent 1 unit on each axis, draw the graph of $y = \dfrac{2}{x}$ for values of x from the completed table.

b Given that $y = x(x-3)$, copy and complete the following table.

x	-2	-1	0	1	2	3	4	5
y		4		-2		0	4	10

On the same graph paper and on the same axes that you have already drawn, draw the graph of $y = x(x-3)$ for values of x from -2 to $+5$ inclusive.

c Write down and simplify the equation in x which is satisfied by the value of x at the point of intersection of the graphs. Use your graphs to solve this equation.   (16+)

4 The railway line from A to B is 25 km long. An engine leaves A at 12.00 and travels towards B at an average speed of 25 km/h. It is stopped for 20 minutes, by signals, at a junction which is 10 km from A and then continues its journey at the same steady speed. Using a horizontal scale of 1 cm to 5 min and a vertical scale of 4 cm to 5 min, draw the distance–time graph of the journey of the engine from A to B. Label the vertical axis 'Distance from A', and mark the points A and B on this axis.

The road from A to B, also 25 km long, runs alongside the railway line and crosses it at a level crossing situated 15 km from A. A car leaves B and travels at a steady speed of 60 km/h to the level crossing which it reaches just as the engine is passing. After a delay of 6 min the car continues its journey at a steady speed so as to arrive at A at 13.22. On the same axes, and using the same scales, draw the distance–time graph for the journey of the car and use it fo find

a the speed of the car when travelling from the level crossing to A,
b the time at which the car left B.   (*CC*)

5 A certain radioactive body, P, has the property that at the end of any hour the number of units of radioactivity of P falls to three-quarters of its value at the beginning of that hour. If at a certain instant the radioactivity is 160 units, calculate the value of its radioactivity three hours later. Express this value as a percentage of the original value, i.e. of 160.

Find also the average rate of decrease of the radioactivity of P during the three hours, in units per hour.

The radioactivity of another body, Q, falls, after any hour, to a fraction $\dfrac{m}{n}$ of its value at the beginning of that hour. At the end of 3 hours it has fallen to 21.6% of its value at the beginning of the 3 hours. Find the value of $\dfrac{m}{n}$. Find also after how many more complete hours the radioactivity of Q has fallen below 5% of its original value.   (*LC*)

6 Write down the four inequalities that define the shaded region (Figure R9).

Find the points in, or on, the boundary of the shaded region

a where $x+2y$ has its largest value,
b where $x+2y$ has its smallest value.

2B-2

1 **a** A toll bridge charges 16p for a motor-cycle, 24p for a car and 40p for a lorry. Express this information as a column matrix **C**.
b The numbers of these vehicles crossing one weekend are given by the matrix

$$\mathbf{N} = \begin{array}{c} \text{Sat} \\ \text{Sun} \end{array} \begin{pmatrix} \overset{\text{M/c}}{134} & \overset{\text{Cars}}{209} & \overset{\text{Lorries}}{21} \\ 65 & 95 & 28 \end{pmatrix}$$

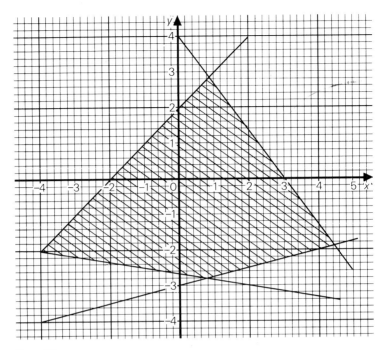

Figure R9

Which of the products **CN** and **NC** can be evaluated?

Denoting this product by **T**, evaluate **T** and state what information it gives.

c To obtain more revenue at weekends, three proposals are made.

I Double the charges on Saturdays only;

II Treble the charges on Sundays only;

III Increase the charges by half on both days.

The matrix **X** is such that the product **XT** gives the actual revenue for the weekend and what it would have been under each of the proposals I, II and III.

Write down **X**, evaluate **XT**, and state which proposal would have been the most profitable.   (*SMP*)

2   The functions f, g and h are defined as follows.

$$f{:}x \to 2x, \quad g{:}x \to x+3, \quad h{:}x \to \frac{1}{x}.$$

a Write down, in the form $x \to \ldots$, the composite functions fg and gf, and the inverse functions f^{-1} and h^{-1}.

b Show that there is no value of x for which $fg(x)=gf(x)$.

c Find a value of x for which $fg(x)=f^{-1}g(x)$.

d Show that the values of x for which $fh(x)=gh(x)$ are the roots of the equation $2x^2+3x-2=0$, and hence find these values.   (*LC*)

3   The petrol consumption of a car varies as the speed increases. It is known that the relationship between the petrol consumption, p litres per 100 km, and the average speed, v km/h, is given by the equation

$$p = 6 - \frac{3v}{100} + \frac{v^2}{2000} \text{ for } v > 50.$$

Find the values of p corresponding to $v = 60, 80, 100, 120, 140, 160$.

On graph paper, draw the graph of p against v, using a scale of 1 cm to represent 10 km/h across the paper and 1 cm to represent 1 litre/100 km up the paper.

From your graph read off the values of p when $v = 70$ and when $v = 90$.

A motorist travelled 20 000 km during the year 1980. Find his total petrol consumption if his average speed was

a 70 km/h,   **b** 90 km/h.

Given that a litre of petrol cost 30p, how much less money would he have spent on petrol during the year 1980 by travelling at an average speed of 70 km/h instead of 90 km/h?   *(LB)*

4   **a** A and B are two points with coordinates $(1, -3)$ and $(11, 2)$ respectively. Calculate (i) the gradient of AB, (ii) the equation of the line AB.
b The two lines $y = -2x$ and $x - 2y = 11$ intersect at C, and the line $x - 2y = 11$ cuts the x-axis at D. Calculate the coordinates of C and D.

Calculate the area of the triangle OCD.

                                                    (OC)

5   The matrix **M** denotes the relation 'is a vertex of' between the domain set of points {A, B, C, D, E} and the range set of equilateral triangles {P, Q, R}.

$$\mathbf{M} = \begin{array}{c} \\ A \\ B \\ C \\ D \\ E \end{array} \begin{array}{ccc} P & Q & R \\ \begin{pmatrix} 1 & 1 & 1 \\ 1 & 0 & 0 \\ 1 & 1 & 0 \\ 0 & 1 & 1 \\ 0 & 0 & 1 \end{pmatrix} \end{array}$$

Sketch a possible arrangement of the triangles, lettering all the vertices.

Compile **M'**, the transpose of **M**.

Form the product **MM'** and explain the meaning of its elements.

Form the product **M'M**. Why is every leading diagonal element 3? Explain the meanings of the other elements.

6 The function f has the property that $f(xy) = f(x) + f(y) - 1$ for any two positive numbers x and y. Show that this implies that $f(1) = 1$.

If, moreover, $f(2) = 2$, find the values of $f(4)$, $f(8)$, $f(\frac{1}{2})$ and $f(\frac{1}{4})$.

Show that $f(0)$ cannot exist.

Express in terms of $f(x)$, $f(x^2)$ and $f(\sqrt{x})$.

Suggest a function that f might be.

On the work of Chapters 6–10, Book 2

Computation practice

Make a rough estimate of the answer to each of the following calculations. Then use your calculator (or logarithm tables) to find the answer correct to 3 significant figures. Given the answer in standard form if appropriate.

1 If $p = 93.72$, $q = 143.6$, $r = 0.482$ and $s = 0.0836$, find the values of

  a $\dfrac{pq}{rs}$ **c** $\dfrac{p+q}{r+s}$ **e** $pr + qs$ **g** $\dfrac{p+qr}{p-qr}$

  b $\dfrac{pr}{qs}$ **d** $\dfrac{q-p}{r-s}$ **f** $\dfrac{q}{ps+r}$

2 If $x = 17.32$, $y = 8.46$, $z = 0.945$, find the values of

  a $\sqrt{xyz}$ **d** $\sqrt{(x^2 + y^2 + z^2)}$ **f** $x^2y^2 + y^2z^2 + z^2x^2$

  b $\dfrac{x}{\sqrt{yz}}$ **e** $\dfrac{x^3 + y^3}{z^3}$ **g** $\sqrt{\dfrac{y}{xz}}$

  c $\dfrac{x^3 + y^3}{z^3}$

3 If $t = 8142$, $u = 71\,900$, $v = 136\,000$, find the value of

  a $\sqrt{(u^2 - 2tv)}$ **d** $\dfrac{1}{t^2u - v^2}$ **f** $\sqrt{\left(\dfrac{t^2 - 100v}{uv}\right)}$

  b $\sqrt{\left(\dfrac{u}{t} + \dfrac{v}{u}\right)}$ **e** $\dfrac{t^3}{u^4}$ **g** $\dfrac{3y - 10t}{(v-u)(u-t)}$

  c $(t + \sqrt{v})^2$

Exercise 3S (Short questions)

1   If $R=\{$right-angled triangles$\}$, $E=\{$equilateral triangles$\}$, express in set language, using the symbol ϕ, the statement 'No right-angled triangle is equilateral'.

2   Repeat Question 1 but without using the symbol ϕ.

3   The sides of a right-angled triangle are 5 cm, 12 cm and 13 cm long. Give the sine and cosine of the smallest angle.

4   Of 20 children who were late for school one morning, 10 were less than 5 minutes late, 6 were between 5 and 10 minutes late, and 4 were between 10 and 15 minutes late. Assuming that all the times were measured accurately and that there were no borderline cases, estimate the mean time of lateness.

5   Give the transformations associated with the matrix

$$\begin{pmatrix} 0 & a \\ 1 & 0 \end{pmatrix}$$ for two different values of a.

6   In triangle ABC, $AB=AC=10$ cm, $\cos \angle B=0.8$ and $\sin \angle B=0.6$. Find the area of the triangle.

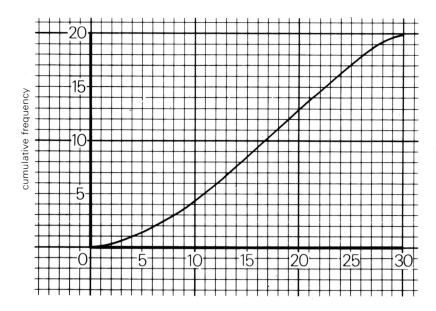

Figure R10

7   The cumulative frequency graph of a certain distribution is shown in Figure R10. Give the median of this distribution.

8   Give the interquartile range of the same distribution as in Question 7.

9   If $n(A) = 17$, $n(B) = 8$, give the largest and smallest possible values of $n(A \cap B)$.

10 If A and B are as in Question 9, give the largest and smallest possible values of $n(A \cup B)$.

11 Give the matrix corresponding to a reflection in the x-axis combined with an enlargement with centre (0, 0) and scale factor 4.

12 In Figure R11, of the lengths b, c, h, x, y, which is equal to $a \sin \theta \cos \theta$?

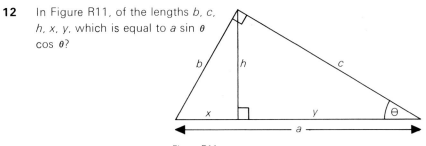

Figure R11

13 Which of the lengths listed in Question 12 is equal to $a \cos^2 \theta$? ($\cos^2 \theta$ means $(\cos \theta)^2$)

14 Between which two of the following statements is it correct to write ⇔?

AB = DC, AB is parallel to DC, **AB** = **DC**, ABCD is a parallelogram.

15 Give the matrix that transforms figure F into figure G (Figure R12).

16 Give the matrix that transforms figure G into figure F (Figure R12).

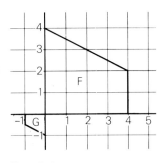

Figure R12

17 Find the median and the interquartile range of the following numbers: 1, 4, 7, 8, 9, 11, 13, 16, 18, 19, 20.

18 If $\angle A = 63.4°$, then sin A = 2 cos A. Find the value of A if cos A = 2 sin A.

19 In a class of 30 pupils there are 22 who sometimes come to school by car and 14 who sometimes come by bus. What is the smallest possible number who come sometimes by car and sometimes by bus?

20 With the same information as in Question 19, but knowing also that there are 9 who come sometimes by car and sometimes by bus, how many never come by either car or bus?

Exercise 3A (Medium length questions)
3A — 1

1 P and Q are subsets of the universal set $\mathscr{E}$. $n(P) = 33$, $n(Q) = 22$, $n(P \cap Q) = 17$.

Calculate $n(P \cup Q)$.

If, moreover, $n(\mathscr{E}) = 70$, calculate $n(P')$ and $n(P \cap Q')$.

2 A regular polygon with 10 sides is inscribed in a circle of radius 8 cm, whose centre is O. Find the length of each side of the polygon, and the perpendicular distance from O to any side of the polygon. Hence find the area of the polygon.

3 A transformation is described by the matrix $\begin{pmatrix} 0 & 1 \\ 1 & 0 \end{pmatrix}$. Describe the set of points which are mapped onto themselves by this transformation.

(JMBC)

4 State what transformation is associated with each of the matrices $\mathbf{M} = \begin{pmatrix} 0 & -1 \\ 1 & 0 \end{pmatrix}$ and $\mathbf{N} = \begin{pmatrix} 2 & 0 \\ 0 & 2 \end{pmatrix}$. If $\mathbf{P} = \begin{pmatrix} 1 & -1 \\ 1 & 1 \end{pmatrix}$, show that $\mathbf{P}^2 = \mathbf{MN}$, and hence, or otherwise, find what transformation is associated with $\mathbf{P}$.

(LC)

5 If M = {mammals}, W = {warm-blooded animals}, write sentences in normal English to express the statements:

a $M \subset W$, **b** $W \cap M' \neq \emptyset$, **c** $W' \cap M' = W'$.

Which two of these statements are equivalent?

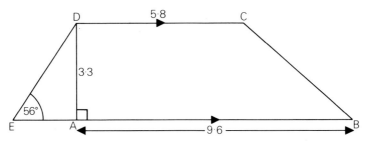

Figure R13

6   In Figure R13, BCDE is a trapezium in which EB is parallel to DC. The
line DA is perpendicular to EB and is 3.3 cm in length. Given that
$DC = 5.8$ cm, $AB = 9.6$ cm and $\angle DEA = 56°$, calculate

    a EA,   **b** ED,   **c** the area of the trapezium ABCD.   (*CB*)

7   The statement 'ABC is a triangle with A a right-angle' is written down
four times, followed by each of the following statements in turn. In each
case, state which of the signs ⇔, ⇒, ⇐ may correctly be written
between the statements, or if none of them may correctly be written,
write 'none':

    a $AB^2 + AC^2 = BC^2$,
    b $AB : BC : AC = 3 : 5 : 4$,
    c A circle can be drawn through A, B and C,
    d $\angle B + \angle C = 90°$.

8   Figure R14 shows the cumulative percentage graph for the marks of
candidates in an examination. For example, 10% of the candidates
gained 70 or more marks.

From the graph estimate

    a the median mark,
    b the lower quartile mark and the upper quartile mark,
    c the inter-quartile range,
    d the probability that a candidate chosen at random had a mark of 80 or
more.

    (16+)

3A — 2

1   Newspapers are delivered to 20 houses. Each house receives either one
copy of 'The Bugle' or one copy of 'The Clarion' or one copy of each. In
all, 16 copies of 'The Bugle' and 14 copies of 'The Clarion' are delivered.
Find the number of houses which receive 'The Bugle' only.   (*LB*)

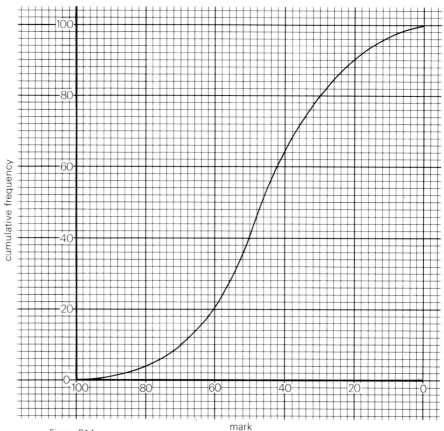

Figure R14   mark

2 On squared paper plot the points (1, 0), (4, 0), (4, 2) and (1, 2), and join them to form a rectangle.

Draw the image of this rectangle under the transformation whose matrix is $\begin{pmatrix} \cos 60° & -\sin 60° \\ \sin 60° & \cos 60° \end{pmatrix}$.

Describe this transformation fully.

3 Repeat question 2 but with the matrix $\begin{pmatrix} \cos 60° & \sin 60° \\ \sin 60° & -\cos 60° \end{pmatrix}$.

4 An aeroplane takes off and climbs in a straight line for 2100 m: by then it is 800 m above the (horizontal) ground. Calculate the angle the flight-path makes with the ground.

Calculate also the *horizontal* distance travelled by the aeroplane.

5 An investigation into the educational programme of a group of 200 fifth-form students produced, among other results, information shown in the following table, concerning the amount of classroom time spent on mathematics per week.

Time (minutes)	0–60	60–90	90–120	120–150	150–180	180–210	210–240
Frequency	13	14	67	56	30	7	13

Use these data to calculate an estimate of the mean time spent on mathematics.   (052)

6 If $\mathscr{E}$={fruit}, A={apples}, R={red fruit}, L={fruit I like}, write the following in set notation.

  a I like red apples,
  b I dislike apples which are not red,
  c The only fruit I like is red apples,
  d The only apples I like are red apples.

Are any of these statements equivalent? If so, which are they?

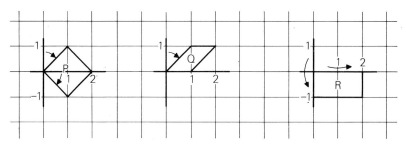

Figure R15

7 Write down the matrices corresponding to transformations that transform the unit square into each of the figures P, Q and R (Figure R15).

8 Each side of a rhombus is 11 cm long, and one of the angles is 54°. Calculate the lengths of both diagonals, and the area of the rhombus.

Exercise 3B (Longer questions)
3B — 1

1 The students in a certain science Sixth Form must study either mathematics and physics, or physics and chemistry, or chemistry and biology.

If $\mathscr{E}$={all these students}, M={students studying mathematics}, P={students studying physics}, C={students studying chemistry}, B={students studying biology}, state which of the sets M, P, C, B, ϕ is equal to each of

  a P' **b** M' **c** $M \cap B$ **d** $B \cap C$ **e** $M \cup P$

Because of restricted laboratory accommodation, the number who can study physics is limited to 50, and the number who can study chemistry to 45. Find

f the largest possible number of students in the Sixth Form, stating the number studying mathematics and the number studying biology if this largest number is accommodated,

g the smallest possible number of students there could be, if all the laboratory accommodation is used, stating the respective numbers studying mathematics and studying biology.   (*LB*)

2   The frequency table below relates to the speeds of 160 vehicles passing a particular point on a main road.

Speed, v m.p.h.	$v \leqslant 15$	$15 < v \leqslant 20$	$20 < v \leqslant 25$	$25 < v \leqslant 30$	$30 < v \leqslant 35$
Frequency	0	2	3	22	30

Speed, v m.p.h.	$35 < v \leqslant 40$	$40 < v \leqslant 45$	$45 < v \leqslant 50$	$50 < v \leqslant 55$	$55 < v \leqslant 60$
Frequency	40	26	22	10	5

Calculate an estimate of the mean.

Prepare a cumulative frequency table, and draw the corresponding frequency diagram. From your diagram write down the median and the upper and lower quartiles.   (051)

3   The vertices of a triangle X have coordinates A(1, 1), B(3, 1), C(1, 2).

a Using a scale of 1 cm to 1 unit draw x- and y-axes taking values of x from -7 to 13 and values of y from -5 to 10. Draw and label the triangle X.

b The matrix of the transformation P is $\begin{pmatrix} a & 0 \\ 0 & a \end{pmatrix}$, and is such that the images of A, B and C under P are respectively A′(-2, -2), B′(-6, -2) and C′(-2, -4). Draw the triangle A′B′C′ and label it P(X). Describe fully the single transformation P and write down the value of a.

c The triangle A″B″C″ is the image of ABC under an enlargement E whose centre is (2, 1) and whose scale factor is 4. Draw and label the triangle E(X), taking care to label the vertices A″, B″ and C″.

d Triangle A′B′C′ can be mapped onto triangle A″B″C″ by a single transformation F. Describe fully the single transformation F.

e D is the enlargement with centre (0, 0) and scale factor 4, and $E(X) = YD(X)$. Describe fully the single transformation Y.   (*CD*)

4   Three points P, Q and A are on level ground, and P is 8 km from A on bearing 040 from A. The point Q is due west of P and is on bearing 330 from A.

a Calculate the distance AQ.

A light aircraft, vertically above P, is at an angle of elevation of 9° from A. Five minutes later the aircraft is 1 km vertically above Q. Calculate

b the vertical height of the aircraft when it was above P,
c the angle of elevation of the aircraft from A when it is vertically above Q,
d the average rate of descent of the aircraft in metres per second, correct to one decimal place.   (16+)

5 **a** Draw a single Venn diagram to illustrate the relations between the following sets.

$P=\{\text{parallelograms}\}$, $Q=\{\text{quadrilaterals}\}$,
$R=\{\text{rectangles}\}$, $S=\{\text{squares}\}$,
$Z=\{\text{quadrilaterals having }\textbf{one and only one}\text{ pair of parallel sides}\}$.

State which one of the sets P, R, S, Z, ϕ is equal to
(i) $R\cap S$,   (ii) $P\cap Z$.
b The 89 members of the Fifth Form all belong to one or more of the Chess Club, the Debating Society and the Jazz Club. Denoting these sets by C, D and J respectively, it is known that 20 pupils belong to C only, 15 to J only and 12 to D only. Given that $n(C\cap J)=18$, $n(C\cap D)=20$ and $n(D\cap J)=16$, calculate
(i) $n(C\cap J\cap D)$,   (ii) $n(D')$.   (LB)

6 The table shows the masses, measured in grams, of 200 oranges in a greengrocer's shop.

Mass (grams)	120 up to 130	130 up to 140	140 up to 150	150 up to 160	160 up to 170	170 up to 180
Frequency	3	9	20	28	24	31

Mass (grams)	180 up to 190	190 up to 200	200 up to 210	210 up to 220	220 up to 230
Frequency	26	22	18	14	5

a Plot a cumulative frequency graph representing the data.
b From your graph estimate the median mass of these oranges.
c The greengrocer decides that the heaviest 25% of these oranges are to be classified 'Grade A'. From your graph find the minimum mass of his Grade A oranges.
d Find the mean mass of his Grade A oranges to the nearest gram. (O52)

3B-2

1 A transformation T is defined by the matrix $\begin{pmatrix} 0 & -1 \\ 1 & 0 \end{pmatrix}$.

a Draw axes of x and y on graph paper, taking values of x and y from -5 to $+5$, and mark on the diagram the points A(0, 3) and B(1, 5) and also their images A′, B′ under the transformation T.

b Describe the geometrical effect of the transformation T.

c Find the gradient of the line segment AB and hence find the equation of the line through A and B.

d Draw on the diagram the line l', the image of l under T, and find its equation. *(JMBC)*

2 In the course of an archaeological dig, the remains of two post-holes, A and B, are discovered, B being 10 m due north of A. It is thought that the next hole, C, will be 10 m from B and that all three will lie on the circumference of a circle whose centre is to the east of AB and whose radius lies between 22 m and 35 m. Assuming that this is so, find the range of possible angles subtended by AB at the centre of the circle, and the range of possible values of the bearing of C from B.

If the further assumption is made, that the post-holes form part of the remains of a complete circle of posts, all equally spaced at 10 m apart, find the set of possible values of the number of posts. *(LC)*

3 A group of children were tested in reading, writing and arithmetic. There were 42 who passed in reading, 40 in writing and 38 in arithmetic. There were 2 children who failed in all three tests. Find the greatest and least possible numbers of children in the group, illustrating your answers by suitable Venn diagrams.

The following two pieces of information are also available.

a 36 passed in both reading and writing,

b 24 passed in both reading and arithmetic.

Copy the Venn diagram (Figure R16), and insert expressions in the remaining four spaces for the numbers in the subsets which they represent. Obtain an expression for the total number in the group, and, by considering the possible values of y, obtain the greatest and least possible values of this total. *(OSI)*

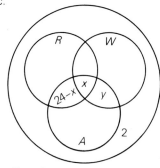

Figure R16

4 At a certain station records were made of the number of complete